A Wanderer by Trade

ALSO BY PATRICK WEBSTER

*Love and Death in Kubrick:
A Critical Study of the Films
from* Lolita *through* Eyes Wide Shut
(McFarland, 2011)

A Wanderer by Trade
Gender in the Songs of Bob Dylan

Patrick Webster

McFarland & Company, Inc., Publishers
Jefferson, North Carolina

Lyrics from the following songs are used by permission: **"As I Went Out One Morning"**: Copyright © 1968 by Dwarf Music; renewed 1996 by Dwarf Music. All rights reserved. International copyright secured. Reprinted by permission; **"Country Pie"**: Copyright © 1969 by Big Sky Music; renewed 1997 by Big Sky Music. All rights reserved. International copyright secured. Reprinted by permission; **"Don't Fall Apart On Me Tonight"**: Copyright © 1983 by Special Rider Music. All rights reserved. International copyright secured. Reprinted by permission; **"Don't Think Twice, It's All Right"**: Copyright © 1963 by Warner Bros. Inc.; renewed 1991 by Special Rider Music. All rights reserved. International copyright secured. Reprinted by permission; **"George Jackson"**: Copyright © 1971 by Ram's Horn Music; renewed 1999 by Ram's Horn Music. All rights reserved. International copyright secured. Reprinted by permission; **"Highlands"**: Copyright © 1997 by Special Rider Music. All rights reserved. International copyright secured. Reprinted by permission; **"I'll Be Your Baby Tonight"**: Copyright © 1968 by Dwarf Music; renewed 1996 by Dwarf Music. All rights reserved. International copyright secured. Reprinted by permission; **"Is Your Love In Vain?"**: Copyright © 1978 by Special Rider Music. All rights reserved. International copyright secured. Reprinted by permission; **"Isis"**: Copyright © 1975 by Ram's Horn Music; renewed 2003 by Ram's Horn Music. All rights reserved. International copyright secured. Reprinted by permission; **"Lay, Lady, Lay"**: Copyright © 1969 by Big Sky Music; renewed 1997 by Big Sky Music. All rights reserved. International copyright secured. Reprinted by permission; **"License to Kill"**: Copyright © 1983 by Special Rider Music. All rights reserved. International copyright secured. Reprinted by permission; **"Sweetheart Like You"**: Copyright © 1983 by Special Rider Music. All rights reserved. International copyright secured. Reprinted by permission.

LIBRARY OF CONGRESS CATALOGUING-IN-PUBLICATION DATA

Names: Webster, Patrick, 1953– author.
Title: A wanderer by trade : gender in the songs of Bob Dylan / Patrick Webster.
Description: Jefferson, North Carolina : McFarland & Company, 2019 | Includes bibliographical references and index.
Identifiers: LCCN 2018046431 | ISBN 9781476674094 (softcover : acid free paper) ∞
Subjects: LCSH: Dylan, Bob, 1941– —Criticism and interpretation. | Gender identity in music. | Sex role in music. | Popular music—History and criticism.
Classification: LCC ML420.D98 W45 2019 | DDC 782.42164092—dc23
LC record available at https://lccn.loc.gov/2018046431

BRITISH LIBRARY CATALOGUING DATA ARE AVAILABLE

ISBN (print) 978-1-4766-7409-4
ISBN (ebook) 978-1-4766-3439-5

© 2019 Patrick Webster. All rights reserved

No part of this book may be reproduced or transmitted in any form or by any means, electronic or mechanical, including photocopying or recording, or by any information storage and retrieval system, without permission in writing from the publisher.

Front cover: Bob Dylan, circa mid–1970s (Photofest)

Printed in the United States of America

McFarland & Company, Inc., Publishers
  Box 611, Jefferson, North Carolina 28640
  www.mcfarlandpub.com

I'm still very patriotic to the highway
Bob Dylan, 1966

Acknowledgments

I would like to thank my colleague and mentor, Terry Gifford, from our days at Bretton Hall College in the 1990s. I would also like to acknowledge the late John Bauldie for his reading of a very early draft of Chapter 2; John Stokes has been ever stalwart and always a fellow partner in crime; Derek Barker was particularly helpful; thanks also to Rod Anstee for his support in the past. In addition, a wide-ranging number of students and staff from the University of Leeds have provided intellectual succor over the years in which this book developed, there are too many to name, but a sincere thank you is offered to all of them.

Table of Contents

Acknowledgments vi
Preface 1
Introduction 3

1. Theoretical Approaches 15
2. Masculinity 31
3. Femininity 64
4. Sexuality 84
5. Identity and Duality 114

Closing Remarks 138
Chapter Notes 151
Bibliography 175
Index 181

Preface

The songs of Bob Dylan provide a unique template on which to map the changes in American society since the 1960s. This book aspires to go at least some way in attempting to map out such changes. In a specific sense, such a map will embrace the construct of masculinity as displayed within Dylan's work; the way in which masculinity would seem to be consistently preoccupied with movement, with exploration, with travel; and the way in which such desultory discourses seem to point towards travel as a gendering experience. In addition to this, the book will offer chapters on femininity, on sexuality and on identity; to present a consideration of the following issues: of the misogyny that would appear to inhabit a significant area of Dylan's work; to present a consideration of the reticence towards sexuality in many of Dylan's songs; culminating in a discussion of the issue of identity in Dylan's work, wherein notions of duality would appear to continually present themselves.

Why choose to write a book on Bob Dylan at this time? One potential response might point towards Dylan's recent award of the Nobel Prize for Literature; there are few acclamations that can accede such an accolade; hence this would arguably seem to point towards a sense of a final achievement. In addition, there is also the point that, as of the time of writing, Dylan is 77 years old—and although the so-called Never Ending Tour would still seem to be in progress—there is the thought that Dylan's career (at least in terms of writing original material) may be drawing towards the sense of an ending. Consequently, this may be an apt point to attempt to delineate the significance of such a career, one now encroaching upon a span of almost 60 years.

In looking at a diverse cross-section of songs, and at 12 particular songs in some depth, the book will aim to assess Dylan's cultural significance. In such a way the book will not desist, where necessary, from adopting a critical and polemical appraisal; for example, the potentially meretricious qualities present in some of Dylan's work. In addition, the book will also take into account the recent allegations of plagiarism and how these charges may serve to lessen the esteem and status of Dylan's work. In this way, this will not be a hagiographic valediction, as so many of the books on Dylan would seem to be; instead the book will look to offer an accurate representation of Bob Dylan's artistic and cultural legacy, whatever a final consideration of his work may be.

Aside from a small number of exceptions, Dylan's work has seldom been viewed within the context of cultural theory. This present book will endeavor to offset this omission, and, in an albeit modest way, it will attempt to remedy such a skewed response. The theoretical focus of the book: the constructs of masculine and feminine identities in Dylan's work, may appear to be overly restricted, but will, in fact, attempt to provide a wider understanding of what Dylan's work may really be saying. Insomuch, the issue of gender relationships will strive to reveal some of the underlying tensions in Dylan's songs, to forge new and previously unspoken areas of discussion. In addition, there is also the argument that complex art forms require a complex means of providing a hermeneutic response; insomuch, while some of the sources used within the book are unlikely to be found in any other books on Bob Dylan, they may, nonetheless, allow for a more thought-provoking reading of the dichotomies that so often pervade Dylan's work.

There has been an almost bewildering array of books published on the subject of Bob Dylan; it is difficult to ascertain the precise number, but several hundred individual monographs would seem to have been published since the 1960s. However, this present book would assert a distinction from those books that have gone before; insomuch as this present work has little if any interest in Bob Dylan the man, it has a great sense of interest in the songs Dylan has written, in the cultural texts he has offered the world, but no interest in Dylan himself. Such a denial of biographical intent allowing a way to eschew the dilemma of retreading of previous criticism, and instead to revel in the polysemantic richness of the songs, to explore the ubiquitous tropes that await such a reading. Finally, in seeking to sketch such new paradigms, the book—in essence—aspires to offer a different way of reading Bob Dylan's work, and, in so doing, to present a new depiction of one of the most significant of American songwriters.

Introduction

Since the release of his first record, in March 1962, Bob Dylan has forged a seminal influence on popular music, and his influence has arguably permeated popular culture as a whole. It is perhaps true to say that Dylan is no longer the commanding figure he once was, and that since the 1960s he has had a much-reduced profile in the world. However, one might argue that the overall body of Dylan's work still represents an impressive object for study. It is within such a context that this present book puts forward the premise that his work is not only eminently worthy, but worthy within the framework of cultural theory. The theoretical framework envisaged here is drawn primarily from the perspective of gender relationships; one of the central questions being: What do the contradictory elements of the construction of masculinity, femininity and sexuality in Dylan's lyrics reveal, and how do we—within a theoretical discourse—envisage the representation of gender within the (love) lyrics of Bob Dylan.

For reasons of both economy and specificity this book looks at, and critically considers, the lyrics of Bob Dylan primarily from 1962 to 1985, although the book attends, when appropriate, to songs from a later period. There were a number of reasons for this decision: firstly, there is an obvious necessity in restricting the field of study when dealing with a living author; secondly, these dates were chosen because they represent what is arguably Dylan's most significant work[1]; and thirdly, the fact that much of the material released since then would only rarely seem to warrant the same level of critical consideration. There were some exceptions—one thinks of a number of songs on the *Oh Mercy* (1989) and *Time Out of Mind* (1997) albums in addition to such later songs as "Mississippi," "Nettie Moore," "Huck's Tune," "Pay in Blood" and so on—but in general Dylan's output since the mid-80s has—from the perspective of at least one opinion—rarely been worthy of the same extensive criticism. Of the numerous albums released since 1985, only a handful have consisted of original Dylan compositions[2]; other than this there has been an increasing and almost bewildering plethora of releases: live recordings, greatest hits compilations, albums of cover versions from the folk and blues tradition, albums of popular music standards, a Christmas album, albums reissued in mono recordings,[3] and then there have been the various releases in the so-called *Bootleg Series*.[4] Here, in the case of the *Bootleg Series*, it would seem as if the ultimate aspiration was to eventually make available *all* of Dylan's unreleased material.[5] The motive for such an aspiration is difficult to ascertain, a cynical response might be to say that—in the absence of sufficient new material—the motive was to accumulate as much financial gain as possible—without concern for Dylan's reputation as a creative artist.[6] Hence, taking this into account, the main perspective of this book will focus on those songs written in the 1960s, the 1970s and into the 1980s.

The first chapter sets out the main theoretical stances to be taken; specifically the ways in which sexual and gendered identities are now perceived; this being attained within a discussion of issues pertaining to homosociality, and the idea of gender as a performative act. The second chapter looks in detail at the construct of masculinity in Dylan's work, examining the way masculinity has often been closely aligned to the idea of movement and travel, and the way the men in Dylan's songs continually appear to be trying to escape, to get "on the road," and hence to distance themselves from a domestic and predominantly feminine environment. The third chapter takes up the various ways in which women and femininity have been represented in Dylan's work; it considers what would at least appear to be a misogynistic discourse running throughout the gamut of Dylan's songs, and attempts to make sense of the complicated and often contradictory roles women play in Dylan's work.

The fourth chapter considers the ways in which Dylan's canon of work deals (or perhaps more pertinently, does not deal) with heterosexual relationships, with the conjoining of the masculine and the feminine; the chapter thus looks towards potentially homosocial and even homoerotic discursive practices, albeit within an almost wholly repressed arena of human sexuality. Finally, the fifth chapter examines the problematical aspect of identity within Dylan's cultural texts, at the common thread of a duality to identity within Dylan's work, and how a perception of this may point towards an explanation of the complicated "nature" of gender construction within Dylan's expansive canon.

In a sense, the study approaches Dylan's work from what might be described as a feminist perspective. The idea of appearing to take such an

Introduction

approach might now seem somewhat dated; nonetheless, it could be argued that it is possible to at least attempt to demonstrate a range of social and historical elements at play within such a theoretical context. For example, Dylan's career began in the early 1960s and proceeded onwards, throughout the twentieth century and beyond, and thus ran on a chronological and parallel track to the development of the contemporary feminist movement. Hence there are a number of parallels to be considered, a number of questions to be asked, a number of arguments to be challenged.

One of the main questions being, in what way does Dylan's work reflect and describe the sexual politics of his time, and what conclusions can be drawn from this? Furthermore, what can we say about the place Dylan's work inhabits within the greater context of gender constructs in Western society and culture, as we proceed through the first decades of the twenty-first century? It would seem self-evident that Bob Dylan's songs have hardly upheld a feminist ideology; however, the way in which his work has reacted to the feminist movement, to the changes inherent within society and culture, is one of the significant areas of discussion herein.

* * *

However, before beginning a discussion of Dylan's work, it would perhaps be important to attempt to determine just what that work might, in fact, consist of; in other words, to attempt to define the textual derivation of Dylan's work. The fact that Dylan has always worked in what is primarily an oral medium raises a number of hermeneutic considerations. Primarily, it means that there is an issue in possessing a complete confidence in the published transcriptions of Dylan's work. In other words, it is problematic to attempt to ascertain precisely how much control the author, himself, has extended over the transcription and the publication of his work. On the one hand, Bob Gottlieb, the publisher of *Writings and Drawings* (the precursor of *Lyrics 1962-1985*), seemed to suggest that Dylan had had a significant role in the editorial process, stating:

> At the time that this [*Writings and Drawings*] came to me as a publishing project the manuscript was complete. Bob demanded, and had every right to have, complete artistic control over his book. No editorial changes were made in the text.... Bob was involved in all its aspects and phases.... I know it wasn't a rushed, overnight piece of hysteria, because too many books happen that way and I can recognise the signs. There was nothing sloppy or careless or rushed or hysterical about this. It seemed to me very carefully worked, and I imagine over quite a period of time.[7]

Introduction

Nonetheless, a careful scrutiny of *Writings and Drawings* (together with its successor: *Lyrics 1962-1985*) would seem to belie this claim. There were numerous inconsistencies and numerous examples of what can only be described as "sloppy" and "careless" transcriptions. While there were some instances in which it seemed Dylan (or at least one presumes it was he) could clearly be seen to be carefully revising his past work; for example, the subtle and circumspectly made changes to "Sad Eyed Lady of the Lowlands" (1966),[8] there were other instances when it seemed clear that other presences, other editorial actors, could be seen as struggling to transcribe an oral performance to the written page, without any kind of guidance other than their own auditory senses. As Clinton Heylin, discussing this same general point, and talking specifically of the song "Caribbean Wind" (1981), commented:

> As a further insult, the version in *Lyrics* has been so badly transcribed that "Redeemed men" have become "Arabian men"—"Were we sniper bait?" actually a great line, has become "Did we snap at bait?" and "chrome brown eyes" are now "lone brown eyes."[9]

There were numerous other such examples, ranging from the risible, in "Precious Angel" (1979), the line "And you torch up the night" being transcribed as: "And you touch up the night,"[10] to the mundane, wherein "Blowin' in the Wind" (1963) had verses two and three somewhat incomprehensibly placed out of order.[11]

It would seem obvious that there was a relationship between performed and transcribed material, and, although it is problematical to be fully aware what this relationship may have been, it is nonetheless important to be aware of such textual ambiguity in Dylan's work. In this sense, one must be clear in recognizing that Dylan's published work—either in book form, or in online format—does not offer a completely accurate written repository of Dylan's oral performances; instead it merely offers an approximation, an approximation deriving from a number of different and indeterminate sources—and not necessarily from Dylan himself. While this need not be seen as being wholly disadvantageous, it does require a certain way of thinking when approaching Dylan's work. As Neil Corcoran has commented:

> We must believe that a collection of published lyrics has little real "authority," even if it has been "authorised" by Dylan himself. The real authority of a Dylan song resides in the moment of its performed utterance, which is always now and always new, a collapsing of past and present, spontaneous and instinctive, happening on the air and in the ear; a change of lyric, a new rhythm, a variation in melody, even an altered inflection, and the song may insist an altogether other meaning and scope ... the song changes, it adapts, it refuses the consolation of the finished in favour of a poetics of process, of constant renewal, of performance rather than publication.[12]

Introduction

One is therefore left with the sense that "a song is always a performance,"[13] and some of the most interesting writers on Dylan have seen his work in this way. Paul Williams' trilogy of books on Dylan eloquently makes the point that Bob Dylan is less a songwriter and more a performing artist,[14] Betsy Bowden refers to Dylan's work as "performed literature," while John Herdman, has commented:

> [Dylan] is one of the first major artists to be emancipated from the visually determined sense of permanence and unalterability in the work of art. His songs are not fixed for all time in the forms in which he first recorded them; but it took critics a while to get used to the extent of the remakings he was ready to impose on them, for the assumption of total freedom which underlies this activity implies the principles of a new aesthetic.[15]

In search of a new aesthetic, we are still left with the question of where does the real text lie. Stephen Scobie, agreeing in part with Corcoran, has concluded that the definitive Dylan text is:

> The accumulation of all performances in the song's total history ... the text is not a fixed set of words or music but a fluid space, a performance area, which sets out a musical and thematic field within which any one version can only be provisional.[16]

There may be some credibility to this approach, but there are practical difficulties and constraints to be considered in accepting such a proposition; one of the most exacting problems relating to the fact that Dylan remains both a living and prolifically performing artist. To put this into some kind of perspective, it has been calculated that, between 1974 and 1987, Dylan performed a total of 485 concerts.[17] According to Clinton Heylin, of these 485 concerts, only twenty-seven escaped being recorded for posterity by members of the audience, the "hardcore fans," whom Heylin described as an "international network of like minded obsessives." As to the number of concerts Dylan performed prior to 1974, a full record is not available; however, it would appear to be in excess of several hundred more live performances. In addition to this, the situation becomes still more problematical insomuch as Dylan has continued to tour since 1987, performing consistently, at least an average of a hundred concerts per year. To put this another way, on average there would appear to be a Bob Dylan concert taking place, somewhere in the world, once every three or four days; and, as the vast majority (if not all) of these concerts rapidly become available, via unofficial recordings—in audio and often video representations—then one has to ask if there is sufficient time available to spend approximately two hours, once every three or four days, to assimilate and critically assess such performances.[18] Thus, without seeming to lack the scholar's sense of zeal towards his or her subject, one might negate any intention of joining this band of "like minded obsessives" and of finding the ultimate Dylan text from this perspective; the "never-ending tour" would here threaten to become the never-ending task of scholarship.

Hence, for the scope of this study, this present book will resist any attempt to encompass such a vastly ambitious arena of interpretation, the extent of such an enterprise simply being too expansive to undertake.[19] Therefore, by way of avoiding such a predicament, this study will restrict a critical consideration of Dylan's work primarily to that of the officially released studio recordings. In addition, whatever its limitations, *Lyrics 1962–1985*—together with its online derivative—would appear to remain at least a rudimentary source of reference, serving as a basic guide in attempting to procure some kind of textual referencing point. However, for the sake of consistency, when the performed text and the published text clearly differ, this will be noted—and the textual variation will be alluded to. It perhaps has to be acknowledged that there is no ultimate text to a Bob Dylan song, but that the closest we can claim to attain, as a definitive text, would be via the original recording and performance itself.[20]

* * *

Incidentally, and by way of a final comment on the textual authority of Dylan's songs, it should be noted that, under the restraints of copyright permissions, all quoted lyrics derive from the transcriptions on Dylan's official website: www.bobdylan.com. This poses something of a problem, insomuch as, from a certain point of view, this online source would seem to be inferior to previous text based sources. It would appear, at times, to be almost partway to being grammatically illiterate; for example, all end of line punctuation would appear to have been deleted, the carefully crafted structure of songs in previously published materials being lost.[21] However, this is the source that must be quoted, and I would beg the understanding of the reader in accepting this compromise. Such a restriction also reduces, for example, the scope of homophonic ambiguity, one of the "little treasures" to be found within Dylan's work. One thinks of "Can You Please Crawl Out Your Window" (1965) wherein the genocide fools were attempting to arrange the religion of the *little tin women*—or were they?—perhaps it was the religion of the *lilting women*. Likewise, in "Shelter from the Storm" (1975) it was ambivalent whether the newborn babies were wailing like *mourning* or *morning* doves. Also, in "When the Night Comes Falling from the Sky" (1985), it was ambivalent whether the thousands who could have overcome the darkness were pre-

Introduction

vented from so doing because of a *lousy buck*—or because of a *lousy book*. In each case the former is sanctioned as the official version, but in each case the latter version might be seen as a viable alternative. In any case, to many listeners Dylan's songs remain oral texts, as they seldom trouble to read the lyrics; the official transcription may suggest one textual signifier—but a significant part of Dylan's audience will merely hear what they hear.[22]

* * *

In attempting to assess Dylan's artistic and cultural significance, as intimated in the opening sentence of this Introduction, the issue of originality would seem to be of relevance. In recent years—with the rise of the Internet—Dylan's work has been increasingly challenged for the lack of just this quality, for its lack of originality; in other words, there have been repeated accusations of plagiarism.[23] In the age of the Internet and online search engines some of Dylan's "borrowings" from other sources have become more and more transparent. Hence to many people, Joni Mitchell included, such changes in the way we can access information has revealed Dylan to be a "fake."[24] How accurate such an estimation may be is open to question, but a recourse to technology might potentially be of use: there is a piece of software, used in higher education, called Turnitin; it was created in 1997, on the cusp of widespread online research, and was aimed at checking student essays and dissertations for unacknowledged citations, this being accomplished via comparison to a vast database of previously published works. At a certain level, it has been successful, acting as a deterrent against blatant plagiarism; and, as such, one might speculate how interesting it might be to subject Dylan's entire corpus of work to Turnitin—the results would no doubt be revealing. However, this would not seem to be justifiable; insomuch as Dylan is not a student submitting an academic assignment, and he has not signed a "Declaration of Academic Integrity," instead he is an artist—working in whatever way he chooses—not bound by the rigor of academic conventions. However, in the age of more efficient plagiaristic detection, it would appear that valid questions have been raised as to the overarching originality of Dylan's work; and hence his reputation has been affected, some would say to a significant extent.

In his liner notes to the album, *The Times They Are A-Changin'*, Dylan famously referred to himself as a "thief of thoughts," and in this sense it is self-evident that all cultural productions derive from an intertextual melange—as will be discussed later in this book. It is clear that Dylan has always participated, like any writer, in such a process. For example, he has used the Bible,[25] he has used the folk tradition,[26] and he has used a wide range of other diverse influences throughout his work. It is not possible to encompass anywhere except a small number of intertextual examples, but nonetheless, the following instances might be mentioned:

"A Hard Rain's A-Gonna Fall" and W.H. Auden's poem "The Witness"
"One Too Many Mornings" and the bush ballad "The Banks of the Columbine"
"Love Is Just a Four Letter Word" and Tennessee Williams' play *Cat on a Hot Tin Roof*
"Stuck Inside of Mobile" and the first century BCE Latin writer Publilius Syrus[27]
"Tears of Rage"/"Too Much of Nothing" and Shakespeare's *King Lear*
"Dear Landlord" and the Greek playwright Euripides[28]
"New Morning" and Wordsworth's "The Prelude"
"Time Passes Slowly" and Thomas Moore's poem "The Last Rose of Summer"
"Forever Young" and Keats' "Ode to a Grecian Urn"
"Lily, Rosemary and the Jack of Hearts" and W.H. Auden's poem "Victor"
"Black Diamond Bay" and Joseph Conrad's novel *Victory*
"Blind Willie McTell" and Billie Holiday's song "Strange Fruit"
"Lovesick" and *Hamlet*

Such a list could go on for longer—much longer—and such a practice would be wholly valid—it is what all writers have always done.

However, a problem arises when one considers some of the other appropriations that Dylan appears to have been making. As Clinton Heylin noted:

It seems Dylan had been dipping into the poetry of that second-rate Civil War wordsmith [Henry Timrod] on his recent chart-topping collection, *Modern Times*. Having in recent years been accused of plagiarizing the works of Jack London and an obscure Japanese gangster memoir, *Confessions of a Yakuza* (1991).[29]

Dylan himself was eventually to comment on the supposed controversy, talking to *Rolling Stone* magazine, in 2012, he said this:

In folk and jazz quotation is a rich and enriching tradition. That certainly is true. It's true for everybody, but me. There are different rules for me. And as far as Henry Timrod is concerned, have you even heard of him? Who's been reading him lately.... Ask his descendents what they think of the hoopla.... It's called song-writing. It has to do with melody and rhythm, and then after that, anything goes. You make everything yours. We all do it.[30]

Dylan claims that "this" was "called song-writing," that "anything goes" and that "we all do it." In fact, it would seem that most songwriters do *not* do this; that is, they at least attempt to produce material with some degree of conscious originality. Dylan has accumulated an estimated wealth of $175 million, derived in large part from copyright properties, properties he rig-

Introduction

orously preserves. However, the question then arises as to whether such copyright properties have been correctly contrived. For example, in writing this book, there have been constant doubts as to whether sections have been fully cited—wherein it is problematical to know if it is one's own work, or whether it is a forgotten source of research. This is part of the process of writing; however, there has been no purposeful attempt to use the work of other authors. From the evidence presented it would seem difficult to deny that Dylan has been doing just this—and, in the age of the Internet, he has been found out—far from being "hoopla," as Dylan calls it, this would seem to have been deliberate misappropriation.

Earlier in his career, when he did not possess such influence and prestige, Dylan was also "found out." There are known instances of successful settlements over infringements of copyright; for example, Dylan's use of Jean Richie's tune and arrangement of "Nottamun Town" for his own song "Masters of War." As Clinton Heylin, in his informative book on copyright usage in pop music, *It's One for the Money: The Song Snatchers Who Carved Up a Century of Pop and Sparked a Musical Revolution*, put it:

> Richie felt no qualms about claiming her share of the spoils; she went after Witmark [Dylan's music publisher in the early 1960s], who wisely settled the matter quietly, according to one of the more unreliable Dylan biographers, for $5,000.[31]

In a similar way, it is well known that Dylan based "Don't Think Twice, It's All Right" on a song Paul Clayton had recorded in 1959, "Who's Gonna Buy You Ribbons," in this case Dylan had used both melody and lyrics; according to Heylin:

> In the end, Clayton settled for a pittance—supposedly no more than $500 ... The spat soured Dylan's and Clayton's relationship for a number of months and was probably due for Dylan's decision to leave another early masterpiece, "Percy's Song," off his third album. The song was another to borrow heavily from a Clayton recording, albeit the resolutely traditional "The Wind and the Rain."[32]

Whether Dylan was subject to other legal action is not clear, no other cases are known; although other offended parties certainly threatened to do so. A famous instance being that of Brendan Behan, who commented, in the 1970s, when Dylan was complaining about being bootlegged, that: "Bob Dylan should know everything about piracy" and that "'With God on our Side' takes music lock stock and barrel and very nearly the words [of my song in what] is a complete parody of 'The Patriot Game.'"[33] Whatever other cases may have existed, it would seem that thereafter Dylan was more circumspect in his acquisition of sources, at least in instances wherein he thought he might be challenged; as Heylin put it: "One thing that could be said in Dylan's defence was that ever since his difficulties at the end of 1963 he had been careful—real careful."[34] In a defense of such charges, one could revert to truisms around the topic; for example, such sayings as: "Anything worth doing has already been done"[35]—"Originality is undetected plagiarism"[36]—and, perhaps most pertinently, "Immature poets imitate, mature poets steal."[37] From a theoretical perspective a more generous word to employ might be that of *bricolage*, a term used in postmodern theory, referring to cultural constructions made from a diverse range of available items, deriving from the French for "do it yourself." Claude Levi Strauss went so far as to suggest that the word *bricoleur* might be a more accurate term than author, in that it did not suggest creation out of nothing, but instead the rearranging of existing materials.[38] Insomuch, the author of the text was no longer seen as the sole arbiter—instead, a mere arranger of materials; an inventive and creative synthesizer of cultural sources—a maker of cultural collage.[39]

However, the latest controversy (at least at the time of writing) concerning Dylan's acceptance speech for the Nobel Prize for Literature (on June 4, 2017—several months late) would seem to have taken the issue of potential plagiarism to a level of almost complete risibility. According to a number of websites, there would seem to be clear and direct evidence that Dylan plagiarized portions of his speech from the SparkNotes from *Moby Dick*. SparkNotes being an online version of CliffsNotes, a series of student study guides; guides that paraphrased literary classics—in other words, a means by which a student might write an essay about a book they had not actually read. The idea that Dylan would do this suggested a mixture of stupidity, arrogance and, indeed, pathos. Using undergraduate study notes to draft a lecture for the Nobel Prize for literature did have an element of pathos—not to say bathos as well; although it should be noted that the speech nonetheless fulfilled the prerequisites for the monetary award that accompanied the prize, some $900,000. Whether Dylan has actually read Melville's epic novel, or whether he merely read the notes, is anyone's guess.

* * *

However, disregarding such reservations, Bob Dylan remains a complex, subtle and eminently serious writer; mercurial and capricious in his art, in his dealings with his audience, with the media and with the world in general; he remains an artist difficult to define; in addition to this, the arena in which he has chosen to work within (song-writing) poses problematical issues for literary and cultural criticism. Nonetheless, disregarding these difficulties and complications, Dylan's work has had much to say about the anxieties and tensions inherent within American society and culture, in the latter half of the twentieth and into the twenty-first century. It must be admitted that much of Dylan's more engaging work derives from early in his career, and yet he remains, one might argue, an artist fully deserving of in-depth study. In his landmark book, *Literary Theory: An Introduction*, Terry Eagleton famously (or perhaps infamously) claimed that: "literary theory can handle Bob Dylan just as well as John Milton."[40] Eagleton did not trouble himself to demonstrate how this might be accomplished in practice; however, one of the aims of this study will be to demonstrate just how this claim might be put into practice; in other words, the ways in which Dylan's work can be "handled" within the discursive practices of literary and cultural theory.

1

Theoretical Approaches

"I would rather model harmonica holders than discuss aztec anthropology and english literature."
—Bob Dylan, liner notes
to *Bringing It All Back Home*

  The history of literary theory, or critical theory, cultural theory, or even simply "theory"—as it has come to be known—is a longer one than might be expected. According to Terry Eagleton, the origins of literary theory, in the twentieth century at least,[1] can be traced back to the publication, in 1917, of Viktor Shklovsky's "pioneering essay" entitled "Art as a Device," one of the earliest works of Russian formalism.[2] Eagleton has also argued that theory had much of its roots in the 1960s, in the age of civil rights, the student movement, the women's movement—together with other political undercurrents; according to Eagleton, in his book, *After Theory*, the women's movement "altered much of the climate of the West almost beyond recognition."[3] In addition, some of the older theories (other than formalism) were still present in the 1960s; the obvious cases in point being Marxist and psychoanalytic criticism, both of which had first been pioneered around the 1930s, but both would be seen afresh in the 1960s.[4] There was also the sense in which literary theory was originally an offspring of developments in linguistics,[5] which had led to the rise of structuralism in the 1950s, and which would eventually lead to poststructuralist and deconstruction theory in the later years of the 1960s.

  From a more specific perspective, the year 1968 would come to be seen as the time when theory took hold, specifically with the advent of what came to be seen as poststructuralist thought. As Eagleton put it:

> Poststructuralism is, among other things, a kind of theoretical hangover from the failed uprising of '68—a way of keeping the revolution warm at the level of language, blending the euphoric libertarianism of that moment with the stoical melancholia of its aftermath.[6]

In other words, with the failure of Marxism as a valid political system in the West, intellectual thought had to find other means of expression. The student uprisings (most significantly in France), in May 1968, had seemed to come close to overturning the state, but in the end did not succeed. Hence Marxist theory seemed of less relevance, and instead of the traditional interest in class struggle, there was an emergence of an interest in sexuality and in the seemingly nihilistic concepts found in deconstruction theory. As Eagleton put it: "The emancipation which had failed in the streets and factories, could be acted out instead in erotic intensities or the floating signifier."[7] In this way, intellectual thought—post 1968—turned to other arenas; theory offering Western intellectual thought a refuge from the reality and seeming squalor of life in the twentieth and into the twenty-first centuries. As such, theory could be interpreted as offering a reflection, in Eagleton's words, of a "guilty self-loathing" of Western liberal thought.[8]

By the early 1980s, university courses in the UK, in America and in Europe had begun to incorporate literary theory into their syllabuses.[9] However, this was not universally accepted in all academic institutions, especially in some of the more traditional universities, so much so that there was something approaching a civil war in the discipline of the humanities, of the arts and of cultural studies.[10] Christopher Ricks was at the forefront of this controversy; to put it mildly, Ricks was not an academic in favor of theory, as he put it: "Obviously, no one objects to the presence of structuralists and theorists of film linguistics in the English faculty. But there is a question of proportion. It is our job to teach and uphold the canon of English Literature."[11] In 1981, Ricks was one of several academics who opposed Colin MacCabe's appointment as a permanent lecturer at Cambridge University. MacCabe was a strong proponent of theory; and, as Peter Barry put it: "The result was a public argument about how English should be taught at universities, with eminent figures from the English Faculty publicly taking sides."[12] Nonetheless, throughout the 1980s theory seemed to gain more and more ground; and it has been suggested that the celebrated "Linguistics of Writing" conference of 1987, at Strathclyde University (where MacCabe had relocated after being denied tenure at Cambridge), may have been the zenith as to the influence of literary theory in academia. As Barry concurred: "In retrospect, the conference seems [to have been] the point when theory reached the height of its glamour and success."[13]

However, three specific events occurred in the late 1980s, and into the 1990s, that appeared to inflict significant damage to the reputation of literary

1. Theoretical Approaches

theory. Firstly, there was the so-called Paul de Man scandal; it was revealed, in 1988, that the Belgium born de Man, then one of the foremost literary theorists in America, had been a Nazi sympathiser during World War II—and that he had written, in "an act of unspeakable moral shabbiness,"[14] a number of blatantly anti–Semitic articles. As Peter Barry put it, although the case was shocking, "it was not primarily the personal guilt or otherwise of de Man which damaged the standing of deconstruction and of literary theory in general, but the grounds on which other theorists attempted to defend him."[15] Barry went on:

> Literary theory ... was seriously compromised by the de Man affair, and thereafter it never quite recovered its prestige, its confidence and its sense of moral and political rectitude.[16]

Writing in the early 1990s, the writer and poet David Lehman concurred, suggesting that the affair had caused "a downturn in the fortunes of critical theory in the academic marketplace."[17] Lehman went on to claim:

> The era of deconstruction is over. It has had its day and we can return with a clear conscious to the warmer more human work of writing about power, history, ideology, the institution of the study of literature, the class struggle, the oppression of women, the real loves of men and women in society as they exist in themselves and as they are reflected in literature.[18]

The second controversial event occurred in 1991, when Jean Baudrillard, then one of the key postmodern theorists, made the satiric claim that the Gulf War of 1990–1991 had not, in fact, taken place at all. Baudrillard's satirical stance was not fully appreciated in the general mass-media—to such an extent that, as Peter Barry put it:

> [Baudrillard] became the whipping-boy of anti-theorists and the target for high-moral-ground condemnations of postmodernism, which was now, in the 1990s, being seen as representative of literary theory in general.[19]

However, the third, and perhaps most damaging scandal to impact on the reputation of theory, was the publication of an article by Alan Sokal, a physics professor at New York University, in 1996. The article was published in *Social Text*, Duke University's postmodern cultural studies journal. Sokal's article, "Transgressing the Boundaries: Towards a Transformative Hermeneutics of Quantum Gravity," was a deliberate hoax, a risible piece of work, designed to ridicule some of the excesses of cultural theorists. On the day the article was published, Sokal published an article in a different journal, *Lingua Franca*, revealing the hoax and "arguing that the acceptance of the original piece exposed the vacuity of postmodernist theory, and, by implication, all cultural theory."[20] Sokal went on to write a book (with Jean Bricamont) about the affair, *Intellectual Impostures*, published in 1997. Peter Barry would comment that:

> The book and the article are not a wholesale attack of postmodern theory (though they were widely taken to be that) but an exposure of the misuse of ideas derived from physics and mathematics by prominent French theorists, notably Lacan, Kristeva, Irigaray, Baudrillard, Deleuze and Guattari and others.[21]

As Barry suggests, in reality the hoax did not lay as much as a proverbial punch on the *intellectual* reputation of cultural theory, but it did succeed in demonstrating some of the more absurd concepts of some theorists; and also, how the editors of such a prestigious journal were unable to see through such a self-evident hoax. In the end the scandal resulted in a "humiliation of postmodern theory"[22] from which it has arguably never fully recovered.

* * *

In a wider and a more general sense, theory might be envisaged as a complex and shifting area of thought, one much more characterized by conflict than by consensus; theory being merely an attempt to understand a world that is perhaps ultimately impossible to fully understand. Theory signals speculation, it suggests difficulty and ambiguity, together with a wholly open-minded way of looking at the world. It challenges many of our so-called common-sense truths; for example, the idea that the meaning of a text resides in the mind of the author; that human beings are independent entities—rather than constructed subjects of social and linguistic forces; it also challenges the absurd notion that *anything* is natural. In the case of the latter claim, nearly everything we accept as natural, when analyzed, can be seen to be a cultural construct—if theory has succeeded in nothing else it has succeeded in providing a "pugnacious critique of common sense."[23] Theory questions everything, the most basic assumptions we have of anything. Theory has little interest in giving "rise to harmonious solutions,"[24] in its own quixotic way theory has always been intent on refusing the idea that there were any solutions, instead theory has consistently offered "the prospect of further thought."[25] However, theory has always allowed a view of the world that is classless, genderless, non-racist, non-sexist—a universal sense of equality for all. In essence, theory has offered a much-needed antidote to all that is mundane, all that is dogmatic, all that is fundamentalist, all that would seek to enchain creative and intellectual enquiry.

1. Theoretical Approaches

Thus it might be fair to say—whether we acknowledge it or not—that we live in a world of theory; or at least this is the assumption that will be made in approaching Bob Dylan's work within this present study. A world of theory in which the following notions are upheld: that politics is pervasive, that language is constitutive, that truth is provisional, that meaning is contingent, and—perhaps most significantly—and as suggested above—that human nature is a myth.[26] In a world upholding such notions, many ideas previously unquestioned and unchallenged can be put into question, and thus it becomes possible to put almost anything into question. Instead of somehow "being there" in the "real world," diverse attitudes can now be seen as mere constructs, constructs dependent on a diverse array of social, cultural and political forces, all mingled together within differing and shifting ways of seeing and thinking. Therefore, if theory can be seen as putting almost anything into question, then logically it can put sexual and gender identity, the main subject area of this study, into question.

* * *

It would seem fair to say that heterosexuality still possesses a putative sense of authenticity within contemporary society; in other words it is still widely assumed to be the ideal of erotic correctness. A powerful component of this argument lies within its link with sexual reproduction; in other words, because heterosexuality appears to be so closely associated with procreation, it also appears to be "normal" and hence, almost inevitable. However, the change of heterosexual behavior away from a "reproductive norm" towards a "pleasure norm" could be seen as at least putting this claim into dispute. It would thus seem valid to say that heterosexual activity has become *almost* as non-productive as homosexual activity. In Jonathan Ned Katz's words: "few people now, except the Pope, judge the quality of heterosexual relationships by their fecundity."[27] Thus, such sexual acts of fellatio and cunnilingus, or vaginal and anal intercourse, would be variously the same, whether they took place between man and woman, man and man, woman and woman, or between transgendered couples; and if these acts were routinely practiced by heterosexual as well as so-called "gay," lesbian and transgendered couples, then a blurring of distinction between these categories could not help but occur. To put this in another way, if the genitals were no longer seen primarily as generative organs, but rather as sources of pleasure, then the binary opposition of heterosexuality and homosexuality would appear to have broken down, at least to a certain degree. Insomuch, heterosexual sex would seem to be as much about pair bonding as it was about reproducing the species, and hence it might be seen as less a biological imperative and more a socially constructed edifice. Furthermore, if reproductive sex as the norm has been replaced by what might be called a "different-sex erotic norm" it would seem fair to agree with Katz when he states:

> If non-procreative heterosexuality is legitimated, it's difficult to understand why a non-procreative homosexuality should not also be approved.[28]

Heterosexuality is a hybrid word, made up of Greek and Latin, from the Greek *heteros*, "other" and the Latin *sexus*, "sex," although it is arguable whether the Greeks would have been able to say quite what it was. In ancient Greek culture it was known that men and women produced children, but it was also openly accepted that sexual desire existed between individuals of the same gender. It was a society and a culture that openly appreciated the corporeal designs of the male body; it was a society and a culture in which sexual relations between males (usually an older and a younger man) were acceptable forms of behavior, a world in which a man could enjoy sexual acts with a wife—but also with fellow males. To take this line of thought further, and to claim that heterosexuality is a relatively modern fabrication, would seem to go against "common sense." Yet if it is possible to argue heterosexuality only has meaning when in binary opposition to homosexuality, then this claim might not seem so illogical. It is now accepted that homosexuality *is* a relatively recent concept, that the idea of a person *being* homosexual dates back only as far as the late 19th century. To be precise: the term "homosexual" is said to have been first coined by the Hungarian writer, Karoly Maria Benkert, in 1869.[29] At this time, it was argued, homosexuality stopped being what people did and became who they were. As Lynne Segal put it:

> Homosexuality and subsequently heterosexuality were not invented as sexual categories and used publicly, until the very end of the nineteenth century. Before then, it is suggested, there were references to various types of sex acts and sexualized parts of the body, but not the idea of sexuality as an inner force or essence.[30]

In a similar manner, Gore Vidal has stated that "heterosexual" and "homosexual" should be considered as adjectives and not as nouns:

> There is no such thing as a homosexual or a heterosexual person. There are only homo- or heterosexual acts. Most people are a mixture of impulses if not practices, and what anyone does with a willing partner is of no social or cosmic significance. So, why all the fuss? In order for a ruling class to rule, there must be arbitrary prohibitions. Of all prohibitions, sexual taboo is the most useful because sex involves everyone … we

1. Theoretical Approaches

have allowed our governors to divide the population into two teams. One team is good, godly, straight; the other is evil, sick, vicious.[31]

Why all the fuss, Vidal asks, but one might also ask: why all the sense of fear and loathing as well? According to French "gay" theorist, Guy Hocquenghem:

> The problem is not so much homosexual desire as the fear of homosexuality: why does the mere mention of the word trigger off reactions of recoil and hate?[32]

This would seem to have been a valid question: why do so many men recoil with disgust at the thought of a man performing a sexual act with another man? Why, for example, is it less acceptable to see two men having sex with each other, than to see two men causing violence to each other; or, in an extreme case, killing each other. On an elementary level this could be explained by the idea that masculinity is defined by little else than by not being feminine. As Terry Eagleton put it:

> Man is what he is only by ceaselessly shutting out this other or opposite, defining himself in antithesis to it. Woman is the image of what he is not, and therefore an essential reminder of what he is.[33]

Thus a man, according to what might be described as a homophobic hegemony, was only a man if he had sex with a woman, a man could not be a "man" if he had sex with another man. In these terms masculinity requires men to be active and not passive, that men must penetrate and not be penetrated. If this was contradicted then the whole sense of masculine identity, the whole sense of being a man, would no longer seem to be tenable.

In addition to such theoretical approaches, some of the field research on sexuality, carried out in the twentieth century, mostly in America, might be of use here. For example, Alfred Kinsey's book, *Sexual Behavior in the Human Male* (1948), was based on a detailed survey of some 18,000 men and women. Kinsey plotted the frequency and incidence of masturbation, premarital coitus, marital coitus, extramarital coitus, homosexuality and other sexual acts. Kinsey's findings proved shocking for traditional moralists: masturbation was "nearly universal,"[34] nine out of ten men had sex before marriage, half of married men had affairs, over one third of adult males admitted to at least one homosexual experience,[35] and 95 percent of respondents had—in some way—"violated the law" on their way to orgasm. Kinsey revealed the reality of human sexuality to be at odds to supposed publicly espoused norms.[36] Kinsey's book, and others to follow, had significant social and cultural effects, if most married couples had extramarital sex then affairs became more socially accepted, the increased divorce rate most likely had a connection with this. Also, the fact that one third of men had admitted to homosexual encounters may have contributed to a greater acceptance of same-sex relationships, to the emergence of so-called gay rights and to the development of a more obvious "gay" subculture.[37] Aretha Franklin may have sung: "You make me feel like a natural woman," but a natural woman was a social and cultural product, "the product of underlying economic relations and ongoing power struggles."[38] In terms of sexuality, there was no such thing as a natural woman, a natural man, or a natural anything for that matter; sexuality was a continuum—not a fixed, static set of binary oppositions, not "a self-evident fact."[39] As Marjorie Garber put it: "The world is flat. The sun revolves around the earth. Human beings are either heterosexual or homosexual."[40]

However, there nonetheless remains a pronounced sense of homophobia inherent within society, not least as present within the songs of Bob Dylan, as will be seen. One of the more subtle ways of explaining this might be to look to the work of Eve Kosofsky Sedgwick. Sedgwick, a highly theoretical, Foucauldian influenced scholar, posited the idea that patriarchy requires intense male homosocial bonding; and the reason why the boundaries between homosociality and same-sex eroticism were so vigilantly maintained was because of the perilously close relationship between the two concepts. In other words, the privilege granted to male and male relations stood in dangerous proximity to the very homosexuality that patriarchal fellowship was obliged to condemn. Furthermore, there was a special relationship, in any male-dominated society, between male homosocial desire (including deeply repressed homosexual desire) and the structures for maintaining patriarchal power, something men within such societies would find discomforting—should they be required to confront this—which, of course, they do not.[41] Thus, for example, male sport manages at the same time to be both intensely homophobic and intensely homoerotic, predominantly such physically tactile sports as boxing and rugby were latently homoerotic, but importantly this latent homoeroticism was deniable.[42] Sedgwick claimed that male-to-male desire was legitimated on a homosocial basis, involving men working in a patriarchal league with one another; but to ensure men retained their social pre-eminence, these structures of oppression had to be firmly maintained.[43]

One of the other influential critics in the area of gender theory, in recent years, has been Judith Butler. In a sense Butler also perceived of heterosexuality as a means by which men retain power in society; her work attempted to "denaturalise the heterosexual matrix," to question and to interrogate the heterosexual matrix, culminating in her famous claim that "sex may have been gender all along."[44] The distinction between the terms sex and gender are now well known, but may be defined as follows: sex was determined by nature while gender was molded by culture; sex being the biological referent, the chromosomal constituents of the body's cellular structure; while gender was the parallel cultural term, the multiple classifications of bodies that occur within a social and cultural space. This was, and is, a significant element in any discussion of gender theory, as Roger Horrocks put it:

> Men and women are not biological brute facts, but social and political constructions ... gender involves the absorption of a set of very complex interlocking unconscious myths about men and women, how they should behave, think, feel, dress, work, make love, speak, and so on."[45]

A whole cultural edifice has been built upon the premise that gender *does* proceed from sex. However, Judith Butler's work has questioned such a seemingly self-evident proposition: does gender proceed from sex or does it proceed from something else, and if so, what might this be? In addition, and within an epicene discourse, Butler has questioned whether erotic identity was, in fact, specific to one's sexed body. Butler argued this may not be the case, and instead argued how one's erotic identity could be described as a fluid phenomenon, a fluid phenomenon that extended across a complex collection of gendered meanings. Butler theorized that a diverse range of sexual identities might be envisaged, that there were different versions of masculinity and femininity; and that these were not necessarily grounded in the anatomical distinction between the sexes. As Butler put it:

> When the constructed status of gender is theorised as radically independent of sex, gender itself becomes a free-floating artifice, with the consequence that man and masculine might just as easily signify a female body as a male one, and woman and feminine a male body as easily as a female one.[46]

Butler suggested that there may be many masculinities, many femininities, casting doubt on the very idea that "sex" should be designated as a phenomena grounded in nature. Insomuch, Butler argued that heterosexuality was a mere impersonation of an original natural form that had, in fact, never existed; and that heterosexuality was a pastiche, a masquerade, "an ongoing process of construction, performance [and] mimicry."[47] In the discursive arena of such an argument heterosexuality became virtually impossible to fully encompass, so much so that it became, in Butler's words: "an inevitable comedy, a constant parody of itself."[48]

* * *

An important issue to consider, when reading Judith Butler, is the difficulty of her writing; Butler's texts are "linguistically as well as conceptually demanding."[49] So much so, that she has previously been voted as one of the worst of academic writers: "for the most stylistically lamentable passages found in scholarly books and articles."[50] However, it is possible to consider her prose style as being "strategically and *deliberately* challenging rather than the symptom of a muddled mind."[51] In other words, while it is often difficult to fully understand what Butler is saying, this could be seen as a part of the "spirit of open-endedness and lack of resolution or closure" in her work.[52] In addition, Butler's work was influenced by such philosophers as Hegel,[53] Foucault, Derrida and Kristeva, all of whom were hardly the most approachable of writers to read, to attempt to understand, to confront. Nonetheless, Butler remains "*the* queer theorist par excellence"[54] no matter how difficult her theoretical models may be, the core of her work providing some of the most convincing arguments with which to approach the complex issue of gender—as in the case of the discussion of Bob Dylan's work here—and in a wider arena as well.

* * *

In terms of a Butlerian reading, it was because heterosexuality was such a "given"—the love that *need* not speak its name—to misquote Oscar Wilde—that it has remained almost invisible. Heterosexuality has seldom been questioned; it has been thought of as "natural" simply because it has always been assumed to be immutably grounded within a biological certainty. In terms of a poststructuralist approach, heterosexuality might thus be seen as one of the last remaining fixed values to be called into question. As Jonathan Ned Katz put it:

> Heterosexuality, we usually assume, is as old as procreation, as ancient as the lust of the fallen Eve and Adam. Heterosexuality, we imagine, is essential, unchanging: ahistorical. That hypothesis is our ordinary, unexamined starting point when we think about heterosexuality—if we think about it.[55]

However, so-called "deviant" versions of sexuality would now seem to be more and more accepted in mainstream society—to the extent of being celebrated for their differences. In fact, celebrated to such an extent that such differing

1. Theoretical Approaches

versions of sexuality could now be seen as acting against, and resisting, the rigid, patriarchal hegemony of sexual politics—a hegemony that has ruled for so long. In this way, heterosexuality could be said to have ceased being accepted as the "natural" state of affairs. In contrast, it has become a fragmented concept, to paraphrase Michel Foucault, it has become a mere ideological maneuver. As postmodernism has been seen as questioning and interrogating the *grand narratives*, all the accepted "big stories" of western culture; in this way "queer theory" could be seen as questioning and interrogating the ideological investments of heterosexuality as "normal," as "natural," as a "given." When the distinction between heterosexuality and homosexuality is revealed for what it is: a mere social and cultural construct, when the idea of something being "natural, normal and given" is stripped away, then a different picture could be seen as beginning to emerge.

In this context, such ideas of sex and gender, of masculinity and femininity, of homosexuality and heterosexuality, will be used, within this study, to inform a discussion of Bob Dylan's textual work. Such a discussion, it might be argued, may reveal a number of significant thematic elements present within much of Dylan's work, thematic elements that have seldom been offered the attention they perhaps deserve. For example, the ways in which sex and gender can now be seen as having more fluid properties, might potentially be seen as a way of expanding an interpretation of Dylan's work, and might therefore assist in undermining the naturalistic assumptions often made in approaching this work, thus creating a more constructive interplay of ideas in which the reader (or listener) approaches Dylan's work. Bob Dylan's songs operate in a dialectical way: a surface ideology wherein the conscious, natural, common-sense and obvious events take place; however, such songs also operate beneath the surface, wherein the silences and absences, the contradictions and inconsistencies, take place. It is here, one might argue, where the flaws of the surface are exposed, where the fractures of the text's unity can be perceived. It is here where we can perhaps reach the central core of Dylan's art. It is an art, one might contend, continually haunted by what was not being said, an art wherein the absent center of the textual body continually constituted new meanings. If such a model is accepted, then it could be argued that only a theoretical approach, to these songs, will fully enable one to de-center the text, and to at least gain some sense of these dialectical practices.

An apt place to start might be with Roland Barthes' celebrated essay, "The Death of the Author," published in 1968, the essay that arguably presaged the beginnings of poststructuralist thought. In his text, Barthes argued against the primacy of authorial intent, for Barthes any cultural text was a mere tissue of quotations; for Barthes it was language that spoke, not the author. A cultural text being seen as a network of ideas, composed of multi-layered discourses, a multiplicity that could not be reduced or distilled into a single, fixed meaning—one reading of a text may privilege one particular reading, but this would be merely one of many potential readings—and the idea of finding an ultimate meaning being futile. Hence any cultural text contains a multiplicity of meanings, of which the author was only aware of a small proportion—and there was nothing to constrain each individual reader constructing whatever meaning he or she might wish to impose—the author being merely one voice among many; the single harmonious reading becoming plural, with the text no longer a site for passive consumption. In this sense, it might be said that traditional criticism has attempted to reduce the literary work to little more than a window on the author's psyche, while theory has attempted to make it seem as if it were: "a window on to the universal mind."[56] In Barthesian terms, we thus become aware that a text's unity lies not in its origin but in its destination; and hence a refusal to acknowledge a fixed meaning will liberate any cultural text under consideration.

In this sense it is interesting to note that the great majority of books, thus far published on Dylan's work, have appeared to take it for granted that Dylan's authorial intent was of primary importance. Such an approach is false, authorial intent, even in Bob Dylan's work, is not of primary importance. The meaning of any cultural text resides with the reader. Once this is accepted, one then experiences a certain sense of liberation; for example, we do not have to know anything of Dylan's life, we need to pay only limited heed to Dylan's numerous comments in numerous interviews,[57] and we do not have to concern ourselves with Dylan's own views on his songs. In a theoretical context, there is nothing behind the veil; a linguistic abyss meets our gaze at the heart of any text, and authorial intent offers no solutions. For example, Shakespeare would not be able to explain why Hamlet delays his revenge, Sylvia Plath would not be able to explain why her protagonist hated her Daddy, Coleridge would not be able to reveal Christabel's sight to dream of not to tell; and likewise, Dylan would not be able to explain any of the ambiguities in his work. Barthes' intent was the rejection of the idea that a text has a single autonomous meaning, created by a single author; instead a text merely has a history of interpretation, with its meaning residing—if it resides anywhere—within its "hermeneutic record."[58] Barthes finished his famous essay with the line: "*la naissance du lecteur doit se payer de la mort*

1. Theoretical Approaches

de l'Auteur"—which translates approximately as: "the birth of the reader must be at the cost of the death of the author."[59] To adopt such a reading strategy, or so one might argue, allows for a much greater appreciation of the text, for the texts of Bob Dylan and for the texts of any other author.

Barthes' ideas corresponded with some of the concepts that occur within reader response and reception theory. For example, Wolfgang Iser put forward the idea that all cultural texts contain gaps or blanks, to which the reader must respond by completing, as in the colloquial phrase: "reading between the lines." Similarly, Hans Robert Jauss put forward the idea that each reader had a "horizon of expectations," that every reader approached every text they read with their own preconceived assumptions, both personal and cultural. In terms of such theories, it is certainly self-evident that a literary text has no real existence until it is read, via the act of reading the reader completes the text's sense of existence; without this a book would simply consist of paper and ink. In essence, such theoretical approaches insist that the reader's role is not passive, as would traditionally be perceived; on the contrary, the reader can be seen as an active agent in the creation of meaning. However, a potential mistake would be to see literary and cultural texts as riddles waiting to be solved—there is no definitive answer to such riddles and it is reductive to believe this to be so. A text is merely a juxtaposition of signifiers; from which a diverse, almost infinite range of interpretations, are produced by the reader. In Mikhail Bakhtin's argument, language itself is in a continual state of flux— it was dialogic—to use Bakhtin's term; there was a continual dialogue with other literary works and authors; there were many voices; in other words, there was a "heteroglossia"; language was not fixed and stable, meaning was not singular and uncontested, it was always plural and contested.

Jacques Derrida famously claimed: "there is nothing outside the text," Derrida's point being relevant here, insomuch as it suggests that any linguistic text can ultimately only refer to itself.[60] At this point the theoretical approaches at play perhaps become more challenging; here we are beginning to confront poststructuralist concepts within deconstruction theory; and Derrida, arguably deconstruction's most significant figure, has never been an easy writer to confront. In fact, he has been described as being both the greatest and least readable of all the theorists; with Stephen Trombley going so far as to call Derrida "the most original" but the "most controversial" of twentieth century philosophers.[61] The difficulty in attempting to engage with Derrida resides in his complexity and in his breadth of knowledge. It would be easy to dismiss Derrida, to claim his work was unintelligible, but it should be remembered that his writings were based on high assumptions of the reader, nothing less than "a lifelong exploration of the entire canon of Western thought."[62] To read Derrida is therefore not an unproblematic undertaking. However, in the context of Roland Barthes' theories around authorial intent, Derrida's argument that meaning is never complete, never fully realized, always deferred, would seem relevant. Words can only be defined by other words, we can never come to an actual meaning, every decoding (in David Lodge's words) is another encoding—this being one reading of Derrida's claim that there was nothing outside the text. Hence the relationship between signifier and signified may not only be arbitrary—as structuralist theory argues—but in Derrida's world that relationship may also be volatile. As we read—or indeed, as we live—it might be said that we are playing a game of which we have no knowledge of the rules. Yet Derrida takes this predicament still further: "There is an intricate structure of rules and conventions which govern the event, but what is behind the rules?"[63]

This is a good question and one that will find a repeated resonance within this discussion of Dylan's work; specifically in relation to the discussion of sexual and gender politics. In terms of specific issues pertaining to deconstruction theory, the one issue that would seem most relevant would appear to be—once again—the idea that a cultural text can never have one central meaning, that it was no longer restricted to a single harmonious and authoritative reading—but instead had a multiplicity of latent, fragmentary and often contradictory meanings—with little linkage to the meaning the author of the text may originally have had in mind. Derrida was incisive in delineating this idea, as Jeremy Tambling put it:

> For Derrida, the idea of some original presence or truth-finding expression in language is the profound error of Western thought … it belongs to a tradition that wishes to operate a hierarchy of absolute truths that actually only have a purely mythical basis—meaning is always deferred.[64]

Meaning *is* always deferred, a cultural text is only experienced, never defined. As Stanley Fish has argued, there is always a gap between the linguistic features identified in the text and the interpretation of them by the reader—what might be called "the hermeneutic gap."[65] Deconstruction theory, at times at least, would appear to suggest that such a gap was too wide and we should not attempt to bridge it, that a search for meaning was beyond our capabilities; as Picasso once said: "The search for meaning is the disease of our society." Susan Sontag's famous essay, "Against Interpretation," published in 1966, made the same point, that interpretation was the revenge of the intellect upon art,

1. Theoretical Approaches

that in place of hermeneutics we needed what Sontag called an erotics of art. In a sense, deconstruction argued for the same proposal—albeit in a somewhat different form of discussion.

In a more general context, deconstruction, as the term might imply, concerns a dismantling of a text in order to look, in detail, at its constituent parts; to contemplate the hidden assumptions of language within the text—what was being said and, perhaps more importantly, what was not being said. Furthermore, deconstruction suggests all meaning is constructed; in other words, no statements or words (including the word "meaning)" have—in fact—any meaning. Such a way of thinking corresponding to the poststructuralist view that language consists of little else but "instabilities and relativities" that were "socially and historically constructed."[66] In particular, the very notion of "nature" was "regarded with extreme suspicion—the very word was taboo."[67] As David Storey put it: "Poststructuralists reject the idea of an underlying structure upon which meaning can rest secure and guaranteed. Meaning is always in process."[68] As intimated here, and above, meaning is always in a state of referral; the simple act of looking-up a word in the dictionary would seem to confirm this idea, the relentless semiotic deferment of meaning as we are led from one signifier to another, from one word to another, with no respite, with no end to such a search, with no final meaning ever becoming available. To recall Derrida's dictum: there is nothing outside of the text, and it is only when language can be located within a discourse, and read within a specific context, that there would seem to be any hope of a temporary halt to the endless play of signifier to signifier.[69]

In terms of Bob Dylan's cultural productions, his wide and diverse range of songs, of oral and performed texts, a poststructuralist approach will attempt to demonstrate just how labile and unfixed such texts can be—as will be seen within the discussion herein. In addition, it would seem valid to suggest that cultural theory, in general, could be seen as a productive contrivance in this context, some of theory's other components: feminism, gay and lesbian (or queer) studies, psychoanalytical theory, structuralism, reader-response theories, some elements of postmodernist theories, some elements of postcolonialist theories and even Marxist theory, will at least allow for the possibility of attaining an understanding of what is actually occurring within Dylan's work. In other words, a theoretical approach, which has seldom been applied to Dylan's work,[70] may at least allow for the possibility of seeing Dylan's songs as something more than merely a play of signifiers interacting with other signifiers. A theoretical reading of Bob Dylan's work will also license, will also allow, will also warrant, a way of approaching Dylan's work without a recourse to a biographical reading of the songs—which, as already intimated, would appear to have unfortunately dominated much of the critical approaches thus far applied to Dylan's work. This arguably resulting in reductive and, at times, even facile readings of the work.[71] As such, the theoretical approaches to be adopted herein will aspire to provide a new and additional way of reading Bob Dylan's diverse and varied body of work.

By way of a final note, there would also seem to be the matter of complex and subtle art-forms requiring complex and subtle critical tools, that cultural productions—even ones as supposedly straightforward and uncomplicated as those of popular songs—were not always amenable to simplification. As Terry Eagleton has argued:

> All propaganda or popularisation involves a putting of the complex into the simple, but such a move is instantly deconstructive. For if the complex *can* be put into the simple, then it cannot be as complex as it seemed in the first place: and if the simple can be an adequate medium of such complexity, then it cannot, after all, be as simple as all that.[72]

In a consideration of this comment, one might be reminded of Eagleton's claim, cited in the introduction, that literary theory can handle Bob Dylan as easily as Milton. A theoretical approach to Bob Dylan's work, whatever its problems and complications, is, one might argue, necessary in order to strive to attain a comprehensive understanding of a complicated writer, artist and performer. In a specific sense, the overarching theoretical stance taken in this study will primarily be based around the ideas espoused by Judith Butler in the 1990s. The theoretical concept that gender was "performative," and that an analysis of Dylan's work, within the constraints of this approach, will expose many of the contradictions towards masculinity, femininity, sexuality and identity. However, in addition to a Butlerian analysis, this study will also be attentive to the ways in which a cross-section of theoretical approaches can also illuminate and enhance an appreciation of Dylan's work, can enhance the multi-faceted complexities found within at least some of his songs. In the following chapter such a theoretical approach will begin by considering the issue of masculinity in the light of the subtle, complex and often contradictory ways in which Dylan depicts, constructs and deconstructs masculinity within his work.

2

Masculinity

"I was born very far from where I was supposed to be."
—Bob Dylan, in the documentary
No Direction Home

The construct of masculinity, in the work of Bob Dylan, remains both a compelling and a contradictory subject area. This might be inferred insomuch as it would seem that the great majority of Dylan's songs were, in fact, more interested in constructs of masculinity than in constructs of femininity; or to put this more simply: Dylan's lyrics employed a much greater interest in men than they did in women. This may appear, on the surface, to be an exaggerated claim, but a careful and detailed reading of the songs would appear to at least go some distance in supporting such a proposal. In this way, the following chapter will put forward a line of reasoning to support this claim; it will argue that many of Dylan's songs demonstrated a desire to escape from a female and a domestic domain, to escape into the world of men, into a world of travel and exploration, into a world of endemic restlessness. In other words, there was a continual dichotomy for the men in Dylan's songs: a desire for women but a need to resist enclosure within that world. A cross-section of Dylan's body of work will be considered in order to support this thesis, in addition to a detailed reading of the song "Isis" (1976). In this song, the relentless desire to both commit and not to commit to the female figure, together with an unwillingness to maintain a lasting relationship with the woman in question, will be used in order to demonstrate the veracity of such a thesis.

In the famous (or perhaps infamous) interview for *Playboy* magazine, in March 1966,[1] Dylan made the following comment: "I'm still very patriotic to the highway." It was a seemingly off-hand remark, Dylan was responding to a question asking whether he still had the opportunity to ride his motorcycle; however, there was a more profound quality to the comment. Dylan has always been patriotic to the highway, insomuch as he has continually—

albeit in metonymic fashion—been loyal to the concept of movement, of travel, of refusing to remain in the same place. One is referring primarily here to the consistent array of discourses pertaining to travel in Dylan's songs, but it could also be applied to the way Dylan, himself, would seem to have structured his life, especially in the last thirty years, on the so-called "Never Ending Tour." Here on this tour, and others before it, a loyalty to the highway, to travel, to touring, would appear to have become a way of life. In another interview from that same year, 1966, Dylan appeared to encompass this whole issue when he told Robert Shelton: "What hangs everybody up is the fact that I'm not stopping."[2] This is, one could argue, one of the most insidiously significant remarks Dylan has made. The remark might be seen as redolent; insomuch as, like Dylan himself, the men in his songs are not stopping, with the idea of constantly resisting containment becoming a template on which to draw a sense of the self, specifically a sense of the self as a man; a "performative" way of constructing a sense of a gendered identity.

Such a scenario could be witnessed from the very beginning of Dylan's career; for example, "Blowin' in the Wind" (1962), arguably one of Dylan's most celebrated and certainly most well-known songs, began with a seemingly simple question: it was a song asking just how many roads a man must walk down before he could be called a man. In one specific sense these lines have been perceived as referring to the civil rights marches of the early 1960s; it was seen as a song asking how many times a *black* man must walk down a road before *he* was called a man. This may be inferred, not merely because the song coincided with the civil rights movement, but perhaps because of the ubiquitous images of African American men, walking down a number of roads, holding up placards proclaiming: "I Am a Man!"[3] Thus it was a song, within the sphere of its own creation and the tensions of its own time, much concerned with issues of race. This may arguably have been the specific inspiration for Dylan's song; however, from a wider perspective, reading these lines over fifty years later, without historical or cultural bias, the song could be read as having a different subtext. In a literal sense, the lines could now be read simply as a definition of masculinity within the body of Dylan's work. The question the song now appears to have been asking was direct and unambiguous; to be called "a man" you were required to walk down a road, to walk down a road a certain unspecified number of times. This being the literal definition of masculinity within the opening lines of the song, at least within a quasi-structuralist reading of the line.

This interpretation may seem to have little significance, were it not for the fact that such a definition of masculinity would appear to have been a widespread trope within Dylan's songs; it was a pattern that occurred consistently throughout the entire span of his work. If one looks, for example, at one of Dylan's earliest lyrics, "Song to Woody" (1962), the song began with the male protagonist a thousand miles away from his home; alone in an unspecified environment, and, perhaps significantly, walking a road that other men had already gone down. Hence once again one was able to recognize the trope of walking a road to define oneself as a man. The narrator of the song went on to compare himself to other men who had travelled the same road, seeing himself as following in their footsteps; striving to place himself "on the road," with some of the great blues singers of the past, with the song citing such instances as: Cisco Houston, Sonny Terry, Hughie Ledbetter—all enveloped within a paean of praise to Woody Guthrie. To Woody Guthrie, Dylan's self-confessed first and last idol, but with the repetitive element consisting of the trope of masculine travel: all the good people who had travelled with Woody Guthrie. Of course, the good people who travelled with Guthrie were predominantly men, men who came with the dust and who were gone with the wind, with the narrative voice in the song seeming to almost offer a eulogy to the hearts and to the hands of these fellow masculine travellers.

Hence one might fairly maintain that there was, throughout the body of Dylan's work, a relentless urge to keep moving, an enduring sense of rambling, of travelling, of wandering; and, most importantly, the enduring sense that this was invariably seen as a wholly masculine endeavor. One could cite a number of early Dylan songs that all dealt, in a clear and unambiguous way, with this idea of masculine travel; for example: "Standing on the Highway" (1962), "Long Time Gone" (1962), "Walkin' Down the Line" (1963), "Down the Highway" (1963), "Dusty Old Fairgrounds" (1963) and "Paths of Victory" (1964). However, this was also a theme that extended throughout the whole of Dylan's career; for example, the songs on Dylan's last album of the twentieth century, *Time Out of Mind* (1997), began, ended, and were concerned throughout, with men walking and with men travelling. It should perhaps be noted, at this point, that to perceive of a notion of travel and movement within Dylan's lyrics, is, in itself, hardly original; a number of other critics of Dylan's work have also pointed this out. For example, David Pichaske commented that "Early Dylan lyrics are permeated with the theme of departure, leaving, clearing out and travelling on, escaping the inadequate present."[4] However, the specific intent within this study will be to link this theme directly with the idea of gender identity. The argument, as expressed here, relates to the idea that Dylan's work explicitly conveys the concept of travel with the concept of being a man, and hence to the performative construct of a gendered identity.[5]

* * *

In this light the question as to whether it would be possible to envisage travel, in itself, as a gendered arena, might be considered. A number of cultural theorists have explored the issue; an apt example being Janet Wolff, who argued that "[T]he practices and ideologies of actual travel operated to exclude or pathologize women, [there was] something intrinsically masculine about travel."[6] As to how convincing such a claim might be remains open to question; but it would seem somewhat problematical to accept that travel was, in itself, intrinsically gendered towards the masculine. It would seem too simplistic to say that men travel simply because they are men; and, in any case, women obviously do travel, both in life and in art.[7] On the one hand, it would appear that historically the ability to travel has had as much to do with such issues as wealth and class, as it has had to do with gender. However, on the other hand, it would seem true to say that, in a certain sense, women have not been as empowered to travel as men, insomuch as the experience of the vast majority of adult females, for a large part of human history, has consisted primarily of pregnancy, childbirth and child-rearing. In such a context, it has been suggested that much of the travelling undertaken by men was stimulated by a reproductive motive. Eric J. Leed has described this desire to travel as a "spermatic journey," that travel is "stimulated by ... a search for temporal extensions of self in children, only achievable through the agency of women."[8] In other words, men travel to disseminate their genes; while women, because of practical necessities, do not.

In a similar vein, the psychologist, Erik Erikson, has argued that it was:

> The physical design of the human body; the inner space of the womb and the vagina, which signifies women's biological, psychological and moral commitment to motherhood, and the possession of the penis predisposes men to be concerned with achievement and exploration.[9]

The idea that many girls tended to make enclosed domestic scenes, led Erikson to claim the importance of "inner space" for women, something that was "deeply rooted in their biological construction."[10] Thus, the physical design of the body: the inner space of the vagina and womb, contrasted against the external penis, offered a predisposal to the gender roles within society. In other words, to place this within a somewhat rudimentary framework: women remain at home and men explore the wilderness; this being at least one way of representing the purported conclusion of Erikson's argument. However, from the perspective of the theoretical approach to be put forward within this present study, an alternate argument will be presented, one that would argue against such a deterministic point of view. One might suggest, in the light of these proposals, (particularly of Janet Wolff's), that travel, rather than being seen as gendered in some unspecified way, could, in itself, be seen *as* a gendering experience. In other words, by travelling one actually derives or performs some sense of masculinity; this argument will be discussed in terms of the constant references towards masculine travel within the discursive practices of Dylan's work.

Some of these practices were played out in an early, unreleased Dylan song, "Ramblin', Gamblin' Willie" (1962); a title that could, in itself, be seen as a pun on movement, freedom and male sexuality. As to whether an American writer would have been attentive to this predominantly British (and somewhat juvenile) wordplay is questionable; however, the somewhat comical idea of a rambling gambling phallic symbol was not without a satiric subtext.[11] In the song, a likable character, named Willie O'Conley, spent the entire narrative rambling and gambling around America, indulging in those things that a man presumably has got to indulge in. We were told that Willie had twenty-seven children, but had never had a wife. The general tenor of the song seemed to imply that such a way of behaving was to be admired, especially as Willie supported his multiple children, as well as their various mothers. What this support may have consisted of was not specified, one assumes it consisted in merely extending some degree of financial maintenance; for it was clear that Willie was either unable or unwilling to give up his rambling and gambling, and to be present with his various extended families in person, at least not for any significant periods of time. The reason why Willie could not be present was left unstated in the song, one assumes that he was simply too busy out in the rambling, gambling world of men, where, unsurprisingly, he eventually met a violent death at the hands of another man. Thus the narrative of the song could be seen as suggesting not only a need to be on the road, but also a need to escape from a feminine and familial sphere of influence. This is, one might argue, a significant constituent in reading the performative element present within the construct of masculinity in Dylan's work. The men in Bob Dylan's songs often had a desire to leave women, in order to confront a wilderness of which women were not a part; in one sense at least, this was what it seemed to mean in order to live up to the idea of being a man.

This idea was readily discernible throughout Dylan's canon. For example, if one looks to the *Blood on the Tracks* period: in "Tangled Up in Blue" (1975), the male narrator felt compelled to seek the wilderness, to confront his inner self, metaphorically represented via the song's great north woods. In "Up to Me" (1975), the masculine narrator of the song was more explicit, telling the woman with whom he was involved, that one of them had to hit the road—and of course it was the male voice to whom this task fell. The road was, one might argue, one of the most important symbolic tropes in Dylan's work; becoming a way of life in itself: "My life is the road that I walk," Dylan told an interviewer in the early 1960s.[12] Thus, within the construct of Dylan's work, the road becomes a way of life, and one way of escaping the dilemma of life was to keep travelling, to keep on moving, to keep on keeping on, as Dylan famously put it in "Tangled Up in Blue."[13] As such, the men in Dylan's songs lived on life's hurried tangled road[14]; they were still on the road heading for another joint[15]; they were walking the road, living on the edge[16]; they were still pushing themselves along the road[17]; and so on, throughout numerous other examples, throughout the whole output of Dylan's work.[18]

One has to be aware of other interpretations; in other words, that there were alternative and perhaps more commonplace reasons as to why men travelled in Dylan's work. One might think, for example, of the blues tradition; a tradition with which Dylan has always been closely associated, a tradition in which travel (and especially masculine travel) has been a dominant motif. In addition to this, there was the obvious idea that men travel in order to search for work, and one could cite the influence of Woody Guthrie at this point. In some of Guthrie's songs it was certainly correct to say that economic factors led men to take to the road in search of employment. A number of Guthrie's songs; for example, "Tom Joad," drawn from John Steinbeck's 1939 novel, *The Grapes of Wrath*, portrayed the plight of men in such a situation. However, one might argue that Dylan's idolization of Guthrie[19] was connected more with the mythological and romantic notions in Guthrie's life and work. Guthrie's celebrated book, *Bound for Glory*, which greatly influenced Dylan early in his career,[20] celebrated the theme of the outcast, the drifter, the man fleeing from convention and conformity, the hobo who found freedom on the highways and railroads of the American landscape. In a sense, Guthrie (or the persona of himself he created) was an outlaw, albeit a morally sanctioned outlaw. Guthrie tapped into the moral relevance of the outlaw in American culture, an idea that would also be repeatedly displayed within Dylan's work. As Wayne Hampton put it:

2. Masculinity

> Bob Dylan's politics, such as they are, involve the romanticisation of freedom, a concern for the social outcast ... sustained by images of hoboes, outlaws, prophets and saints on a slow train bound for glory.[21]

One might thus argue that the road, for the men in Dylan's work, was primarily a place with a romantic, visionary and often mythological ambition. Furthermore, the men most admired in Dylan's work were often outlaws, or at least outsiders; men who had moved beyond the constructed confines of conventional society. I might look like Robert Ford, Dylan had intimated in the appropriately titled song "Outlaw Blues" (1965), but adding, that he felt just like Jesse James. In other words, the masculine protagonists in Dylan's work would much rather hold and embrace the romantic idea of the masculine-self as outlaw. Of course, this was something of a conceit; this was something that significantly suggested artifice and play-acting. In other words, there was an obviously transparent suggestion of there being a knowingly paradoxical element to such a construct of masculinity.

Aside from Woody Guthrie, other obvious influences, in such a context, were the Beat writers, most specifically Jack Kerouac. Kerouac's seminal work, *On the Road* (1957), arguably informed a similar pattern of male desire, a pattern propounding a significantly gender-specific quest for self-discovery via the road. As such, Kerouac's work might be described as putting forward the idea of a male outsider escaping the narrow confines of society in search of a lost frontier, making a celebratory escape from responsibility; and, in so doing, exerting a significant influence in Dylan's sighting of romance and visionary experience "on the road."[22] The prerogative of which, one might argue, pointing again towards a sense of the construct of gender in Dylan's work. In the reverentially titled song, "On the Road Again" (1965), Dylan's male narrator wanted to be on the road, wanted to be in the wide open spaces, wanted to be in the wilderness, wanted, in fact, to be anywhere as long as he was not with the woman in the song and with the rest of her family. The familial context here seemed significant, here the intent of the song was both satiric and comic: with the singer waking up with frogs inside his socks, with his lover's mother hiding in the ice-box, and with his lover's father having paranoid delusions of being Napoleon Bonaparte. In the song, the narrative clearly demonstrated, after all of this familial chaos, that the masculine protagonist could not prevail within such an environment, he needed to get on the road—again. The song was only one example of a number of songs Dylan wrote in the mid–1960s that positioned a male character desperately attempting to avoid the onset of familial constraints. Other examples included:

"Motorpsycho Nitemare" (1964), "Maggie's Farm" (1965), "Tombstone Blues" (1965) and "Highway 61 Revisited" (1965). These songs portrayed men who did not want to settle down with the farmer's daughter, who did not want to work for brother's or pa's or ma's, men who wanted to get away from Mama's in the factory and Papa's in the alley, and men who wanted nothing to do with fifth daughters and first fathers and seventh sons. All these songs portrayed male protagonists who needed some means of escape, men who did not want to be constrained within the worlds in which they found themselves.

In one of Dylan's seminal works of the 1960s, "It Ain't Me Babe" (1964), a similar intent could be more explicitly inferred. The famous refrain, with its thrice-repeated denial of, No, No, No—could be read as both a political and a personal statement. In a political sense the line could be read as a retreat from a world of social protest, but, in a different and more individual discourse, the line could be read simply as a repudiation of confinement within a feminine domain. Thus the refrain of the song, It ain't me babe, it ain't me you're looking for, became a message from a man to a woman, or even from men to women, a message repudiating the idea of any kind of permanent commitment. In a later song, "The Groom's Still Waiting at the Altar" (1981), Dylan again put forward the idea of a retreat away from commitment, but here included a possible reason why—with the masculine voice in the song confessing he had to give up the woman—named Claudette—at exactly the moment she began to want him. The fact that the male protagonist was compelled to give up the woman, in the very moment she expressed a desire for him, was significant; and hence there was a clear sense that some part of the masculine self must be kept inviolate from a feminine sphere of influence.

In an earlier song, "Don't Think Twice, It's All Right" (1963), the reason for the break-up of the relationship was contiguous with this same concept:

> I'm thinkin' and a wonderin' all the way down the road
> I once loved a woman, a child I'm told
> I gave her my heart, but she wanted my soul
> But don't think twice, it's all right[23]

This was an idea that would culminate in the later song, "Sweetheart Like You" (1983):

> You know, I once knew a woman who looked like you
> She wanted a whole man, not just a half
> She used to call me sweet daddy when I was only a child
> You kind of remind me of her when you laugh[24]

2. Masculinity

The male figure here would only offer half of himself, with the implied suggestion that he must preserve some aspect of himself outside of the female domain. This being a thematic element that would be apparent within other aspects of Dylan's work, and hence it could be argued that the men in Dylan's songs, however hard they tried, often failed in their attempts to live up to the expectations of the women with whom they were involved. An idea personified by a line in "One More Night" (1969), wherein the male voice eventually had to admit that he just could not be what the woman (he was addressing) wanted him to be. The point at stake here revolved around the hollowness and fragility of the construct of masculinity that haunted some of the unconscious elements in Dylan's work; in other words, there was a sense that the men in Dylan's songs could never quite bring themselves to confront the dichotomy of both wanting and not wanting the women with whom they were involved. In this light it is perhaps significant that even in songs that purported to describe happily ensconced marital relationships, even in songs that have generally been perceived as extolling the pleasures of life within a settled monogamous relationship, even here there was still a sense of skepticism and doubt. For example, in "Sign on the Window" (1970), Dylan ended the song with a vision of supposed domestic bliss: of building a cabin in Utah, of marrying a wife, of catching rainbow trout, of having children who called him Pa; summing all of this up by proclaiming that this must be what life was all about. However, there was a sense here of a male voice striving to convince itself of the conceit it was proposing. While the idea of making sense of the world by placing oneself within such an arena of domesticity was one obvious means of defining oneself as a man; there seemed, nonetheless, an element of self-imposed coercion being utilized, almost a sense of desperation in the hope such a conceit had some meaning. At the end of the song we were told that—this must be what it's all about—but the fact that Dylan felt the need to state this twice suggested he might have been protesting too much. As Michael Gray put it, the closure of the song was "made less positive by its being repeated, as if for self-reassurance."[25]

* * *

There are a wide range of theories to account for the masculine fear of engulfment in the female and the subsequent loss of the self. For example, Julia Kristeva has explored the masculine fear of the abject nature of the female, while Nancy Chodorow's work has identified how women's universal responsibility for mothering creates asymmetrical factors between the genders; in addition, Hélène Cixous' concept of *écriture feminine* would seem to suggest that, in an albeit extreme scenario, men might not be required at all. However, one might argue, in the case of the specific discourses within the songs of Bob Dylan, that his texts offered a relatively simple response; the men in Dylan's work feared engulfment within the female domain because it would force them to confront the inconsistencies in the construct of their own gendered identity. Hence the concept of movement and the freedom to travel becomes a means of evading such an engulfment; and to keep moving, to refrain from stopping, to preserve a patriotism to the highway, at least offered a way out of such a dichotomy. Insomuch, it provided a means of evading a sense of confronting the problematical discursive maneuvers involved in posing the question: what does it mean to be a man?

* * *

There were, it must be accepted, some isolated examples of songs in which Dylan placed a male protagonist out in the wilderness in the company of a woman. For example, in "John Wesley Harding" (1968), the narrative of the song began with the singer down in Chaynee County,[26] with the male protagonist of the song's title taking a stand,[27] but here, in this case, with his lady by his side. One might also think of the unnamed protagonist and his companion, Magdalena, who travelled together in "Romance in Durango" (1976), and also the sister who was on the highway with the steel driving crew in "Tough Mama" (1974). However, these were rare exceptions, and the one other example would appear to have been the song "Gypsy Lou" (1963). This was a significant song in Dylan's canon, a song in which the gender roles were entirely reversed; this was a song about a rambling woman with a rambling mind who left a large number of masculine lovers behind her. The fact that Dylan did not release the song for nearly fifty years was perhaps significant, as if it was a self-aware anomaly and hence excluded from the main body of Dylan's work.[28] In any case, these songs were very much the exception that proved the proverbial rule; the wilderness in Dylan's work was predominantly defined as the place where males, usually heroic males, escaped to allude the domain of women.

In his book, *America in the Movies*, Michael Wood speculated upon the motives behind the male heroes of Hollywood westerns in the 1940s and 1950s; and, as such, this theoretical conjecture, which had a convincing degree of credibility, may possibly illuminate the question as to why so many male

2. Masculinity

protagonists in Dylan's work had an attraction for the road and such an equivocal attitude toward women. According to Wood:

> [T]he hero secretly fears women—women and the civilisation, compromise and settled life they represent; he sees them as sources of corruption and betrayal, luring him away from independence and a sure sense of himself, as well as from the more comforting company of men.[29]

Wood went on to argue that: "women [are] a form of entanglement, a dark snare almost always eclipsed by the glamour and loneliness of wandering."[30] It would seem fair to argue that such fears and desires also operated (often to an exaggerated degree) in Dylan's work, thus further enhancing the argument that the portrayal of masculinity had a diverse range of slippages, a diverse range of labile qualities, a diverse range of unspoken emotions, all beguilingly portrayed throughout the ambiguous discursive practices of the songs. One of the songs that most reflected these fears and desires, was "Isis," from the 1976 album, *Desire*; this was a song that explored ideas of freedom and escape, a song that mixed the surreal and the allegorical, the mythic and the real, in a sophisticated melange of gender politics—and a song that will be considered in some detail here.

* * *

In terms of a reading of "Isis," as far as can be ascertained, the song has not commonly been seen as deriving from the Western genre. However, taking into account Michael Wood's argument, as discussed above, one could reasonably suggest that the song could be read in the context of ideas very much redolent of the Western, albeit a Western genre Dylan and Jacques Levy[31] revisited with a postmodern sense of parodic irony. Furthermore, and perhaps of greater significance, when the song is read within the Western genre then the implication for the construction of masculinity, within its creative discourse, achieves a still greater level of interest. While the Western has rarely been seen as an important or typical theme within Dylan's work, it does, or so one might argue, deserve a certain degree of attention. For example, one might consider the first words Dylan gives the world, or at least the first words found in his first collection of lyrics: *Writings and Drawings*.[32] The first song in the collection was "Talkin' New York" (1961), and the opening lines of the song found the protagonist rambling out of the wild west, leaving behind the towns he loved the best, going through some ups and down, before finally making it to New York—town. Thus, in a certain sense, and within a consciously quixotic reading, Dylan could be seen as appearing to the world as if appearing out of the wild west; in an imaginative literal sense, together with a geographical, historical and cultural context, Dylan therefore appears to the world as if he was emerging from this genre, from the wild west.[33] In addition to this, Dylan has written a modest, but significant, range of songs that were positioned (either in whole or in part) within the Western genre, one might think of the following examples, the aforementioned "Rambling Gambling Willie" (1963) and "John Wesley Harding" (1968), also:

"The Ballad of Frankie Lee and Judas Priest" (1968)
"Wanted Man" (1969)
"Lily, Rosemary and the Jack of Hearts" (1975)
"Patty's Gone to Laredo" (1975)
"Romance in Durango" (1976)
"Senor: Tales of Yankee Power" (1978)
"New Danville Girl" (1985)[34]
"The Man in the Long Black Coat" (1989)

together with the collection of songs from Dylan's soundtrack of Sam Peckinpah's film *Pat Garrett and Billy the Kid* (1973).

As a genre, the Western—in film and in the novel—has generally been regarded as a somewhat lightweight and escapist form of popular culture. However, as Jane Tompkins has argued, in her book: *West of Everything: The Inner Life of Westerns*, there is nothing lightweight or escapist about the needs the Western answers, "the desires they arouse and the vision of life they portray."[35] The overarching argument Tompkins makes is that the Western provides an environment in which men can find a reality, a reality that might otherwise be lacking in their lives, that the Western functions as:

> a symbol of freedom, and of the opportunities for conquest. It seems to offer escape from the conditions of life in modern industrial society: from a mechanised existence, economic dead-ends, social entanglements, unhappy personal relations, political injustice.[36]

What would appear to have been at stake in Tompkins' argument was the lack of a sense of challenge; the Western being a method of getting away from the triviality of life into something that at least seemed to be real. Hence the hunger that the Westerns satisfied was a hunger, not so much for adventure, but for meaning. In a general sense, the Western was a genre in which something really was at stake. Thus the genre was not so much an escape from reality, as an attempt to get as close as possible to something that was real. As Tompkins put it: "In the Western nothing stands between the man and

2. Masculinity

the world,"[37] and of course, the use of the word "man," in this quotation, was relevant, insomuch as the Western was, and is, almost universally a genre about men; this being a point to bear in mind when discussing the Western in relation to Dylan's work.

Thus it would seem, bearing the above in mind, that the Western may provide a cogent metaphor for the representation of masculinity within the song under discussion here, "Isis," arguably one of Dylan's most revealing depictions of masculinity. The song was revealing, insomuch as Dylan—albeit most probably with little conscious awareness—succeeded in providing at least a partial explanation as to why the men in his work so often behaved in the ways they did. In the song, there was a clear and unambiguous portrayal of a man, of a male protagonist, acting out the solitariness of the Western hero; a hero who was courageous, self-reliant, independent and, above all, free of female dependency. This was apparent from the beginning of the narrative, wherein the hero married an exotic woman (with the exotic appellation of an Egyptian goddess),[38] but then, for reasons wholly unexplained, felt compelled to leave her:

> I married Isis on the fifth day of May
> But I could not hold on to her very long
> So I cut off my hair and I rode straight away
> For the wild and unknown country where I could not go wrong[39]

The song itself would appear to have deliberately refrained from offering little in the way of a direct answer of why this should have been so; why this man could not stay with this woman, why he could not hold on to her for very long. The song merely expressed a need for the woman, while also expressing a need for adventure and freedom, together with the paradox of needing them both at the same time.

From his public comments it would seem that Dylan perceived of the song as having marriage at its core. In concert performances he often prefaced the song by referring to it from this perspective:

> Listen closely, this is a true story, it could happen to any man. This is about the marriage ceremony between man and woman, it's what happens when you get married. It's called "Isis."[40]

However, in terms of the textual content of the song, the inherent ideological maneuvers at play within the song, this would hardly seem to have been Dylan's actual intention; if the song was about marriage it would seem to have been about a marriage of a wholly different kind. Thus, far from being a song about a conventional marriage, the song seems to have been more concerned with what befell the narrator after he had married the woman called Isis, with what happened when he was absent from the company of women, and with what happened when he was in the company of other men. One might recall here Leslie Fiedler's famous phrase: "the holy marriage of males,"[41] Fiedler's much misunderstood argument that a marriage of a different kind was portrayed throughout American literature, and this, one might suggest, was closer to the actual nature of the marriage within Dylan's song.

The first act the narrator carried out, after removing himself from Isis's feminine influence, was to cut off his hair. A number of critics of Dylan's work have speculated over the meaning of such an action; to Aidan Day it implied a loss of creative energy and a sense of purification[42]; similarly, Stephen Scobie saw it as undergoing a ritual purification[43]; Wilfrid Mellers perceived the removal of the hero's hair as asserting a male dominance before embarking on a heroic adventure[44]; while to John Herdman the act was a shedding of complexity and a way of seeking simplicity.[45] All these readings would seem valid, and there was certainly a ritualistic element to the act; in addition, it would seem fair to say Dylan's protagonist cut off his hair to prepare himself for some unstated ordeal ahead, as if he were a penitent readying himself for the trials to come. However, within the context of a more uncomplicated and semiotic reading, one could simply see the act as pointing to a masculine archetype, insomuch as it is culturally the norm for men to have shorter hair than women. In addition, the cutting of one's hair, and especially shaving, demonstrates a control over one of the main visible masculine indicators of maturing sexuality; shaving being an initiation into manhood. Thus, in a sense, the act of the protagonist cutting off his hair can ultimately be seen as emphasizing (or even performing) a gendered identity, a masculine identity.

The narrator may have decided to leave the heterosexual embrace of a newly married wife, but—like the act of cutting off one's hair—the song seems to have had a continual anxiety to hold to the dominant ideology of a "normal" heterosexual identity. As the first verse tells us, the narrator rides *straight* away, and while the protagonist may have been heading for a wild unknown country (arguably the wild and unknown country of his sexuality) there was still the insistence that he could not go wrong. In other words, one reading of the song suggested the hero was determined he would not stray from a rigidly defined heterosexual structure, he would not go wrong—he would remain "straight." This was an idea emphasized in the song's second verse:

2. Masculinity

> I came to a high place of darkness and light
> The dividing line ran through the centre of town
> I hitched up my pony to a post on the right
> Went into the laundry to wash my clothes down

There were clearly apparent binary oppositions presented within the verse: darkness and light, high and low places, right and left, or perhaps even right and wrong.[46] Insomuch, what appeared to be decisive was the fact that the song's hero chose the right hand option. In other words, he was insistent on following the rational, dominant and conventional ideological route. To choose the post on the right might be read as suggesting the normal over the perverse, and hence, at least within the context of a "Fiedlerian" reading, it might be seen as suggestive of stating an insistence to maintain a loyalty to a heterosexual matrix. Furthermore, the narrator then went into a laundry, to wash his clothes down; this, like the cutting of his hair, could be seen as a way of suggesting cleanliness and righteousness; in other words, the opposite to any kind of transgression.

In the laundry, in the song's third verse, an encounter occurred which significantly augmented the narrative:

> A man in the corner approached me for a match
> I knew right away he was not ordinary
> He said, "Are you lookin' for somethin' easy to catch?"
> I said, "I got no money." He said, "That ain't necessary."

The nature of the meeting was redolent with ambiguity, the words "match" and "catch" both seeming to possess dualistic connotations. On a literal level the word "match" simply appeared to suggest that "the man in the corner," the stranger, might merely have wanted help in lighting a cigarette; however, on another level the short incident could have been seen as a somewhat blatant proposal to enter into a relationship of a reciprocal kind: the stranger was arguably asking for a match to correspond with his own desires. In a similar way, the word "catch" resonated within a decidedly equivocal discursive arena. In one sense it could have been seen as an economic invitation to make a quick profit, but the word also resonated forward within the narrative, to a line later in the song, in verse eight: "When he died I was hopin' that it wasn't contagious." The song was written in the pre–AIDS universe of 1975, but it nonetheless somehow managed to retain a subversive quality redolent of fears of contamination. There was a sense of infraction in the words "contagious" and "catch," of some kind of unknown exchange having taken place, an exchange that had implications for both of the men; and it should perhaps be noted that the song had already told us that one of the men was "not ordinary." This is not to say that the song was in any way predictive of the AIDS epidemic, only that some sense of the panic to come over the disease, in the 1980s, was insidiously present in such a later reading of the verse. In any case, there was certainly a feeling of tension within the relationship between the two men; these men were not simply "two drifters off to see the world," there was a sense of anticipation, a sense of anxiety that pointed towards something both hermetic and impenetrable.

It should be noted that few critics of Dylan's work have, as yet, shown an awareness of the ambiguous tensions within the song. However, Paul Hodson was one exception, writing, in the early 1990s, that: "'Isis' is one of several [Dylan] songs shot through with sexuality about men" and that "the relationships between Dylan's men are complex, developing and rarely summed up."[47] One might well concur with this statement, and, in such a context, Jane Tompkins' description of the repressed, covert sexuality between men in Westerns might be seen as applicable to the two men in the song:

> the hero frequently forms a bond with another man—sometimes his rival, more often his comrade—a bond that is more important than any relationship he has with a woman and is frequently tinged with homo-eroticism.[48]

One could thus argue that it is possible to see a connection between the actions of the men in many Westerns and the men in Dylan's song. As Hodson suggests, the relationship between the two men in "Isis" (as with other men, elsewhere in Dylan's work), was rarely summed up, there was an ambivalence that the reader or the listener to the song could not define.

In the fourth verse of the song, the two men began their journey:

> We set out that night for the cold in the North
> I gave him my blanket, he gave me his word
> I said, "Where are we goin'?" He said we'd be back by the fourth
> I said, "That's the best news that I've ever heard."

One notes that the two men left at night and that they headed for the cold and the north, these being harsh, masculine images that stood in opposition to Isis's feminine southern world of lightness and warmth. Insomuch, there was a sense that these were men braving the elements, undergoing ordeals that would exact superhuman effort. As in the Western, what was at stake here was a getting away from the triviality of life, escaping into something that seemed real, something that called "the whole soul of man into being," that called for a sense of action that "totally saturate[d] the present moment,"

2. Masculinity

that totally absorbed the body and mind, and directed one's life to "the service of an unquestionable goal."[49] The goal of the two men in "Isis" would appear to have been a search for treasure, but, within the discourse of the adopted Western genre, the goal could be interpreted as having a greater significance. To borrow again from Tompkins, the two men were in:

> ... a world without God, without ideas, without institutions, without what is commonly recognised as culture, a world of men and things, where male adults in the prime of life [found] ultimate meaning in doing their best together on the job.[50]

Further to this, the sense of bonding between the two men, as they appeared to search for an ultimate meaning together, was enhanced by the exchange of possessions, as quoted above, in verse four. The narrator gave the stranger his blanket and received, in return, the man's word. The gift of a blanket suggested a certain sense of intimacy, what might be seen as almost a feminizing gift indicating comfort and warmth. While the gift of "his word" offered a further element of ambiguity; in a sense the song could be read as a tract concerning the male ownership of language. One man giving another man "his word" could be read not merely in the sense of swearing a promise, but also describing the ownership of language itself. Allen Ginsberg may have described Isis as a "Lady Language Creator,"[51] however, the discourse of the song, together with contemporary poststructuralist theories of language, betrays this idea.

* * *

To look in detail, for a moment, at the narrative at play within the song, it is interesting to note that while the narrator could remember some information about Isis; for example, the way that she smiled; he could not remember her words, her use of language, he could not remember the best things she said, as will be seen, shortly, in verse six. Isis, as a woman, did not own language, her gender lacked the universal signifier of language and thus her words were relatively unimportant and easily forgotten, whereas the male gift of "the word" *was* of significance. In both a symbolic and a literal sense, both of the men in the song, the narrator and the stranger, possessed the phallus, Jacques Lacan's universal arbiter of sexuality, the key signifier of meaning, the ultimately privileged signifier. Thus there was a sense here in which men owned language, they gave each other their word, and hence appeared to use language to control women. In the context of such a Lacanian reading, the gift of the word from one man to another, raised what was albeit an unintentional, but still entertaining lampoon of Lacan's ideas. This could be seen via the narrative detail that the two men in the song were heading north, encountering a frozen landscape—which offered obvious indicators of masculine adventurers undertaking polar expeditions. Hence this idea of a polar adventure, when overlaid with Lacanian resonances of the phallus as the ultimate signifier, could not help but bring to mind an almost risible search for "the pole."

* * *

In the fifth verse, a materialist motive for the journey was suggested:

> I was thinkin' about turquoise, I was thinkin' about gold
> I was thinkin' about diamonds and the world's biggest necklace
> As we rode through the canyons, through the devilish cold
> I was thinkin' about Isis, how she thought I was so reckless

As indicated previously, there was an implication that a quest for treasure, for fabulous wealth, may have been the real purpose of the journey, hence putting the song within a common genre of adventure story. However, material greed would seem to have been an incidental incentive, far from a prospect of gold and diamonds, it was the idea that Isis would find the narrator "so reckless" that appeared to be of primary importance.[52] Once again a contradiction was therefore inferred, the male narrator may have achieved his wish of finding himself within an exclusively masculine environment, but nonetheless his thoughts were still concerned with the female presence he had left behind. As if to compound this, in the sixth verse there was a sophisticated variation to the narrative, a rare example of analepsis in Dylan's work, wherein the narrator paused to reflect on a previous memory of Isis:

> How she told me that one day we would meet up again
> And things would be different the next time we wed
> If I only could hang on and just be her friend
> I still can't remember all the best things she said

Within the main narrative, the two men continued their journey and eventually reached the pyramids, which were, somewhat improbably it must be said, buried in ice:

> We came to the pyramids all embedded in ice
> He said, "There's a body I'm tryin' to find
> If I carry it out it'll bring a good price"
> 'Twas then that I knew what he had on his mind

2. Masculinity

It was at this point in the song, in verse seven, that the narrator's companion revealed that it was a body he was actually looking for. As such, there was an ambiguity and a sense of tension to this information, as depicted in the words of the narrator: "'Twas then that I knew what he had on his mind." However, as to what the man may have actually had on his mind was left unspoken. In a conspicuous gap in the narrative, in an elision, in an aporia, in what might be described as an "Iserian blank," the following verse, the eighth verse, offered some unexpected narrative exposition:

> The wind it was howlin' and the snow was outrageous
> We chopped through the night and we chopped through the dawn
> When he died I was hopin' that it wasn't contagious
> But I made up my mind that I had to go on

There was a typically "Dylanesque" quality in the descriptive phrase: "the snow was outrageous," albeit most probably occurring in order to provide a rhyme for contagious; in addition, the idea of chopping through the night and chopping through the dawn had a beguiling ambiguity. After which came the final line of the verse, the unexpected narrative ellipsis: with the stranger dying and the narrator quickly burying him.[53] At this stage the narrative became overtly compressed—with the cause of the stranger's demise remaining undisclosed. All that could be discerned was an anxiety on the behalf of the narrator, a sense of unease with the cause of the fatality, and a hope that it was not communicable.

Roger Horrocks, writing of masculinity in the Western, noted that the desire men may feel for each other, within the genre, could be attained only through violence and death, when there was nothing to lose in betraying one's true feelings. According to Horrocks, the Western novel and film were "phallic discourses" taken to an end point; they were "end-time discourses" in which the only thing that one man could give another was death, a dissolution back into the universe, a merging back into everything else. As Horrocks put it: "Men yearn for death. And they yearn for death in each other's arms, finally babbling of their forbidden love for each other."[54] Something of this could be felt in the emotional interchanges between the two men in "Isis." There was an unspoken, understated and underdeveloped attraction between the two men in the song, one that could only be alluded to via the death of one of them.

In the ninth and tenth verses, the narrator continued on his quest, alone:

> I broke into the tomb, but the casket was empty
> There was no jewels, no nothin', I felt I'd been had
> When I saw that my partner was just bein' friendly
> When I took up his offer I must-a been mad
>
> I picked up his body and I dragged him inside
> Threw him down in the hole and I put back the cover
> I said a quick prayer and I felt satisfied
> Then I rode back to find Isis just to tell her I love her

As detailed here, the narrator returned to Isis, to tell her he loved her, which was not, one might note, quite the same as actually loving her. The succeeding verse, verse eleven, offered further narrative detail:

> She was there in the meadow where the creek used to rise
> Blinded by sleep and in need of a bed
> I came in from the East with the sun in my eyes
> I cursed her one time then I rode on ahead[55]

The detail offered here was significant: Isis was in the meadow, where the creek used to rise. The subtle phrasing here, of where the creek *used* to rise, might be seen as suggesting a lost fertility, pointing to a number of possible readings. For example, if one continues to read the song within the Western genre, then the sense of sexual deprivation found in the Western could be perceived, as Jane Tompkins put it:

> Like the absence of greenery, it [the cowboy's denial of sex] is a turning away from fertility, fluidity, propagation and an affirmation of what is hard and dry and takes a long time to come to fruition.[56]

However, the song also at least claimed to be embedded within a narrative of Egyptian myth, and, if only on a much reduced level, the dry creek could hence be seen as evoking the dried-up Nile of the original Isis-Osiris story.[57] In the original myth it was a failure of fertility that called for a sacrificial death and rebirth. Seth, the son of Isis and Osiris, killed his father and scattered him, in fourteen pieces, up and down the Nile. Isis searched until she had found thirteen of the pieces to rebuild her husband, lacking only the fourteenth piece: the phallus. If one relates this to the narrative embedded within the song, it thus becomes significant to note that when the narrator breaks into the tomb he finds the casket empty, as the song put it: "There were no jewels, no nothing." Disregarding the potential testicular reference in the phrase: "no jewels,"[58] the word "nothing" could be deconstructed, in Shakespearian terms, as "no thing," in other words, no phallus.[59] In a sense,

2. Masculinity

as with the aforementioned search for the pole, the song became a search for the phallus. There was "no thing," there was only an empty tomb and a dried up creek. Dylan's technique here (together with the input of Jacques Levy) was impressive in its complex overlay of myths, all of which succeeded in suggesting a sense of sexual aridity that was present, just beneath the surface of the lyric.

In the penultimate verse of the song, the narrator and Isis had a short, surreal conversation in which the narrator, somewhat unconvincingly it must be said, appeared to agree that he would stay with Isis, that he would seal his commitment to her:

> She said, "Where ya been?" I said, "No place special"
> She said, "You look different." I said, "Well, not quite"
> She said, "You been gone." I said, "That's only natural"
> She said, "You gonna stay?" I said, "Yeah, I jes might"

It should be noted here, that the lyrics quoted above were not those of the recording, the version of the lyric with which most listeners would perhaps be most familiar. It would seem that there was a textual revision, of verse twelve, some time between the release of *Desire*, in 1976, and the subsequent publication of the song in *Lyrics 1962–1985*, in 1985.[60] The verse, as published in *Lyrics 1962–1985*, had a number of subtle revisions, textual revisions that most probably remained obscure to most *listeners* of Dylan's work; insomuch as, and as far as can be ascertained, Dylan has never performed the *Lyrics* version of the song either in concert or elsewhere on record. Yet, from a certain point of view this is the officially sanctioned version; as such, and as discussed in the introduction of this study, this merely representing another indication of how problematical the search for the authentic Dylan text can be.

However, attempting to offer an analysis of the text of the song, in its performed version, would not seem to be without its difficulties. As previously intimated in the introduction, the license to reprint Dylan's lyrics, from Special Rider Music, states that: the lyric quotation must be printed exactly as it appears on the song's lyric page at www.bobdylan.com. Hence a direct transcription of the performed version would appear to be proscribed from analytical, critical and hermeneutic debate. As the textual alterations in question are crucial to a discussion of the song, one might suggest the reader listens to the recording of the song to witness the actual textual construction; alternatively, one might attempt to suggest here (albeit somewhat clumsily and in an indirect fashion) what that textual construction consisted of. The changes to the lyric occurred at the end of the second and fourth lines of the verse in question, the twelfth verse; in the second line, instead of "Well, not quite" Dylan sang: "Well, I guess" and in the fourth line, instead of "Yeah, I jes might" Dylan sang: "If you want me to, yes." This final word, "yes," as will be seen in the discussion below, was of some significance, hence the need for clarification here. As to the reason for the change in the verse, it is impracticable to attempt to ascertain how this lyrical variation occurred; it could have been a careful literary amendment by Dylan himself, or it could have been a mishearing or a misquoting via an anonymous editorial action. In whatever way, it arguably applied a somewhat detrimental action to the verse as originally performed.

As intimated, the narrator's final quoted word, in the performed version of the lyric, was a life affirming, Joycean: "yes," thus offering the song a subtle intertextual resonance. "Yes" was the last word of spoken dialogue in both "Isis," as reconstructed above, and also in James Joyce's novel, *Ulysses* (1922), wherein Molly Bloom's final words—the final words of the novel—were as follows:

> I put my arms around him yes and drew him down to me so he could feel my breasts all perfume yes and his heart was going like mad and yes I said yes I will Yes.[61]

The narrator of Dylan's song, like Leopold Bloom in *Ulysses*, had returned to his beginning, and, after a period of wandering, had found no answer, no solution, no meaning with which to confront the sense of futility, frustration and loneliness he had had before he left. Furthermore, Isis, like Molly Bloom, had remained at home, waiting for her husband to return, as she knew he would. Both Dylan's unnamed narrator and Leopold Bloom were, in a sense, subjugated by the women they were involved with; there was a sense that both Isis and Molly possessed a certain understanding of the fears and desires of the men they were married to; and that, as women, they knew how to use this power. Isis's lover and Bloom may have been in possession of the universal male signifier, they may have had the ability to travel in the world; but, for all of this, these men: the narrator of Isis, Leopold Bloom and even the Homeric, Odysseus, ultimately seemed dependent on the female presence and were thus continually drawn back towards them.

This sense of futility and ultimate dependence on the female could be seen in a narrative detail, found within the ninth verse, that the tomb was empty. The journey made by the narrator could thus be seen as an allegorical account of a search which ultimately led only to the place where the journey had begun. For example, John Herdman has commented that the narrator of "Isis" has:

> ... been through hell and back again, has gained nothing and learned nothing, and now finds himself once more in the very situation which drove him forth. We can visualise a nightmare-like eternal recurrence of this cyclic movement.[62]

This was an accurate comment, Dylan's hero had found no solution, no meaning, and his only option would seem to have been to return and to attempt to find some meaning in life via a woman's love. This, one might argue, was the underlying contradiction of the construct of masculinity in this text and perhaps elsewhere in Dylan's work as a whole.

Aidan Day, one of the few critics of Dylan's work to have discussed the implications of masculinity within the song, at least in any detail, noted that the narrator's return "with the sun in his eyes" played upon the association of Isis with the moon:

> In the speaker's return to Isis is imaged again, as in the opening of the lyric, a sacramental conjunction of sun and moon: a creative union of masculine and female principles. As a parable of a psychic split, the speaker's journey away from Isis exposes the inadequacies of too one-sided a development of the conventionally masculine aspects of identity. The much prized attributes of the heroic ego—all will and active self-determination—are stripped to expose an aggressive, imaginatively barren and ultimately life-denying acquisitiveness.[63]

In an otherwise carefully measured book—sometimes to the point of aridity—Day presented an intellectually stimulating argument. However, and perhaps more pertinently, the song could also be read as an allegorical construct encircling the impossibility of ever reconciling gender differences, the impossibility of man and woman ever fully comprehending one another. The question the song appeared to be asking was whether Isis, and her reckless, masculine lover, could ever live happily ever after: or indeed, whether any man and woman (as positioned in Dylan's work) could ever truly live happily ever after. The song derived from an album called *Desire*, and there would seem to have been a desire to achieve a union between the masculine and feminine spheres of action. However, whether this could ever be achieved within the performative construct of gender in this song, and many others in Dylan's canon, seemed uncertain.

In the thirteenth and final verse, at the *denouement* of the song, we were offered this final scene:

> Isis, oh, Isis, you mystical child
> What drives me to you is what drives me insane

> I still can remember the way that you smiled
> On the fifth day of May in the drizzlin' rain

The narrator, forced back into a feminine domain, appeared to recall the contradiction of needing Isis and not needing her, together with risking his life and possibly his sanity in the process of so doing. Thus the song ended, in a completely circular fashion, ending as it had begun: on the fifth day of May in the drizzling rain. The fifth day of the fifth month was perhaps relevant—once again—to a Joycean reading, insomuch as there would appear to have been an inherent complexity in the numerical patterning within the song, perhaps with the deliberate intent of the song's authors, a complexity of which James Joyce may well have approved. For example, it might be noted that the song had thirteen verses, perhaps alluding to Osiris, whose body was found in thirteen pieces. In addition, the number thirteen might have also been linked to the fact that this was a song about a great moon goddess.[64] Thus it was perhaps valid to perceive of a reference to the lunar cycle of thirteen menstrual months; to the old "feminine" calendar of thirteen lunar months: thirteen times twenty-eight adding up to 364 days, one day short of a year, possibly alluding to the "year and a day" of myth and legend. Thus the fact that Dylan's song seemed to end exactly one day short of the year in which it began,[65] cannot help but suggest at least the possibility of a certain numerological patterning on the part of the song's design.

* * *

From a different but related perspective, the story as told within the song could also be seen as encompassing the tradition of the American quest narrative. Joseph Boone has argued that the American quest narrative was a genre written by men, about men, for men: "a genre that valorises ideological concerns in a patriarchal social structure."[66] Furthermore, that the ambivalent attitude towards sexuality, what Boone called: "a rebellion against the ethos of sexual polarity pervading the countless tales of love and seduction,"[67] suggested that the journeys undertaken by these men could be seen as a way of exploring the enigma of sexual identity. Boone wrote of:

> the outward-bound voyage to confront the unknown, that by definition constitutes quest narrative, simultaneously traces an inner journey toward a redefinition of self that defies social convention and sexual categorisation.[68]

Boone suggested a difference in the American version of the quest-romance formula, a shift from the European goal of "a fair lady's love," to goals that

2. Masculinity

had more to do with "metaphysical objects of truth, absolute reality and the nature of authority."[69] This idea would seem to echo Leslie Fiedler's concept of asserting one's virility via heroic acts rather than genital acts, and that "manly friendships" acted as a substitute for marriage.[70] All of this may be seen as at least one explanation for the ways in which many of the men in Dylan's songs acted; and, in this way, also adding weight to the argument (as expressed within this study) to the ways in which the performative nature of gender might be seen to operate within Dylan's work.

* * *

"Isis," like other American texts as diverse as: *Moby Dick*, *The Adventures of Huckleberry Finn* and *On the Road*, not to mention a multitude of other examples in both literary and cinematic forums, found a masculine couple embarked upon a quest narrative. One might, for example, compare the two men in "Isis" to Ishmael and Ahab in *Moby Dick*; with the narrator of the song being envisaged as an equivalent to Ishmael, a man ensconced in both the feminine and masculine worlds,[71] while the man the narrator encountered in the song, could be seen as representing Ahab, a figure with a one-sided definition of his masculinity, as his "tragically fixed purpose and fixated personality attest[ed]."[72] Leslie Fiedler has written that *Moby Dick* can be read not only as an account of a whale-hunt, but also as "a love story, perhaps the greatest love story in our fiction."[73] In an analogous sense "Isis" could be read as being more than a mere account of a search for the world's biggest necklace; in its own way it was also a love story—although a love story perhaps outside of the conscious intent of its authors—and, one could argue, outside of the hermeneutic expectations of the majority of its listeners. Nonetheless, in the textual body of "Isis," as in *Moby Dick*, one can perceive and read, in greater and lesser ways, an exploration of Fiedlerian ideas of manly friendships acting as a substitute for marriage. It is important that this was deniable, but it is a theme that nonetheless runs throughout *Moby Dick* and, one might argue, throughout the song in question here, one of Dylan's most beguiling creations: "Isis."

As has been seen, the masculine journey often entailed a man leaving a woman, departing on a journey of great importance, a quest, often in the company of another man. As intimated, this could be seen in texts as diverse as: Homer's *The Odyssey*, Joyce's *Ulysses*, Melville's *Moby Dick*, Twain's *The Adventures of Huckleberry Finn*, Stanley Kubrick's film *2001: A Space Odyssey*—and so on—such texts could be linked with Dylan's song, "Isis," all telling much the same story. These were decidedly masculine and homosocial stories; with Dylan's songs repeatedly suggesting that there was an intrinsic maleness about travelling. Camille Paglia, in her book *Sexual Persona*, concurred, seeing men in the same way, as sexual exiles, wandering the earth seeking but unable to find satisfaction, never achieving contentment. For Paglia man was the *homme fatal*, a rambler, a cowboy, a sailor, who would constantly move on—while the *femme fatale* would remain. As Paglia put it: "Woman does not dream of transcendental or historical escape from natural cycles, since she is that cycle. Her sexual maturity means marriage to the moon, waxing and waning in lunar cycles."[74] Paglia was not referring here, either generally or explicitly, to Dylan's song, but her argument was so specific that she might well have been doing so.

Paglia was, however, interested in the Western genre in its relation to masculinity, and in the case of its use here, in "Isis," there was a beguiling metaphor in the idea of the West as a New Eden, wherein a male couple could allow "visions of love" amid "deserts, horses, huge skies and the far country."[75] Instead of an acceptance of domesticity, the cowboy, the drifter, the wanderer, the rambler, the traveling man—and so on—were all able to hold to the impossible romance of constantly traveling, of constantly moving on, of constantly heading for the next town. There was an echo here, in the sense of the iconic figure of the cowboy, of a man who was able to live, once again, within nature, to have no responsibility—and instead to have the ability to confront his own nature, found within a lost paradise, with the promise that the yearning for a New Eden might be achieved. In this way, as Jane Tompkins put it, men were able to dream of a home that was literally "on the range," with the Western hero seeking the solace of the open space of the wilderness, a home within of vastness and magnificence and emptiness and, above all, the silence of the wilderness. As the song had it: "Where seldom is heard a discouraging word, and the skies are not cloudy all day."[76]

As by way of a final comment on the homosocial and Fiedlerian readings found within "Isis," it might be of interest to consider the ethnic identity of the stranger (the "man in the corner") the narrator of "Isis" encounters in verse three of the song. Few physical details were offered in the text; however, it might be reasonable to speculate that few listeners of the song might have imagined the stranger, the "man in the corner," to have been black; yet, from a specific arena of speculation, this may arguably have been the case. In other words, the stranger in "Isis" could just as easily have been black as white, the fact that few of the listeners and readers of the song have ever explored this possibility merely betraying the underlying prejudices of the song's predominantly white audience. Toni Morrison, in her short monograph, *Playing in the Dark*, a book that remains one of the key works of race in American literature, discussed, at one point in her text, some of the characters in Ernest Hemingway's novel, *To Have and Have Not*; during her discussion of one of the characters, Eddy, Morrison made the comment: "Eddy is white, and we know he is because nobody says so."[77] This simple sentence spoke eloquently about many of the assumptions we make when reading American literature. In just the same way, we know that the "man in the corner" is white—because nobody has said he is. However, the "man in the corner" may well have been black—and, if so, then here one can perceive of a return to Leslie Fiedler's key argument, to one of Fiedler's key phrases, the edict that in American literature: "a white and a colored American male flee from civilization into each others arms."[78] In addition, and to quote Fiedler at his most extreme, and in an albeit an out of date nomenclature: "In dreams of white men, psychologists tell us, the forbidden erotic object tends to be represented by a colored man."[79] It is here, within Fiedler's almost prophetic argument, that we can read the actual intent of the narrative in Dylan's song; or at least we can read of one hermeneutic supposition.

* * *

Leslie Fiedler has often been seen as something of a "loose cannon" in American criticism[80]; and to the casual reader of *Love and Death in the American Novel* it might have seemed, as intimated above, as if Fiedler was suggesting that American novels were fundamentally about white American boys in love with African American men. However, as Charles B. Harris, in his introduction to the 1997 edition of the book, put it: "What Fiedler had really meant to say, however, is that this chaste 'anti-marriage' of male companionship frees the protagonist of classic American fiction from the adult entanglements of heterosexual passion, marriage and domestic obligations."[81] In this way, Fiedler's book denoted the lack of women in such American novels as: *Moby Dick, Huckleberry Finn, The Last of the Mohicans, The Red Badge of Courage*, the stories of Edgar Allan Poe and so on; as Fiedler contended, these were: "books that turn from society to nature or nightmare out of a desperate need to avoid the facts of wooing, marriage and child bearing."[82] According to Fiedler: "the typical male protagonist of our fiction has been a man on the run, harried into the forest and out to sea ... anywhere to avoid civilization, the confrontation of a man and woman which leads to the fall to sex, marriage and responsibility."[83] Fiedler went on to offer this summation of his ideas:

> Through the corrupt city, the innocent tough guy ... moves on an immaculate journey. The undraped daughters of the rich, tight-breasted virgins and nymphomaniacs tempt him with their proffered bodies; but he is faithful only to his buddies ... a chevalier of the city streets, blasting down the female he never quite manages to possess, and who, dead in one book, rises up in the next, phallic and aggressive, deadly whether clothed or nude.[84]

Insomuch, Fiedler's book, with its chevalier of the city streets, might be seen as providing a template for the portrayal of men within Bob Dylan's "Isis," Fiedler's book delineating the profoundly homosocial discourses at play within the text of the song.[85]

* * *

By way of a temporary digression, while on the topic of race, it might be noted, that although Dylan wrote a number of songs in the early 1960s that described the plight of African Americans, he seldom confronted the issue of slavery itself. Perhaps the closest instance in which he was able to do this occurred in a song he did not write, his performance of "No More Auction Block"—performed at the Gaslight Café in October 1962, and released on *The Bootleg Series Vol. 1–3: Rare and Unreleased 1961–1991*. A possible reason for this might lie in the simple fact that slavery would seem to be seldom discussed in American artistic productions as a whole; there are relatively few films, plays, novels and so on that deal with the subject. In other words, there was a sense in which Dylan had as little ability to encompass the grotesque history of slavery in America as anyone else, insomuch as it has been seen as a site of such unspeakable horror. As Fiedler put it: "the ultimate Southern horror, the unmitigated terror of conscienceless and brutal slavery."[86] There was also the issue of having to conspire in the upkeep of a patriotic hypocrisy, the duplicity and double standards in claiming, at America's very beginning, that *all* men were created equal; in Toni Morrison's words: "the inherent contradiction of a free republic deeply committed to slavery."[87] Or as Frank Pembleton (played by the African American actor Andre Braugher), the fictional detective in *Homicide* (the precursor to *The Wire*), commented: "Everyone was an immigrant at some point in this country—some even by choice." This inability to deal with slavery could be seen in Dylan's song "Mississippi," one of his more significant works of the 2000s, it was titled after one of the most racist states in the United

2. Masculinity

States, but it possessed a complete lack of interest about race; instead it merely offered a repetition of the ubiquitous trope of masculine travel; for example, the protagonist had been in trouble since he set his suitcase down; the only thing he did wrong was to stay in Mississippi a day too long; his heart was not weary—it was light and free—and so on. In the 1960s, Dylan had written several songs set in Mississippi: as in "The Death of Emmett Till," "Oxford Town" and "Only a Pawn in Their Game"—all of which dealt with racial issues—he had also appeared at a voter registration rally at Silas McGee's farm, in Greenwood, Mississippi, this occurred in July 1963, and was a rare instance of Dylan seeming to place his own personal safety at risk. However, in the one song named after Mississippi, a song that came much later in his career, he was unable to include any suggestion of a discourse pertaining to race.

* * *

To return to the main area of discussion: Bob Dylan may have written, in one of his most intriguing but most overlooked songs of the 1960s, "I Can't Leave Her Behind" (1966),[88] of the impossibility of ever leaving the company of a woman. However, such a sentiment was betrayed, not merely by the sexual innuendo of the title (possibly a deliberate intent on Dylan's part), but in the way such a sentiment was displaced by the general discourse of his work. In other words, while the song seemed to express the absolute need of female companionship, this was very much the exception and there were numerous other songs to contradict such a conceptual model. To cite one example, in "Tight Connection to My Heart" (1985), the male narrator told the woman he was getting his coat, as if to brave an oncoming storm, going on to further inform the woman that there was something he had to do (perhaps whatever it was "a man's gotta do") and that she should go inside and stay warm. As in "Isis," once again there was a sense in which the male protagonist was shown with an inexplicable desire to leave the warmth of a feminine environment, to travel into a cold masculine world, to accomplish something unstated, presumably to do—as intimated above—whatever it was a "man's gotta do." The issue as to whether there was something innately feminine about the home and something innately masculine about wanting to leave it, was not open to discussion, at least not within the overarching discursive practices of Dylan's songs. It was simply accepted as a given; with the men in Dylan's songs continually demonstrating a need for freedom, a need to separate from a feminine influence, arguably because this was the blueprint of masculinity they were both destined and condemned to act out, in order to fulfill their idea of what it meant to be a man.

If one returns to the song "Don't Think Twice, It's All Right" (1963), a song that arguably remains one of Dylan's most impressive love/anti-love songs, here a male voice told the woman he was addressing that it was pointless to sit and wonder why he had left her:

> When your rooster crows at the break of dawn
> Look out your window and I'll be gone
> You're the reason I'm trav'lin' on
> Don't think twice it's all right[89]

The phrase "You're the reason I'm trav'lin' on" must be seen as one of the most significant phrases in Dylan's work, in his entire lyrical lexicon. In a sense the phrase summed up why so many of the men in so many of Dylan's songs were still on the road, why so many men embarked on so many seemingly self-important, if ultimately meaningless adventures and pursuits.[90] To restate the point: it could be argued that these men were on the road, were in a continual state of movement, because of women, because of the need to escape from the domain of women. Furthermore, this was the primary way in which they constructed a sense of masculinity, to find a means of being men. These men were on "the dark side of the road," where they were bound they "[could not] tell,"[91] but if they were on the road at least they were not shackled to the very thing they seemed to fear.

In one of Dylan's many other songs with a Western theme, "Wanted Man" (1969), the male protagonist of the song was wanted in a wide range of the cities and states of America: in California, in Kansas City, in Colorado—even in Georgia by the sea. However, whether he was wanted in the clichéd Western sense of being an outlaw was open to interpretation. The wanted man in the song was also wanted by a collection of women, by Lucy Watson, by Jeannie Brown and by Nellie Johnson, and hence there was the idea that the wanted man was an outlaw, as much from a female domain, as he was from the law and from the judicial system. In "Billy" (1973), a similar motif could be seen at play, with the song persistently posing the question of why Billy could not be free. An undefined "they" did not want the outlaw to be free; but to whom the line may have been referring was ambiguous; in a literal sense, the line may have been referencing the lawmen and the bounty hunters on Billy the Kid's trail; however, the line could also have been referring to the women who would lay claims to the outlaw's spirit—to his soul—hence

2. Masculinity

raising an analogous proposition. Throughout the song the character of Billy the Kid was described as figuring a way to get back home, but it was questionable if he would have been able to define where, or what, that home might have been. In the song's fourth verse, Billy was described as: walking all alone, a line that might arguably bring this discussion back to the beginning, to the issue discussed at the start of this chapter, to the image of a man walking down a road alone, as if there were something essentially masculine about the desire for such a solitary and ultimately meaningless way of life.[92]

The road, when taken to its logical conclusion, led to just one destination; this could be seen to plain and specific effect in the song "Let Me Die in My Footsteps" (1963). Herein the male narrator had a resolute determination to keep on walking, even if it meant it would be necessary for him to die, in his said "footsteps." In other words, if he were to die, he would die proactively on the road, he would not, as Dylan's supposed namesake put it, go gentle into that good night.[93] It has been said that "Let Me Die in my Footsteps" was written around the time of the 1962 Cuban Missile Crisis; and, in another song written at about the same time and on a similar theme: "A Hard Rain's A-Gonna Fall" (1963), the same idea was more famously expressed. The song began with a maternal voice asking where her blue-eyed son had been, where her darling young one had been. To which the blue-eyed son replied that he had been stumbling on misty mountains, walking on crooked highways, stepping into sad forests, standing in front of dead oceans—and so on. However, even under the threat of total annihilation, what one might interpret as the threat of a nuclear holocaust, the blue-eyed son would keep on walking, would keep on walking even towards his death, such was the significance of masculine travel—and the way it was so prevalent within the philosophy of the men in Dylan's work.

This sense of a near death-wish was expressed, still more explicitly, in the song "Goin' Goin' Gone" (1974), wherein the narrator closed by claiming, in ubiquitous fashion, that he had been walking a road, that he had been living on the edge, and finally, in a somewhat ominous light, he was (as the title of the song put it) going, he was going, he was gone. Similarly, in the song "I and I" (1983), the male protagonist found that he was pushing himself along the road, and, once again, there was an ominous note insomuch as the protagonist was on the darkest part of the road; a phrase that recalled the dark side of the road in "Don't Think Twice, It's All Right," a phrase that suggested, far from this song's spirited claim of: "Where I'm bound I can't tell" that these men knew exactly where they were going; they knew exactly where they were ultimately bound, where such desultory and peripatetic wanderings would take them.[94] The heroes of these songs, like the archetypal heroes of the Western, ended up walking from civilization, walking into the wilderness, walking on into an "infinite America," walking on towards the horizon, walking towards the sunset, walking into a "dying star."[95] They appeared to be relentlessly "going west," and to go west, as Jane Tompkins put it, was to go as far west as one could, and to go "west of everything," was to die.[96] However, as Michael Wood put it, such heroes, such men "live happily ever after—as long as they keep walking,"[97] or to paraphrase Bob Dylan, as long as they refrain from stopping.[98]

Therefore, and by way of approaching a summary to this chapter, one might conclude by restating that such a compulsion to take to the road was clearly gender related within Dylan's work. Furthermore, one could suggest that this argument could be positioned as implying this made up a significant aspect of the underlying structure of masculinity, as expressed in many of Dylan's songs, a structure, it might also be suggested, that was constructed upon a wholly assumed artifice. In a final consideration, it might therefore be assumed that there was no logical reason why these men, in these songs, felt compelled to do this; in other words, the many men in many of Dylan's songs felt compelled to travel for no other reason than that they unconsciously felt the need to do so. In one of the most iconic films of the 1950s, *The Wild One* (1953), a young woman asked Marlon Brando's character, Johnny, "Where are you going when you leave here?" To which Brando's character laconically replied, "We just go." In a similar way, in Jack Kerouac's seminal work of masculine travel, *On the Road* (1957), a similar nihilistic notion was expressed:

> "Sal, we gotta go and never stop going till we get there."
> "Where are we going, man?"
> "I don't know, but we gotta go."[99]

In a sense, this exchange in Kerouac's book, as with Brando's comment in *The Wild One*, significantly informed much of the philosophy behind masculine travel within Dylan's work. Insomuch, it would appear that this seemingly nihilistic notion had, in fact, a more rational and logically constructed foundation. In other words, while the men in many of Dylan's songs appeared to "just go," while it appeared their primary impulse was merely to "get away," there was, in a certain sense, a more logical reasoning in play. The men in the narratives of Dylan's songs may have appeared to be wanderers by trade, to have had no direction home and to have been continually heading for

2. Masculinity

another joint; however, one might argue here that they were simply acting out a concept of gender as a performative construct. In the world according to Dylan, these wanderers by trade, within the multiple discourses of the songs, were, in fact, acting out a role that defined their construct of masculinity, acting out a role that defined them as men.

3

Femininity

"The new woman is nothing without a man."
—Bob Dylan, the *Playboy* interview, 1978

Betty Friedan's book *The Feminine Mystique*, published in 1963, could be seen as the beginning of the modern feminist movement. The book argued against the assumption that women enjoyed being wives and mothers, and that they had no ideological, political or intellectual point of view about the world.[1] Friedan's book coincided with the beginning of Dylan's career, but it is doubtful if he read it, Dylan may have been aware of the book, but at least on the evidence of some of his songs it would seem highly doubtful if he agreed with the argument being made. In a wider sense, feminism might be described as follows: it was a conscious movement to resist patriarchy, to disturb the complacencies of a patriarchal culture, to assert a belief in sexual equality and to eradicate sexist domination in society.[2] In this sense feminism could be said to be attempting to deconstruct the androcentric hegemony; to refute the right wing ideology that has always sought to mobilize against women's sexual autonomy. As Lynn Segal put it, such a right wing ideology argues against: "abortion, against homosexuality, against divorce, against sex education, indeed against everything which has helped undermine men's control over women's sexuality."[3] For example, the American evangelist, Pat Robertson, went so far as to claim that feminism was "a socialist, anti-family movement that encourages women to leave their husbands, kill their children, practise witchcraft, destroy capitalism and become lesbians."[4] There was nothing quite so extreme in Dylan's work; albeit at the time of the so-called "born-again" period, Dylan came close to at least seeming to agree with some elements of such a misogynistic discourse.[5] In the light of this, a reading of Dylan's work from a feminist perspective, as found within a diverse range of his lyrics, will be made in this chapter.

From the perspective of adopting a feminist critique towards his work, Bob Dylan's career begins in an apposite way. The first song on his debut

3. Femininity

record, *Bob Dylan* (1962), opened with an unashamedly chauvinistic discourse, with the singer in deprecating mood, decrying his supposed lover within a misanthropic and overtly sexist discourse. The song, Jesse Fuller's "You're No Good,"[6] suggested more than just an antagonism towards the woman addressed in the text; the male voice demonstrated a significant distrust of the female subject. The song made a number of generalizations about her, comparing her to an evil deity and a man-eater, giving the overall impression that she was someone to be feared. This was merely the initial sense the world had of Dylan on record; however, one might argue that these views, from the very beginning of Dylan's recording career, were not wholly unrepresentative, and that, throughout his career, Dylan has often depicted the women in his work in a comparable fashion. The question: as to why so many of his lyrics would at least appear to demonstrate what might be described as a misogynistic approach, will be one of the main issues to be explored in this chapter.

The persona of Bob Dylan, as a famous singer of the early 1960s, has typically been seen as that of a radical voice of youthful protest, an advocate of the under-privileged, a champion of the oppressed. One might see this as a legitimate view in terms of Dylan's approach to a certain range of issues. For example, the civil rights movement, the threat of nuclear war, the social injustices done to specific individuals and so on. However, on what were arguably two of the most important political issues in America in the 1960s, which one might reasonably assume as being that of the Vietnam War and the feminist movement,[7] in these areas Dylan was profoundly silent. There were few if any songs about the Vietnam War,[8] and there were certainly very few songs about the feminist movement. As Christopher Ricks put it:

> You have to wrack your brains to find a Dylan song about women's liberation ... women's liberation seems to me the biggest domestic change in America that Dylan has been resistant to, hostile to, suspicious to.[9]

One might concur here with Ricks and maintain that Bob Dylan, the supposedly tolerant and liberal protest singer of the 1960s, often had a less than tolerant and liberal attitude towards women, and certainly towards the feminist movement. One might suggest that Dylan's attitude to women has often been one of suspicion and hostility, that the women in Dylan's songs were seldom seen as fellow, equitable human beings; in fact it would seem clear that women were often seen as a threat to the structure of masculinity within Dylan's work.

Some sense of such an argument could be seen in the song "Don't Think Twice, It's All Right" (1963). This was a work that has been described as Dylan's first love song,[10] yet one might suggest this may have been a somewhat erroneous claim. In the chronology of Dylan's recorded work it was arguably one of the first songs written with a woman as the sole subject, but in many ways it was much more of an anti-love song than a love song. As discussed in Chapter 2, this was a song in which a man was unable to wholly commit to a woman, but it was also a caustic, derisive and sarcastic exercise in which the woman (or "gal" as she was called) was informed she had simply not come up to expectations:

> I ain't sayin' you treated me unkind
> You could have done better but I don't mind
> You just kinda wasted my precious time
> But don't think twice, it's all right[11]

There was a sense of dominance and mastery to the discourse of the text as presented here; a sense of dominance that was, in a sense, typical of Dylan's work in general. The male voice tells the woman she could have done better, but the sense of arrogance might have prompted the listener of the song into turning the question around, to ask if the male voice, himself, could not have done better. It was clear that a relationship of some kind had failed, but it was also equally clear that the masculine narrator was putting the blame totally on the woman. There seeming to be no hope of a rapprochement, the gap between the singer's desires and the woman's being too great to bridge.

Hence in this way there was an interesting dichotomy apparent. To the majority of commentators "Don't Think Twice, It's All Right" was a great love song, while at the same time it could also be seen as a slanted, resentful and gender-biased song. Dylan has been described as the great love songwriter,[12] and yet at the same time, and as will be argued here, he also at least appears to have been the great misogynistic writer. It is a mark of Dylan's faculty for artistic complexity that he can appear to be both of these things at the same time. Thus it is important, when dealing with a writer as subtle and as enigmatic as Dylan, to be aware of the potential for these contradictions. The men in Dylan's work are often suspicious and hostile towards the women they are involved with, but they are irredeemably drawn to them as well. One potential answer to this contradiction is, one might suggest, connected to the artifice of gender in Dylan's work, to the performative nature of gender, to the sense in which gender is constructed in Dylan's work: as the argument herein will attempt to establish.

* * *

There are, it must be admitted, some examples of straightforward love songs to women in Dylan's work, which should come as no surprise as the love song is, after all, the core topic of popular music. And yet, a straightforward love song, from a man to a woman, is perhaps surprisingly rare within Dylan's canon. As Craig Snow put it:

> Only rarely does passionate love [occur] in the midst of a healthy and ongoing relationship.... The most common subject Dylan returns to throughout his career is love ... [but] few of his love songs can be accurately described as expositions of heartfelt, sustaining, and mutually satisfying love.[13]

Such songs do exist, one might think of:

"Girl from the North Country" (1963)
"Tomorrow Is a Long Time" (1963)
"Boots of Spanish Leather" (1964)
"To Ramona" (1964)
"Sad Eyed Lady of the Lowlands" (1966)
"If Not for You" (1970)
"Wedding Song" (1974)
"Sara" (1976)
"Precious Angel" (1979)
"Covenant Woman" (1980)
"Emotionally Yours" (1985)

and finally:

"Love Is Just a Four Letter Word" (1965)

However, even in these few examples there were compromising factors. "To Ramona" would seem to have been very much a platonic love song; both "Girl from the North Country" and "Boots of Spanish Leather" were songs in which the love object had departed; both "Precious Angel" and "Covenant Woman" were songs in which the woman was worshipped and adored only for the fact that she had led her lover to salvation through Christ. Finally, in the case of "Love Is Just a Four Letter Word," it is somewhat ironic that, in what was arguably *the* ultimate love song in Dylan's canon, a song in which a man expressed total and unqualified love to a woman, this was a song that has never been released. It remains the one acclaimed, prestigious and celebrated song of which no Dylan version, either official or unofficial, studio version or live rendition, is known to exist, it is the one famous song in which Dylan's voice is literally voiceless.[14]

All of this is not to say that Dylan's songs did not, at times, have an overtly sensual and erotic quality. There are, for example, a significant number of songs in which women were seen as objects of unadorned sexual desire. Once again this would not be wholly unexpected, insomuch as this has always been a common theme in popular music and certainly a consistent and pervasive trope in the predominantly male blues tradition. Yet, within Dylan's work, one can perceive that such erotic descriptions rarely occurred without a tendency to add a demeaning context to the object of desire. For example, in the opening song on *Under the Red Sky*, "Wiggle Wiggle" (1990), the woman was unashamedly sexualized: being informed that she should wiggle on her hands and knees. Similarly, in "New Pony" (1978), the pony/girl was seen merely as someone to be climbed on top of and ridden. In "Blind Willie McTell" (1983), the nubile black women, who were presumably freed slaves, were depicted as strutting their feathers, raising a number of questionable issues, some almost racist in nature, as well as the implied sexist discourse.[15] One of the most excessive cases, in such a context, could be seen in "Dirty World" (1988), a song Dylan contributed to the first Traveling Wilburys album. Here the woman in the song was objectified in a particularly salacious context, and, unusually for Dylan, the language possessed a much more explicit quality. There were, for example, a number of crude clichés: a variation on the American saying of putting something where the sun doesn't shine; together with phallic references to pick-up trucks, and so on, all of this overlaid within a sense of mock anal sadism. In such a way the song was as crude and as "dirty" as the title of the song itself. It is possible to write about women in this way, and—as intimated—this is hardly rare in both popular music and the blues tradition,[16] but such a scant regard for a respectful attitude towards women then becomes clearly apparent.

A better-known and more subtle example of such a tendency to sexually objectify women could be seen in "Lay, Lady, Lay" (1969), a song in which the love object was given the following instructions:

> Lay, lady, lay, lay across my big brass bed
> Lay, lady, lay, lay across my big brass bed
> Whatever colors you have in your mind
> I'll show them to you and you'll see them shine[17]

3. Femininity

In this case, there was a woman (or a lady, as she was alliteratively described) whose only function, it seems, was to make her man smile, presumably by pleasing him sexually—on the big brass bed. Furthermore, the man was seen as all-powerful, with an innate knowledge of the colors that existed within the lady's mind, this seeming to be concurrent with the ability to make them explode, presumably into the metaphorical bliss of *jouissance* or of sexual ecstasy. "Country Pie" (1969), a song from the same record, *Nashville Skyline*, offered a more exaggerated version of this burlesque of skewed sexual stereotypes. On the surface the song may have seemed a rather lightweight and light-hearted work; however, in contrast to this, it could also be read as a song with a darkly satirical undertone. The title of the song punned on a number of levels. It was a country pie because the song appeared on what was a self-confessed country music record, albeit a conscious parody. It was also a country pie because of all the ingredients present:

> Raspberry, strawberry, lemon and lime
> What do I care?
> Blueberry, apple, cherry, pumpkin and plum
> Call me for dinner, honey, I'll be there[18]

However, disregarding the vaguely sexist assumption of the man being called for dinner, it was a country pie because, at a somewhat more invidious level, there was a potential satire that involved taking the "o" out of country pie. When this was accomplished the intent of the line: "Oh me, oh my, love that country pie" became less ambiguous and more suggestive. The male protagonist in the song loved one particular part of the female subject, the object of desire was positioned as little more than a vaginal wedged shape of pie; the same bawdy word play Shakespeare had used in *Hamlet*—the somewhat infamous "country matters" scene.[19]

At times the sheer verve and wit of Dylan's writing tended to disguise the slanted gender discourse taking place. This could be seen to good effect in an unused song of 1964, "Denise," in the song, via the use of two common idioms, the masculine voice asked the eponymous Denise whether she was on sale or whether she was merely on the shelf. What was really being asked here was whether Denise was a prostitute (for sale), or whether she was an old maid (on the shelf), all enveloped within a sarcastic metaphor of sexual commerce.[20] The idea of woman as a sexual commodity, as a prostitute, was, perhaps unsurprisingly, a recurrent feature in Dylan's work. One might think of the street-walker in "Simple Twist of Fate" (1975), the woman who was a prostitute (and a hot one) in "Billy" (1973), the specific number (twenty-four) of women in the brothel in "The Ballad of Frankie Lee and Judas Priest" (1968), the woman of shame in "Jokerman" (1983), the woman who claimed she could fix the male protagonist up fast in "Bob Dylan's New Orleans Rag" (1964), the prostitute (or whore, as she was referred to in the song) passing the hat in "Foot of Pride" (1983) and so on, throughout a diverse number of other examples. In contrast to these numerous instances, it was not surprising to note that male prostitutes—men using their bodies for sexual commerce—hardly appeared at all in Dylan's work.[21]

In a further context, one can perceive, in Dylan's work, of a sense of a masculine voice on the defensive, and therefore going on the offence to ward off an implied threat. There were a number of songs in which this idea, of a woman menacing a man in a physically threatening way, could be seen, this occurring most often in songs overlaid within a comedic and satiric framework. For example, it occurred via the black humored, Hitchcockian parody, "Motorpsycho Nightmare" (1964), a song in which a woman, somewhat miraculously it must be said, threatened to turn into Tony Perkins in order to murder the male protagonist. In a similar sense, the unused, "Hero Blues" (1963), was a song in which the woman wanted the man with whom she was involved to find a heroic death; this being merely to allow her to tell all her friends. In "Down the Highway" (1963), the issue was straightforward: the way the singer loved the woman was bound to get him killed. While in the case of "Long Distance Operator," an unused song that was performed live in 1965 and then released on *The Basement Tapes* (1975), here the woman had no need of a shotgun or a knife, here was a woman who could kill with merely a smile.[22]

A variation on this theme occurred in songs from the mid-1960s that dealt, albeit obliquely, with the use of drugs. Women in these songs were often seen as equating metaphorically to the dangers inherent in drug taking. For example, in "From a Buick Six" (1965), Dylan spoke of a graveyard woman, a junkyard angel who would provide the male narrator with the *junk* he needed, no matter how harmful it might prove to be. In "Sitting on a Barbed Wire Fence" (1965), the assimilation of women and drugs was made more explicit; in the song the masculine voice was involved with a woman (arguably another cipher for narcotics) who was killing him even while he was still alive, ageing him prematurely past his age of twenty-five. Finally, the one Dylan song from the 1960s that was unquestionably and famously about drugs was named not after just one woman, but after a number of women, in fact, a very specific number of women: "Rainy Day Women #12 & 35" (1966). It would seem that there was an obvious implication here, in linking women with drugs, insomuch as both of them possessed not only the promise of bliss and euphoria, but also the ultimate threat of death and decay. Hence what could be ascertained here was that women were both dangerous and powerfully attractive, offering further evidence of the ambivalent contexts in which women were presented in Dylan's work.

A number of Dylan's songs from the so-called "born-again" period (approximately 1979–1981), took this idea further. Here the predominantly bleak presence of a feminine influence was further bolstered via a belief in the masculine figure of Christ as savior, thus enabling the male protagonists of these songs a further excuse to evade the confines of a feminine domain. For example, in "Heart of Mine" (1981), the male narrator warned his heart against placing his trust in the woman he was involved with, or perhaps even women in general; knowing she would not be faithful, that she would betray his love to others, that she would never be true. Women in Dylan's "born-again" songs were frequently portrayed as calculating temptresses, as treacherous sorceresses, leading men away from the path of righteousness, misleading men and leading them astray. The culmination of such a way of thinking came in the song "Trouble" (1981), where Dylan appeared to go so far as to suggest women were responsible for *all* of men's troubles, that since the very beginning man had been cursed by the trouble women had made. This way of thinking resonated (most probably deliberately) within a fundamentalist Christian discourse, to the extent that it seemed to recall the story of Eve tempting Adam to sin in the Garden of Eden. In other words, with the implied suggestion that the original "trouble," referred to throughout the song, had been caused by a woman, that a woman, Eve, was ultimately responsible.

In an earlier song, "As I Went Out One Morning" (1968), Dylan had deliberated further upon this idea, offering an allegorical and "Americanized" version of the Garden of Eden narrative:

> As I went out one morning
> To breathe the air around Tom Paine's
> I spied the fairest damsel
> That ever did walk in chains[23]

It was a song that suggested its female subject, its fairest damsel, was unearthly and demonic, as well as being both rapacious and defiant:

> I offer'd her my hand
> She took me by the arm
> I knew that very instant
> She meant to do me harm

The mere touch of a woman here suggested danger and menace, so much so that by the second verse something akin to an exorcism appeared to be taking place:

> "Depart from me this moment"
> I told her with my voice.
> Said she, "But I don't wish to"
> Said I, "But you have no choice"

However, the damsel railed against this, begging the man, descending into what appeared to be subterfuge and trickery:

> "I beg you, sir," she pleaded
> From the corners of her mouth
> "I will secretly accept you
> And together we'll fly south"

The damsel spoke from the corners of her mouth, suggestive of deceit, and then proposed, in a conspiratorial manner, that she and the narrator should fly south. One could see here how the sexual tensions, inscribed within Dylan's text, began to emerge. To fly south had a number of connotations, if one imagines the song as being set in some imagined time and setting connective to Tom Paine (who will appear at the end of the song), then to fly south could be seen as suggestive of geographical spaces; for example, the southern states of America, with Mexico beyond. However, if the song was read in a more metaphorical way, then the geographical reference might be interpreted in more human terms, and the "fairest damsel" could be seen as tempting the man to fly to the southern regions of her own body; in other words, to the sexual areas of her body, hence she was tempting the male protagonist with her sexuality. Thus the "fairest damsel," in this interpretation, becomes Eve personified, and, in a repetition of Biblical tradition, was aligned with sin, flesh and the devil.

* * *

However, there were still further and still more explicit examples of what could be seen as misogynist discourses at play within Dylan's work. For example, the song "Is Your Love in Vain?" (1978), might be said to have had an

3. Femininity

exaggerated notoriety in Dylan's canon; especially in view of the following stanza:

> Can you cook and sew, make flowers grow
> Do you understand my pain?
> Are you willing to risk it all
> Or is your love in vain?[24]

The placing of women in such a clichéd and sexist position would seem to have been almost deliberately designed to provoke a feminist backlash. John Herdman has described the song as Dylan "contriving to cock a satirical snook at Women's Lib," and noted that it was "possibly an intentional parody."[25] However, in contrast to this view, one might argue that Dylan had no such parodic intent; that he was making an intentional critique on the Women's Movement. In a 1978 interview with journalist, Barbara Kerr, of the *Toronto Sun*, most likely around the time he wrote the song, Dylan had commented:

> You give me a woman that can cook and sew and I'll take that over passion any day ... the new woman is nothing without a man ... that comes from people who think women should be karate instructors or airplane pilots, a man is looking for a woman to hold one end up while he holds up the other.[26]

One notes here that Dylan appeared to take it for granted that women should be viewed as a mere adjunct to men; within this way of thinking it scarcely seems possible that karate instructors and airplane pilots could just as easily be women. It would seem female karate instructors and female airplane pilots, within Dylan's construct of gender politics, were simply looking for men to "hold the other end up."

David Griffiths was perhaps correct when he suggested that Dylan's songs: "rarely feel as misogynistic as they read out of context."[27] Yet, in the further example to be looked at here, the opening of the third verse of "Sweetheart Like You" (1983), it is hard to see this as anything but a deliberate piece of misogynistic hyperbole—whether in or out of context:

> You know, a woman like you should be at home
> That's where you belong
> Watching out for someone who loves you true
> Who would never do you wrong[28]

This could be viewed as the nadir of Bob Dylan's reactionary sexual politics. This was telling the woman in the song, perhaps even women in general, and certainly the Women's Movement in particular, exactly where she and they belonged. One has to be aware that, in Dylan's work as a whole, there was often a knowing sense of irony and sarcasm, a property present in at least some of the diverse ways in which Dylan's work constructed differing attitudes towards women. For example, in "Just like a Woman" (1966), to say someone ached like a woman but, at the same time, broke like a little girl, might be interpreted as being both clichéd and sexist—but this would only be so if the listener was inattentive to the satirical quality such a text possessed. Nonetheless, from a wider perspective, one could argue that there is a consistently held misogynistic attitude to women, one such as found here in "Sweetheart Like You," one that seems to have had no element of intentional satire and that these lines therefore had a deliberately literal intent.

To support this claim one might refer to the significant number of other songs, apparent throughout Dylan's canon, that appeared to express such an intentional misogynistic discourse. There are too many instances to list in any degree of entirety, but the following examples might offer at least a suggestion of such a range of instances. For example, the little less than insulting content in "Bob Dylan's Blues" (1963), wherein the female subject was denigrated as a five and ten cent woman with nothing in her head. In "If You Gotta Go, Go Now" (1965), the woman was represented as little more than a sex object, the whole song being built around the question—albeit in a mildly amusing satiric mood—of whether the woman was prepared to stay and spend the night with the singer. The obscure song "Champaign Illinois," co-written in 1969 with Carl Perkins, consisted of little more than a male protagonist bragging about the number of women available to him. In the song "Mozambique" (1976), the women present within the text, the pretty girls in the exotic space of the eponymous location, did not seem so far removed from a sense of sexual tourism. In "Am I Your Stepchild" (1978)—the woman was represented as being like a noose around the singer's neck; the title of the song "The Ugliest Girl in the World" (1988) required no further comment; and finally, in the song "Sugar Baby" (2001), the culminating effect of the lyric was to put forward the idea that there was no limit to the amount of trouble women could bring.

In looking at Dylan's work, and in attempting to offer an accurate representation, it must be admitted that there were a number of songs in which women were unambiguously and clearly positioned in a compassionate light. For example, the compassionate if overly alliterative line in "Chimes of Freedom" (1964), wherein there at least appeared to be a genuine concern for the woman in question; however, one might note that, even here, the mateless

3. Femininity

mother and the mistitled prostitute were masculine constructs within the song, and hence there may have been little actual understanding of the plight of the woman so described. In addition, there were a number of other Dylan's songs in which women were portrayed as helpless victims at the hands of men; for example, in "Seven Curses" (1963), wherein a condemned man's daughter sold her body to a corrupt judge in a vain attempt to save her father's life, and, in so doing, the song demonstrated a considerable degree of empathy for the plight of the female subject. In "The Lonesome Death of Hattie Carroll" (1964), in what was perhaps Dylan's most impressive song of social protest, an older, impoverished, black woman was callously killed by a younger, rich, white man. While in "North Country Blues" (1964), here one found a unique song, insomuch as it was seemingly the only instance in which Dylan spoke directly and significantly from the perspective of a female voice; it was an autodiegetic text told from the perspective of the widow of an iron ore miner in Minnesota, and in so doing offered an eloquent and empathetic view of its female protagonist.

There were also a number of instances in which women were placed within an enigmatic discourse, wherein the female presence was presented as a mystery, as an intriguing riddle, a riddle which the men in the songs could seldom seem to resolve. For example, "One More Cup of Coffee" (1976), was a song that reached its enigmatic closure with an intertextual allusion to Joseph Conrad,[29] wherein the heart of the woman, whom the singer had been addressing throughout the song, was described as being both mysterious and dark. In the song "Something There Is About You" (1974), Dylan once again resorted to cliché, finally admitting there was something about the woman, for whom he had been extolling his love, that he could not quite put his finger on. Or in the often misinterpreted song, "Sara" (1976),[30] in this already enigmatic song the masculine voice found it easy to look at a woman called Sara, but found it much more difficult to offer a way to define her. In these songs, and in several others, there was a sense of there being a gap sufficiently wide between man and woman—as to render any genuine understanding between the two as almost unachievable. This inability to define woman has, at times, given Dylan the maturity to admit to a certain masculine incomprehension. For example, "One Too Many Mornings" (1964), was a song in which a kind of grudging reciprocity entered the gender discussion, the song ending with the singer admitting that both he, and the woman he was addressing, possessed an equally balanced parity of esteem, each being right from each other's side. A similar reciprocity occurred at the end of "Idiot Wind" (1975), wherein the male narrator had the maturity to accept a sense of ignorance about the woman he had been berating for the four long stanzas of the song. In the final chorus, the coruscating criticism of the woman was lessened, with the masculine voice now admitting both he *and* she were idiots, as if to suggest that he too, as a man, shared an equal proportion of culpability. The song ended with the singer admitting he would never wholly know the woman he had been singing about—as she would never wholly know him—as if acknowledging a gender divide in the song that neither the male nor the female voices would ever be able to cross.

However, it is important to note that even in songs that appeared regretful, that seemed aimed towards an act of contrition between the genders, even here there was often a predisposal towards a masculine or even patriarchal authority. To cite just one example: in "Oh Sister" (1976), this was a work generally seen, at the time of its release and up to the present day, as a great song of gender reconciliation, a song that seemed to be a clear essay on the rights of women, on woman subjugated by law, by state, by marital relationships and by patriarchal culture in general. Yet a careful reading of the song suggested that even this supposed work of reconciliation had a covert perspective, insomuch as it ended with what seemed like an inferred threat. The closing line of the song putting forward the implication that the singer would not be present in the future; in other words, the female protagonist, the sister, would not see him (the male protagonist) tomorrow. In this way there was a sense of an almost coercive male dominance at the end of the song, no matter how benign the overarching sentiment of the text may have seemed. The male voice may have been feigning sexual equality, but there still seemed to remain a certain sense of anxiety that seemed to require a show of strength.

* * *

In looking at the differing ways in which Dylan's work approached relationships with women, one might argue it was possible to perceive of a common factor. There would appear to have been a different attitude toward women with whom there may have been the prospect of a sexual relationship, and with women with whom there was no such prospect. In other words, women with whom the men in Dylan's songs did not have to prove themselves within a sexual arena tended not to present the same kind of tensions. In the light of this, one might note a number of songs in which women were placed in the role of either refuge or savior, songs such as "It's Alright Ma, I'm Only Bleeding" (1965), "Shelter from the Storm" (1975), "License to Kill" (1983) and others. It is perhaps significant that the feminine presence here took on something akin to a maternal role, rather than a role of a man-woman relationship, and hence the atmosphere was much less charged and arguably much less hostile. The question that then arises is why this should be so, and thus, in the latter part of this chapter, the song "License to Kill," will be considered in some detail in relation to this question. In addition to this, an interpretation of the song will attempt to further illuminate one of the central arguments in question within this study: the overarching issue of gender constructs in Bob Dylan's work.

In "License to Kill" the ideological base of the song seemed to derive from an ecological stance; it castigated "man" for believing he could rule the earth and misuse it in any way he desired. As the opening lines put it:

> Man thinks 'cause he rules the earth
> He can do with it as he please
> And if things don't change soon, he will[31]

However, the word "man" was not used here in a generic sense. It did not embrace the whole of mankind; it was gender specific, it was a trenchant and definitive reference to the masculine gender. This was made clear in the song's first chorus:

> Now, there's a woman on my block
> She just sit there as the night grows still
> She says who gonna take away his license to kill?

In contrast to "man," the "woman" was portrayed as a passive observer who merely asked when man's killing would stop. Hence the conclusion might be drawn that the woman here was seen as the life-giver, and man as the life-taker; these were traditional, almost clichéd roles, but roles not commonly found to a great extent in Dylan's work.

There were further contexts in play; the song contained a complex array of contradictory elements, which offered some degree of illumination as to the fractured nature of gender constructs within Dylan's work. We might note, for example, the contradictory stance the song adopted in relation to masculine travel. As discussed in Chapter 2, men can be seen to travel, to journey and to explore, within Dylan's work, in order to define their construct of masculinity; however, here in "License to Kill," the ideological stance was different, the first verse closed with what was arguably one of Dylan's most naive couplets, an eccentric and even reactionary view of the contemporary world of space exploration:

A Wanderer by Trade

> Oh, man has invented his doom
> First step was touching the moon

A few months after the release of *Infidels* (which included the song in question) Dylan was asked, by a journalist from *Rolling Stone* magazine, to explain these lines:

> I have no idea why I wrote that line, but on some level it's like a door into the unknown. I mean, what's the purpose of going to the moon, who's going to benefit?[32]

This point of view was somewhat confusing, given the consistent and almost unswerving predilection for masculine travel in Dylan's work. There was a contradiction in the song, insomuch as the space race and the Apollo missions have been seen—for example, in Tom Wolfe's *The Right Stuff*—as the embodiment of American masculinity and frontier machismo. Thus Dylan's attitude to such a venture, what David Griffiths called: "that damning curious critique of Apollo 11,"[33] had a certain equivocal connotation. The 1960s, the apex of Dylan's career, was the period when space travel seemed to have a genuine resonance within American culture: a decade that began with the shock of Yuri Gagarin's first trip into space and closed with Neil Armstrong's triumphant first steps onto the moon. The individual astronauts who ventured into space were predominantly male, thus extending Dylan's notion of masculine travel. Therefore, why Dylan should have had such a negative attitude to this issue raises a number of intriguing questions.

The fact that the moon has been traditionally so closely equated with the feminine might offer a possible reason for the contradictory attitudes towards space travel in Dylan's work.[34] This premise being supported by other such "superstitious" attacks on space travel as found on the *Infidels* record. For example, in "Neighbourhood Bully," a song that has usually been interpreted as a sympathetic manifesto for the rights of the Israeli state, also asked whether the neighborhood bully had contaminated reaches beyond the earth, if "he" had polluted the moon and the stars. While in the song "Union Sundown," matters became almost risible, with Kansas being cited as a previous source of plentiful bounty, but with the moon now seen, in absurdist terms, as an alternative site of food production. It was difficult to understand the logic of Dylan's thinking, why he would suggest growing food on the moon; insomuch, as far as can be ascertained, no one has ever suggested this might be an option. As such, one might note that the moon was the common factor, thus Dylan's argument may have been associated with the fact that this great symbol of the feminine influence, had been reduced to little more than a lump of rock: to be polluted, to have food grown on it, and to have men walking on it. One might thus perceive, in the underlying narrative discourses of these songs, a concern with the inviolate nature of a female goddess, and with the potential desecration of her by man. However, as seen in the case of "Isis" (another moon goddess), there also existed a sense of unease, an apprehension, a desire to pull away from a feminine influence; in other words, once again there was the dichotomy of both wanting and fearing the female presence.

Further to this, there were elements, in "License to Kill," that dealt with ideas of feminine passivity and masculine violence, linked with the worship of a feminine goddess, together with a retreat into a Christian ideology. In each chorus the middle line had a subtle change of emphasis:

> She just sit there as the night grows still …
> She just sit there facin' the hill …
> Sitting there in a cold chill …
> She just sit there as the night grows still …

In each the common factor was passivity, in each the woman was sitting, and in each she seemed powerless to have an effect on what was occurring before her. She waited as the night grew still, she waited facing the hill, she waited in a cold chill, and then, in a resolution back to the original chorus, she waited again as the night grew still. The word 'hill' could arguably be seen as acting as a symbol for Calvary, as it sometimes tended to do in Dylan's work,[35] thus not only was the woman passively watching man despoil the planet, she also became associated with the women who watched passively as Christ died on the cross. In this sense, one element of the song's discourse could be interpreted as offering a feminine perspective on the "crucifixion" of a planet's whole ecology, with the woman of the song passively observing the coldness of death that was soon to consume the environment.[36] Man was "hell bent for destruction," with the implied suggestion that masculinity was, in itself, dangerous, that men were violent simply because they were men.[37] However, one could also argue against such a proposition, and, in a much wider context, suggest that such a mistakenly adopted biological imperative was germane to the argument as expressed in this study: the argument that masculinity is an artificial and performative construct. Furthermore, that it added weight to the suggestion that the construct of gender was significantly fractured in Dylan's work; for example, as discussed in Chapter 2, Dylan's apparent reverence of the outlaw figure, as expressed in many of his songs, demonstrated this; in songs like "Joey" or "Hurricane" the act of being a man often involved the use of violence at some level—this demonstrating, one could argue, a falsity and an artifice in such a construct. In other words, one could argue that men have been brainwashed into behaving the way they do, by the society they find themselves living in. As "License to Kill" put it:

> Now, he's hell-bent for destruction, he's afraid and confused
> And his brain has been mismanaged with great skill
> All he believes are his eyes
> And his eyes, they just tell him lies

* * *

The material in this chapter has sought to offer an accurate picture of the way women are represented in Dylan's work. Germaine Greer, writing in the 1960s, found the categories of women in Dylan's work to be relatively straightforward:

> Even a poet as now as Dylan has two kinds of female character in his imagery—the sad-eyed lady of the lowlands, the girl from the north country, who is inviolate and inviolable ... and the others who are human, confused and contemptible.[38]

However, one might suggest Greer's view, although valid at the time, could now be seen as having a somewhat narrow perspective. It would appear that Dylan's embodiment of the female character in his work was more complex and more nuanced, and could not be defined within such generalized terms. The women in Dylan's work were not simply set in binary opposition to each other; they were more than simply angelic or demonic, more than the inviolate and inviolable, more than the confused and contemptible. The discursive materials cited in this chapter, drawing on a wide-ranging cross-section of Dylan's published work, has aimed to demonstrate this. The culmination of this analysis would appear to suggest that the women in Dylan's songs were frequently depicted as deceivers, castrators, temptresses, often unfaithful, often seen as little more than sex objects and, in general, all too rarely viewed in a sympathetic light. The women in the songs were sometimes elevated to the level of enigma, or were sometimes viewed as a maternal refuge, although this was seldom more than the exception. Thus Dylan's attitude to women often inhabited what might be described as a misogynistic discourse. As previously suggested, this was explained, at least in part, by the sense of a fear of women, as so ubiquitously found among the songs Dylan has written; however, in this he was not alone, instead Dylan's work could be seen as akin to

3. Femininity

that sense of a misogyny institutionalized within our culture; as Ursula K. Le Guin put it:

> The misogyny that shapes every aspect of our civilization is the institutionalised form of male fear and hatred of what they have denied and therefore cannot know, cannot share: that wild country, the being of women.[39]

Enclosed within the argument this study espouses, one could suggest that this was getting close to explaining the attitude Dylan's songs adopt towards women. Betsy Bowden has talked of Dylan's "vicious attitudes toward women,"[40] and Bowden was surely correct when she stated: "Like most men, like Freud, like the knight in the 'Wife of Bath's Tale,' he [Dylan] doesn't know what women want."[41]

In adopting such a viewpoint, this chapter will conclude by looking at a song that arguably exemplifies this argument, a song that perhaps comes close to offering an authentic insight into the construct of femininity in Bob Dylan's work. The album, *Time Out of Mind* (1997), ended with a song titled "Highlands," a song that, in one sense at least, could be read as a text offering a version of Dylan's artistic and creative attitudes towards feminism. The central scene of this long song consisted of an extended incident in which a masculine persona (who for the sake of argument we might perceive as being at least similar to the performative persona we think of as "Bob Dylan") had a long conversation with a waitress he meets in a restaurant in Boston. It was a significant song in that, like "License to Kill," it represented a rare instance in which Dylan allowed a female voice to challenge and interrogate its masculine protagonist. The woman here had an authentic voice, a voice that was able to mount a viable challenge to the patriarchal ideology the "Bob Dylan" persona seemed to advocate.

The scene within the song, stretching over seven verses, is worthy of quoting in full; the scene proceeded as follows:

> I'm in Boston town, in some restaurant
> I got no idea what I want
> Well, maybe I do but I'm just really not sure
> Waitress comes over
> Nobody in the place but me and her
>
> It must be a holiday, there's nobody around
> She studies me closely as I sit down
> She got a pretty face and long white shiny legs
> She says, "What'll it be?"
> I say, "I don't know, you got any soft boiled eggs?"

She looks at me, says, "I'd bring you some
But we're out of 'm, you picked the wrong time to come"
Then she says, "I know you're an artist, draw a picture of me!"
I say, "I would if I could, but
I don't do sketches from memory"

"Well," she says, "I'm right here in front of you, or haven't you looked?"
I say, "All right, I know, but I don't have my drawing book!"
She gives me a napkin, she says, "You can do it on that"
I say, "Yes I could, but
I don't know where my pencil is at!"

She pulls one out from behind her ear
She says, "All right now, go ahead, draw me, I'm standing right here"
I make a few lines and I show it for her to see
Well she takes the napkin and throws it back
And says, "That don't look a thing like me!"

I said, "Oh, kind Miss, it most certainly does"
She says, "You must be jokin.'" I say, "I wish I was!"
Then she says, "You don't read women authors, do you?"
Least that's what I think I hear her say
"Well," I say, "how would you know and what would it matter anyway?"

"Well," she says, "you just don't seem like you do!" I said, "You're way wrong"
She says, "Which ones have you read then?" I say, "I read Erica Jong!"
She goes away for a minute
And I slide up out of my chair
I step outside back to the busy street but nobody's going anywhere[42]

There was a convincing veracity to the exchange, almost as if the scene, as presented, may have occurred within Dylan's own historical record. As the scene proceeded the male voice appeared defensive, awkward and even inadequate; as such, there was a sense of vulnerability and very nearly a sense of innocence to the masculine subject represented here. One could witness the "Bob Dylan" persona resorting to a variety of tactics in an attempt to bolster itself; the woman was patronizingly called a "kind miss"; there would seem to have been an attempt at irony in the "I wish it was" comment; similarly, there was an attempt to lessen the woman's words in the line, "Least that's what I think I heard her say," but then eventually the "Bob Dylan" persona had to respond and he claimed that he did read feminist authors, although (in a final defensive move) he sensed it would not matter to the woman anyway. However, the woman called his bluff and the masculine protagonist was finally forced into coming up with a name: he had read Erica Jong. But this was all that occurred, the confrontation ended in a decidedly anti-climatic

3. Femininity

fashion; with the waitress going "away for a minute," and with the male protagonist sliding out of his chair and stepping outside to the busy street, where, paradoxically, "nobody [was] going anywhere." Hence at the end of the encounter, one notes that, once again, the solution for a masculine protagonist in Dylan's work resided with the idea of movement, with travel and with escape; as discussed in the previous chapter, here was a man once again intent on what appeared to be a meaningless flight from a woman. Therefore, to move towards a summary of the scene, it might be read within a metaphorical context; with the attempt by "Bob Dylan" to draw the waitress in the Boston restaurant becoming a metaphor for the attempt by Bob Dylan to draw women in his work as a whole: attempting and perhaps ultimately failing to fully understand the female presences before him.[43]

As part of a final summary to this chapter, one might suggest that this scene, the interpretation of it presented here, together with the general discussion of the feminine presences in Dylan's work, offers further evidence—towards the argument made within this study—that the construct of femininity (like masculinity) can be seen as an artifice, a construct, a performative edifice, in which cracks and inconsistencies often become visible. One of the issues that make Dylan's love lyrics so "potent" are the multiple paradoxes inherent within them. It would seem clear that there was a consistent obsession with women—Dylan has several hundred songs to his credit with which to prove this—and yet women also unswervingly seemed to be the "dark snare" threatening to entrap the "masculine heart." Hence, what would seem clear from the diverse range of songs Dylan has written about women, was that while the female presence remained an endless source of fascination, this presence was also a source for a wide range of tensions, of fears and of anxieties. As such, this arguably told us much about Dylan's sense of a construct of femininity, and, at some remove, of masculinity. Therefore, after looking separately at the ways in which the masculine and the feminine spheres of gender were constructed in Dylan's work, the following chapter will look towards what happens when these two were conjoined, at what happens in those instances when Dylan's work dealt with sexuality, at the ways in which sexual relationships were framed, forged and fabricated within Dylan's work.

4

Sexuality

"Sex is a temporary thing."
—Bob Dylan, the *Playboy* interview, 1966

In 1966, Dylan discussed his attitude to love and sex during a conversation with Robert Shelton; Dylan's comments were revealing, expressing a subtle and considered evaluation of human sexuality:

> Love and sex are things that really hang everybody up. When things aren't going right and you're really nobody if you don't get laid in one way or another, you get mean, you know. You get cruel. Now, why in the world sex should force this is beyond me. I truthfully can tell you that male and female are not here to have sex, you know, that's not the purpose. I don't believe that that's God's will, that females have been created so that they can be a counterpart of man's urge. There are too many other things that people just won't let themselves be involved in. Sex and love has nothing to do with female and male. It is just whatever two souls happen to be. It could be male and female, and it might not be male and female. It might be female and female or it might be male and male. You can make fun of it and be snide, but that's not really the rightful thing.[1]

Fourteen years later, on stage in Hartford, Connecticut, in May 1980, Dylan would appear to have had a somewhat different opinion about the freedom of individuals to experience sex and love with whomsoever they wished. The concert in question took place during Dylan's so-called "born-again Christian" period, a time in which Dylan was in the habit of delivering what can only be described as a series of sermonizing diatribes: the main subject areas being God, the Devil and the evils of man. In Hartford that night Dylan was talking about Joshua and the iniquities of certain towns in Canaan, after which he began to deliver a sarcastic critique against "homosexuals" living in modern-day San Francisco:

> But God said those cities were defiled; God said to Joshua, do not go in there. And Joshua asked why, and God said because their iniquities are not yet filled. So, nowadays, when you look around today—you know, we started this tour in San Francisco. San Francisco, it's a unique town these days, I think it's one-third or two-thirds of the pop-

4. Sexuality

ulation there are homosexuals. Guess they're working up to a hundred per cent. I don't know—well, I guess their iniquity is not yet filled; I don't want to be around when it is. San Francisco, city of brotherly love! The Bible says men will become lovers of themselves, ain't that right, proud and holy! You pray for ungodly vice and you'll get it, ungodly vice and lust. But God's got other things in store for you—in these end days.[2]

To espouse such a point of view might be seen, by some at least, as an ignorant and disingenuous display of fundamentalist bigotry, of moralizing rhetoric writ large; an inept proselytizing of otiose and jejune prejudice; a tendentious use of sophistry that failed to register within a moral discourse, a shabby polemic that now—and at the time—seemed merely meretricious. From a liberal, tolerant and open-minded perspective, for Dylan to have publicly expressed such blatantly homophobic views was unacceptable, both as a performer and as a man. This was made all the worse via the fact that Dylan's implied threat, that God had other things in store for "homosexuals," appeared to come true (at least for those with a similar bigoted mindset) via the onset of HIV/AIDS, just a few years later. In the interim between the two quotations, as referenced above, there would seem to have been a major change in Dylan's way of thinking about the world. Prior to the time of Dylan's infamous comments in Hartford, his approach to religion had always appeared to be more visionary than fundamental, not the eschatological fascination with death and salvation on the "holy slow train,"[3] as would seem to be implied by Dylan at this stage in his professional and personal life.

The above quotations were personal opinions of Dylan's and one should always be wary of relating an artist's life to an artist's work. However, in this specific instance, one could argue that such an extreme change of view had some bearing on Dylan's work, insomuch as one can perceive of clear and corresponding changes in the differing attitudes adopted, at different times, within the landscapes of Dylan's songs. Thus, taking this into account, this chapter will explore some of the reasons that might explain the markedly differing attitudes Dylan has adopted towards sexuality, in all its variant and diverse forms. Furthermore, the chapter will examine such concepts through the theoretical frameworks expressed within this study, the contention that gender is a constructed artifice, a performative action. Insomuch, such an approach will seek to support the view that such contradictions, as inherent within the differing attitudes to sexual relationships in Dylan's work, further advances the argument that constructs of gender have fractured inconsistencies and incongruities.

A Wanderer by Trade

* * *

One might begin by suggesting that the overarching temper of Bob Dylan's lyrics has rarely expressed an overtly sexual content. It would appear that although Dylan's work coincided with a time of so-called sexual liberation, his work would seldom seem to have made use of such new freedoms. If one compares Dylan's work to a writer such as Allen Ginsberg, a writer to whom Dylan has often been compared,[4] then it would seem fair to say that Dylan's work has not offered the same sexual candor Ginsberg's work exhibited. While Ginsberg's work has expressed an openness and an honesty, in contrast, Dylan's work has mainly depended on restraint and understatement.[5] In other words, in terms of the erotic, the sexually explicit and the self-confessional,[6] Dylan has always remained a reserved and conservative writer. One even finds, for example, songs of a specific puritan attitude to sex and sexuality; in such early songs as "Troubled and I Don't Know Why" (1963), "Playboys and Playgirls" (1963), and then in later, so-called "born-again" songs, such as "When You Gonna Wake Up?" (1979) and "Slow Train" (1979). These specific examples may be rare; however, one might argue that such a puritan attitude towards sex and sexuality extended throughout the major part of Dylan's canon.

Such a reticence would appear to have extended to the actual vocabulary used by Dylan in his work, wherein he would seem to have generally adopted a restrained lexicon in terms of explicit expression. For example, one notes that the songs were almost wholly devoid of "four letter words," with Dylan perhaps able to comment on this via his song, "Love Is Just a Four Letter Word" (1965).[7] There were some rare exceptions to the absence of explicit language: for example, the ubiquitous four letter faecal noun appeared in both the songs: "George Jackson" (1971) and "Hurricane" (1976).[8] In addition, it has been said that the most famous of four letter words appeared in the song "I'm Not There" (1967); however, as the song has never been officially published and as the extant vocal performance lacked sufficient articulation, this is difficult to ascertain.[9] One might speculate here that the lack of a usage of explicit language may have been due to commercial as well as artistic considerations; in other words, the fact that Dylan was writing within the restrictions and confines of popular music. However, one could also presume that there was simply an inherent reticence and reserve within Dylan's work towards the use of an explicit sexual vocabulary.

It should perhaps be accepted that there were a number of exceptions

4. Sexuality

in terms of songs that did appear to have an overtly sexual content. For example, a number of songs on the *Basement Tapes* collection have generally been seen as having a "bawdy demeanour." One might think, for example, of the scatological burlesque within the song "Please Mrs. Henry" (1967), replete with its somewhat juvenile imagery of cranes about to leak and stools about to squeak. Alternatively, there was the overtly suggestive "Odds and Ends" (1967), here within a comedic discourse, the song's determined narrator was insistent he would not get any "juice" spilt on himself—within the song it was readily apparent what this "juice" was referring to. In another instance, in the opening line of the song "Million Dollar Bash" (1967), there was reference to a big dumb blonde, whose wheel was gorged: leaving the listener to make what they would of this somewhat crude innuendo. Also, the song "All You Have to Do is Dream" (1967), contained some unmistakable phallic imagery, with the female presence in the song, referred to as a little girl, being invited to blow a horn, a horn as hard as any horn she might have seen. However, it must be remembered that the *Basement Tapes* were not initially intended for public consumption, and it could therefore be argued that Dylan was allowing himself the freedom of writing and performing material he may have imagined the world at large might never hear.[10] In addition, and by way of a final note on this topic, there may have been other songs that went still further, that were too lascivious or licentious; as Cameron Crowe, discussing the *Basement Tapes* in the liner notes to the album, *Biograph* (1985), commented, there were "a number of songs too bawdy even to record."[11]

In addition, there were a limited number of other instances of Dylan intentionally releasing work with an explicitly sexual or erotic content. One such instance has already been mentioned, the song "Country Pie" (1969), as discussed in Chapter 3. Among the other instances, one might cite the song "Spanish Harlem Incident" (1964); in the case of this song, within an openly hedonistic discourse, there were only marginally concealed allusions to fellatio; here the gypsy gal of the song had the singer swallowed, while he fell beneath her pearly eyes and her flashing diamond teeth. There were a number of other songs with similarly knowing references to oral sexuality; for example, in "Where Are You Tonight? (Journey Through Dark Heat)" (1978), the male narrator, borrowing from the idiomatic blues influence of Robert Johnson, admitted that he had, albeit metaphorically, bitten into the root of forbidden fruit, with the juice running down his leg. From a more literary source, the Lawrence-esque idea of fruit or flowers as a vaginal symbol was also used in "Sad Eyed Lady of the Lowlands" (1966), wherein Dylan created the surreal image of a group of kings, from Tyrus, waiting in line for a geranium kiss.[12] Also, as Betsy Bowden has noted,[13] a couplet from the second verse of "She Belongs to Me," had obvious and similar sexual connotations, with the narrator of the song, down upon his knees, peeking through the keyhole of his beloved. The obvious allusions to cunnilingus were readily apparent here, at least within a certain reading of the songs in question, and albeit expressed in a guileful and metaphorical manner by Dylan. Finally, one might think of a number of other diverse instances, such as the eroticism of the entwined lovers in "Visions of Johanna" (1966), the lover's lips that were watery and wet in "I Don't Believe You (She Acts Like We Never Have Met)" (1964), the exaggerated and ingenious sexual innuendo of "4th Time Around," (1966), the flippant references to sadomasochistic sex in "All I Really Want to Do," (1964), and lastly, the onanistic references such as the rainman coming with his magic wand in "I Wanna Be Your Lover" (1965)—not to mention the narrator of "Goin' to Acapulco" (1967) pumping on his meat.

However, this would seem to sum up the greater sense of eroticism within the corpus of Dylan's work; and as to why there should have been such a sense of reticence elsewhere in this corpus poses a certain paradoxical situation. One way of responding to this quandary might be to point, once again, to the apparent artifice within the construction of gender identities in Dylan's work. In other words, to suggest that the awkwardness inherent within Dylan's attitudes to sexual relationships may have been caused, may have arisen, by the fractures and inconsistencies that existed within his perspectives on masculinity and femininity, and upon the way they interacted with each other. In adopting such an approach, such a line of thought, there is one further song that should perhaps be mentioned. It is arguably of some significance that the one song where one finds a preponderance of critics commenting upon the sexual content of a Bob Dylan text, wherein a specific song would appear to have been discussing sexuality in an explicit way, here in this case one finds a song that would seem to have been dealing with a differing kind of sexuality.

The Bob Dylan text in question, as may have already been surmised, was the song "Ballad of a Thin Man" (1965). The key point here, and what would seem to have been of most interest, was that this was a text that has been seen, almost without exception, in a homoerotic rather than what might be termed a "heteroerotic" light. A number of the most authoritative and most well-known names in the world of Dylan criticism have passed comment on the song, and all in a uniformly similar way. For example, Craig McGregor wrote that:

> "Ballad of a Thin Man," deals openly with homosexual experiences. When Dylan was in Australia [in 1966] I criticised it as an "in group" song, and he quickly defended it as dealing with "something else altogether."[14]

While according to the author and theologian, Steven Goldberg:

> In "Ballad of a Thin Man" Dylan … uses a homosexual encounter to deal with man's search for realisation.[15]

The more populist writer, Michael Gross, speculated:

> Is the sword swallower of the sixth verse gay? A veiled reference to sodomy? Is Dylan trying to tell us something about homosexuality?[16]

Michael Gray claimed that:

> "The Ballad of a Thin Man" [sic] has Mr. Jones propositioned, or mock propositioned, by a sword-swallower (meaning cocksucker?) who kneels (confirming the idea?) and "clicks his high-heels."[17]

John Herdman likewise claimed:

> The situation in which Mr. Jones is lost involves a homosexual propositioning.[18]

Even Sy Ribakove and Barbara Ribakove, fan-orientated authors of the first published book on Dylan: *Folk Rock: The Bob Dylan Story,* found the song: "cluttered with obvious phallic symbols."[19] And, Robert Shelton, arguably the most rewarding of Dylan's many biographers, but also arguably one of the most enthusiastic apologists of Dylan's many apologists, admitted that: "Some of Mr. Dylan's lyrics are obviously camp fantasies."[20] In addition, it might be interesting to note that some of Dylan's comments to the press, around this time—the mid-1960s—also seemed to have elements of what Shelton described as "camp fantasies." For example, asked by a popular British music paper in 1965 what was his personal ambition, Dylan replied: "To be a waitress."[21] A year later, in the famous *Playboy* interview, Dylan made the following admission: "Well, I've always wanted to be Brigitte Bardot too. But I don't want to think about that too much."[22] Such remarks, along with others, would appear to have offered both a sense of the sophisticated satirical pose Dylan adopted with the media at the time, but also evidenced the fluidity and ambiguity with which he approached issues of gender and sexuality. These being issues worth bearing in mind in relation to Dylan's art, especially in the case of the song currently under discussion.

However, notwithstanding such interpretative opinions, together with Dylan's own deadpan comments, one has to be somewhat dubious in confining the song, as with any cultural text, to such a restricted and dogmatic interpretation. In a sense, the various critics quoted above were only offering an individualistic point of view; in other words, they were merely offering their own particular reader response to the song in question. To leave this unquestioned may be problematic; as Terry Eagleton put it: "There is no single determinate truth to any particular narrative or event, just a conflict of interpretations."[23] Thus one has a sense of reluctance here to restrict a single meaning to the song under discussion. Dylan's songs, like all texts, are labile and constantly subject to change, their polysemantic qualities will always resist such one-dimensional interpretations; they will strive to preserve a sense of universality, they will strive to avoid a diminishment of a sense of openness, they will strive to achieve whatever sense of expression is available. For example, a one-eyed midget could be interpreted as having phallic connotations, as could the title of the song itself for that matter. However, within another interpretative context, a one-eyed midget could simply be read as a monocular carnival performer, just as it is possible to presume that Mr. Jones may have simply been a thin man. Similarly, it is possible to perceive of the sword swallower, replete with his (camp) high heels, as kneeling to offer Mr. Jones oral stimulation, that the milk demanded was a simile for semen, that the bone mentioned was an erection. However, it is also possible that the sword swallower was another circus performer, and the milk and the bone were literal and not symbolic representations.

The point at issue here being a subtle one; while it was of interest that such a wide range of critics should have sought to read a significant preoccupation with a homoerotic subtext in this particular song; at the same time it would seem important to attempt to preserve Dylan's work from such restrictive and reductive interpretations. However, in contrast to this, one might attempt to make the point that there *was* an overall ambivalence towards gender roles in Dylan's writing of this period. It might seem as if the comments above suggested that the song "Ballad of a Thin Man," was the exception that proved the rule,[24] but whether or not "Ballad of a Thin Man" was interpreted as portraying a "homosexual" experience, one could argue and maintain that the *milieu* of Dylan's song-writing from this specific period (the middle 1960s) was suggestive of a sense of fluidity towards sexuality, one aptly demonstrated by Dylan's open-minded and liberal comments to Robert Shelton, as quoted at the start of this chapter. It would seem that at this period

4. Sexuality

in his writing (and sometimes beyond) Dylan had a significant selection of songs attentive to the fluidity of sexual identity; in other words, songs that were open to a range of erotic possibilities and erotic ambiguities.

An appropriate place to begin would arguably be with the song "Jet Pilot," a song not released until 1985, on the *Biograph* compilation, but a song recorded in October 1965, at a recording session in New York City, at what would come to be seen as the first of the many sessions that would eventually lead to the *Blonde on Blonde* album.[25] It was not much more than a fragment of a song, not much more than one verse building to an unexpected punch line. However, it was a punch line whose surprising outcome revealed something of the fluidity of sexuality within Dylan's work, or at least a fluidity in the use of pronouns within Dylan's work. The song ended with a couplet guardedly warning that one had better watch "her" closely because "she" was not a woman, "she" was a man. In other words, the "she" was not a "she" at all, and this, one could argue, was cogent evidence that gender—at least in a certain sense—could be seen here as a performative construct. However, this was not a rare exception, a number of similar instances could be found in a significant number of Dylan's songs from around this time. These were songs with a degree of gender ambiguity that would appear to have been routinely been misinterpreted because of preconceived assumptions.

For example, one might take the song "Most Likely You Go Your Way And I'll Go Mine" (1966); insomuch as this was a song written by a man and sung by a man, the love object in the song has routinely and habitually been assumed to have been a woman. For example, Michael Gray, in one of the earliest and most thoughtful monographs of Dylan's work, argued that: "On *Blonde on Blonde* ... the image of a particular woman is deliberately established by the one sided dialogue in 'Most Likely You Go Your Way.'"[26] Notwithstanding Gray's wide and diverse knowledge of Dylan's work, this could be seen as an erroneous reading; insomuch as a reading of the text without such gender specific preconceptions allowed the "you," as addressed in the song, to become a much freer construct. At the opening of the song there was a "you" whom the narrator of the song claimed was in love with him,[27] and was thinking of him, but who could have been wrong; furthermore, the "you" stated a desire to hold the singer—but he knew this "you" was not that strong. One of the strengths of this song, and others of the time, was this sense of gender ambiguity. A liaison was occurring in a song sung by a man, but the "you"—the love object—did not necessarily have to be a woman, there were no gender specific pronouns anywhere in the text, only a cryptic reference, in the final verse, to some other kind of lover. All of this is not to necessarily suggest that Dylan had intentionally written a song that addressed a male subject, a man, instead the point here would be to simply suggest it was a false assumption to automatically read the song in a gender stereotyped way. Thus the fact that a critic as perceptive as Michael Grey was able to make such a misdirected reading, unsupported by any actual textual evidence, is redolent of one way in which Dylan's work has been misread.

This sense of gender ambiguity could be seen elsewhere in Dylan's work. For example, such an ambiguity was apparent in a song from a slightly later period, in as well known a love lyric as "I'll Be Your Baby Tonight" (1968), a song that was seemingly completely secure within its own discourse of normative heterosexuality. This may have been the presumption; however, if one considers the actual text of this song then there is, in fact, nothing to suggest the gender of the love object. The complete text of the song is worthy of quoting in full:

> Close your eyes, close the door
> You don't have to worry any more
> I'll be your baby tonight
> Shut the light, shut the shade
> You don't have to be afraid
> I'll be your baby tonight
> Well that mockingbird's gonna sail away
> We're gonna forget it
> That big, fat moon is gonna shine like a spoon
> But we're gonna let it
> You won't regret it
> Kick your shoes off, do not fear
> Bring that bottle over here
> I'll be your baby tonight[28]

It was a love song, this much was evident, but once again there was nothing within the textual discourse of the song to suggest it was a love song from a man to a woman, this was a mere assumption on the part of the reader/listener, to interpret the text in this way. As such, it would seem to be a valid assumption that the majority of listeners to the song heard a normative heterosexual story. Hence, in a certain sense, this could be seen as further demonstrating the conventional and fixed attitudes towards a textual object, albeit within a normative socio-cultural order; in other words, outside of a Butlerian reading of gender constructs. In the song there was a room; there were two people; there was a bottle, a big fat moon and a bird that was about

4. Sexuality

to sail away. This was all the information the reader/listener was offered. However, there was also an air of secrecy and subterfuge suggested within the text: the eyes of the lover had to be closed, as the door had to be closed, as the light and the shade had to be shut out. In addition, the specific information that the bird was a mockingbird could have been seen as at least intimating a burlesque of normality; finally, the passivity the male voice expressed throughout the song appeared to set up at least a suggestion of ambiguity. Of course, there was an alternate explanation, perhaps the two lovers were involved in an illicit tryst, and had to keep their affair, their lovemaking, discreet. This would certainly have been a valid reading, but this would purport to represent only one potential reading, and hence would not preclude the alternative reading, as offered here.[29]

In the particular context under discussion here, such a reading was perhaps sanctioned and endorsed by the fact that *John Wesley Harding* was, for the most part at least, predominantly male-focused, it was overwhelmingly homosocial within its discursive practices. In other words, "I'll Be Your Baby Tonight" ended a collection of twelve songs that had dealt almost exclusively with masculine protagonists, with the world of men: a collection concerned with wild west outlaws, War of Independence revolutionaries, dead saints, jokers and thieves, Frankie Lee's and Judas Priest's, drifters, landlords, hoboes, immigrants and messengers: all of them masculine to a fault. Thus the song "I'll Be Your Baby Tonight," came as a contrast to all that had gone before it, and the placement of a love song, in such a location, thus seemed somewhat incongruous and out of place. In addition, one might allude to a further song, the eleventh track on the collection, "Down Along the Cove," which came between the ten songs about men and the final song on the album, "I'll Be Your Baby Tonight." However, "Down Along the Cove" was a song whose supposed erotic charge was so insipid and artificial as to render it almost meaningless within the discussion here. A.J. Weberman once speculated that the song's little bundle of joy may have been drug related, rather than love related; of course, Weberman often read drug references into Dylan's work; yet here the love song element was so bland as to make this reading seem almost credible.

There were a number of further instances in which Dylan's work seemed to deliberately subvert gender stereotypes. For example, the figure of Achilles, who was hungry like a man in drag in "Temporary Like Achilles" (1966)[30]; the five believers, who were all dressed *like* men in "Obviously Five Believers" (1966); the (masculine) waitress in "Bob Dylan's 115th Dream" (1965), who was handsome in a powder blue cape. While there is no intent here to deal with cross-dressing in Dylan's work in detail, there were a number of other instances of transvestism that might also be mentioned; for example, such songs as: "Black Diamond Bay" (1976),[31] "Foot of Pride" (1983) and "Tweeter and the Monkey Man" (1988). Cross-dressing obviously raises the issue of gender as performance in a literal way; it raises the issue that there is nothing inherently feminine about a dress, or anything inherently masculine about a suit, that these were mere social constructs. Further to this, Judith Butler has argued that cross-dressing has the virtue of showing that gender is imitative in structure; in other words, being male or female, masculine or feminine, entails a performance that requires certain specific bodily signals. The question then arises: are we required to learn how to become men or women, to become masculine or feminine, and hence could masculinity just as easily signify a female body as a male one; in other words, was this merely a performance, was this merely an act? In terms of the discussion of the fragile structure of masculinity, as presented in this study, it is perhaps significant to note that cross-dressing is more easily tolerated in women than in men.[32] In other words, it would seem less of a taboo for a woman to dress like a man; for example, a woman can wear trousers, a suit, or even a tie; however, if a man were to wear a dress there would be a clear sense of breaking a coded barrier.[33] The corollary of this being that male dress could be seen as mere pastiche; as Judith Butler has shown, this constant dressing up by men to be men, and the drag artist's effortless mockery of this, demonstrates the fragility of this sense of gender identity.

In taking this into account, one might consider the way Dylan seemed, at times, to be deliberately experimenting and playing with such concepts. For example, in an albeit somewhat obscure song, "What Kind of Friend is This?" (1966), Dylan delivered this "arch" couplet: What kind of man is this/Who loves me behind my back?—with the reader/listener of the song making whatever they wished out of such a comment.[34] It must be admitted that songs from outside of this period, around the time of *Highway 61 Revisited* and *Blonde on Blonde,* did not tend to offer the same degree of sexual ambiguity. However, there were exceptions, for example, "You're Gonna Make Me Lonesome When You Go" (1975), from the *Blood on the Tracks* album. This was a song that has invariably been misread as a song written by a man to a woman. This was to ignore the fact that the text could just as easily have been read in such a way that pointed towards a same-sex relationship. Once again it was a song that was gender neutral in terms of the use of pronouns and vocabulary. In addition, and to offer just one textual example, the song's confessional references to Verlaine and Rimbaud could not help but raise issues of erotic ambiguity. It would seem that such hetero-sexist misreadings therefore acted to constrain the text's full potential, to deny a discussion of what was actually occurring within the textual contents of the song. Here we had a clear example of a superficial biographical reading of a Dylan text completely missing the subtle gestures of gender performativity. One might therefore argue that the song, insomuch as it derived from the *Blood on the Tracks* collection, was misread, as the songs on that album were almost universally perceived as being autobiographical, there was an almost unchallenged notion that these songs concerned the breakdown of Dylan's relationship with his wife.[35] In a hermeneutic and reader response approach this was a mistaken and somewhat facile assumption; hence a song as textually rich and diverse as "You're Gonna Make Me Lonesome When You Go" was stripped of much of its creative capabilities in the rush towards a biographical interpretation.

John Herdman was one critic and author of Dylan's work who would seem to have been alert to some level of gender ambiguity existent in Dylan's songs. Discussing Dylan's love songs, or what he described as "that large body of songs that deal with personal relationships,"[36] Herdman obliquely suggested that these songs were " not simply those which are addressed to lovers or former lovers ... but which find their subject in the infinite varieties of human confrontation."[37] Herdman, seeming to concur with Christopher Ricks,[38] referred to such songs as "the centre of Dylan's achievement,"[39] but noted that many of Dylan's so-called love songs were in fact "after-love songs," and that many of them were also songs that at least gestured towards a fluidity regarding gender roles. Herdman claimed that: "From *Desire* onwards the excitement of Dylan's lyrics lies for the most part in areas other than the songs of personal relationship."[40] This was a significant comment, what Herdman would seem to have been pointing towards, albeit somewhat carefully, was the suggestion that the subject of heterosexual love no longer provided sufficient material for Dylan to write songs with the same enthusiasm. This would appear to be a reasonable proposition; however, it could be argued that the natural division, concurrent with the time of the *Desire* record, as Herdman suggested, was not the case, and that such a situation had been apparent for some time before. For example, "Desolation Row" (1965), was an apt example to support such an argument; "Desolation Row" was a song that dealt with a variety of human confrontations, it was one of Dylan's most ambitiously complex compositions, presenting a sinister, carnivalesque parade of figures, what Robert Shelton perceptively described as a "grotesque Mardi-Gras."[41] This motif suggested a disruption of the hierarchical discourse, a "Bakhtinesque" turning upside down of authority. Mardi-Gras: a "fat Tuesday"—the day before Ash Wednesday—the start of lent, wherein transgressions were legitimized and the perverse could parade in a sanctioned manner. Furthermore, as will be demonstrated, the song transgressed in terms of its portrayal of gender stereotypes, as much as it did with anything else. Hence one might maintain that the most significant way this freedom to transgress could be perceived, within the song, was via the arena of sexuality. As Ellen Willis remarked, describing the song as being: "An eleven-minute freak show whose cast of losers, goons and ghosts wandered around in a miasma of sexual repression and latent violence."[42] In this way, one might concur that "Desolation Row" was a song much concerned with the repression and inversion of sexuality. However, it is possible to take this further and to interpret this feature of the song predominately as an analysis of masculinity, as an attack upon the confident structures of masculinity. This could be seen, for example, in the way Dylan put forward two of the great male lovers of western culture: Casanova and Romeo—one historical, one fictional—and how both of these figures seemingly came to particularly sudden and unpleasant endings. Casanova was simply killed with self-confidence, while Romeo came to an unspoken but most probably grisly ending: it would seem Romeo had been in the wrong place at the wrong time, nothing was explicitly stated, but the verse in question, verse two, ended with the ambulance leaving and Cinderella sweeping up—what this might have been was not made clear, but the implication was that Cinderella was sweeping up Romeo's grisly remains—as they lay upon the ground in Desolation Row. The song further inverted male sexuality by presenting the reader/listener with such predominantly virile and manly figures as fisherman and sailors in decidedly ambiguous and ultimately feminizing settings: the fishermen were holding flowers, while sailors were frequenting beauty parlors. And finally, an even more direct attack on masculinity occurred in verse six, wherein Dr. Filth appeared to be metaphorically, or even literally, castrating his sexless patients.

Such anxieties could be seen in some of Dylan's later songs; written, of course, by an older masculine voice. Here male sexuality became still more marginalized, still more burdened and possessing still greater levels of anxiety. In the song "Don't Fall Apart on Me Tonight" (1983), from the *Infidels* album, we were offered a text about a relationship between what appeared to be an older man and a younger woman; with the two protagonists inhabiting what

4. Sexuality

seemed to be a dysfunctional liaison. It was a song full of agoraphobic anxieties, beginning with what appeared to be an oblique reference to the then recent assassination attempt on Pope John Paul II,[43] then transferring these anxieties towards the outside world in general. However, and perhaps most interestingly in this context, the song went on to frame such fears around the narrator's own doubts about his masculinity and, more specifically, what appeared to be fears about his own virility:

> Just a minute before you leave, girl
> Just a minute before you touch the door
> What is it that you're trying to achieve, girl?
> Don't you think we can talk about it some more?
> You know the streets are filled with vipers
> Who've lost all ray of hope
> You know, it ain't even safe no more
> In the palace of the Pope
> Don't fall apart on me tonight
> I just don't think that I could handle it ...[44]

Thus the song could be interpreted, at least within one specific reading, as a text about anxiety over male prowess; with the title, itself, thus providing one potential reading: an unembellished message directed towards the narrator's own fears surrounding his virility. In the song, the narrator wished he could take the young woman (or "girl" as she was described) "to the mountaintop," in other words—again in one reading—to the heights of a sexual climax. In addition, the narrator wanted to build the "girl" what was described as "a house made out of stainless steel," that is: to give her a rigid structure of some kind. However, he could not—unlike the millionaire with the (phallic) "drumstick in his pants"—he would seem to have had no rigid structure to offer her. All of this acted to enhance the feelings of paranoia, the feelings of mistrust, the feelings of agoraphobic anxieties apparent within the text; culminating in the second line of the chorus, with the almost risible *double-entendre* of "I just don't think that I could handle it."[45]

Of course, this in itself could be seen as a "rigid" interpretation; however, it could be argued that it was possible to perceive of a recurrent theme developing around this topic, especially in some of Dylan's later work. For example, the need for a shot of love, in the song "Shot of Love," (1981), or more explicitly in a song from the same time, the almost bathetic echo of impotent rage in the song "Dead Man, Dead Man" (1981), with its follow-up question of when will you arise? Alternatively, one could go backward in time to a song such as "Visions of Johanna" (1966), with its quixotic juxtaposition of both virility and impotence in the phrase: it's so hard to get on. In another way, one might go forward to a later song, such as "Lovesick" on the album *Time Out of Mind* (1997); it was of interest that the material on this collection was almost entirely devoid of active sexuality; in *Time Out of Mind* love would seem to have literally become sick. The first-person protagonist of these so-called "love songs" would appear to have grown sullen and morose, with an overarching sense of an older voice looking back to the vitality of youth with a sense of longing and envy.

Hence once again, it is possible to argue that, within a specific body of Bob Dylan's work, one can perceive of a reservation, a sense of unease, a series of disparate concerns—all connected with issues of masculinity, most particularly with anxieties around the phallus. In much of Dylan's work, especially in his later songs, there was a sense that virility was one of the attributes men valued above all else; providing a sense of what it meant to be a man. This concern for the power of the phallus may not seem overly conspicuous, but it was there if one were to look closely. For example, in a satiric context, this sense of concern could be seen in the song "Bob Dylan's 115th Dream" (1965), herein, when the masculine narrator was asked for some collateral, he simply pulled down his pants, as the song colloquially put it, as if this would suffice. Alternatively, in the song "Lily Rosemary and the Jack of Hearts" (1975), a sense of phallic anxiety could be seen at a cumulative moment in the narrative. This occurred in verse thirteen, at the moment of Big Jim's killing, the moment when a cold revolver clicked.[46] In other words, a cold gun misfired; a subtle narrative detail that seemed to undermine the notion of the gun as a phallic symbol, a notion so redolent within the culture as to be almost clichéd, but nonetheless a line that could be read as suggestive of a dislocation of potency.

* * *

This preoccupation with elements of masculine physicality, together with phallic performance, may arguably be confirmed via a linguistic examination of certain elements, as found within the canon of Dylan's work. For example, although Dylan has often been viewed as being predominantly a writer of love songs, a significant proportion of Dylan's songs have been written to, and about, men. To evidence this, it might be noted that of the 429 texts in *Lyrics*, the main core of Dylan's writing c. 1962–1985, arguably the key period in Dylan's artistic output,[47] forty-nine were entitled in an epony-

4. Sexuality

mous way. Of these, thirty were named after men while only nineteen were named after women. In this sense, it could reasonably be argued that Dylan's concern with men was more significant than was his concern with women. In addition, a glance at a concordance of Dylan's work would appear to bear this out; to cite just one example, in 2007 it was noted that Dylan's work, his then extant collection of published songs, had a vocabulary of some 8,170 words, of which the most commonly used lexical noun was "man," this appearing some 425 times throughout the then assembled collection of songs.[48]

* * *

In a different context, one of the other ways in which Dylan's work has looked at issues of masculinity has been from the perspective of race. As discussed in Chapter 2, from the very beginning of his career, at the apposite time of the early 1960s, Dylan has shown a concern for the plight of African American men. A wide range of Dylan's songs dealt with the dangerous and often violent way of life that was the common experience for many black men in America.[49] For example, the song "The Death of Emmett Till" (1962), was an early didactic protest song about a fourteen year-old black youth who was beaten, tortured and murdered in Mississippi, for simply whistling at a white woman. "Ballad of Donald White" (1962), was another early protest song about a black man, ironically named White, who could not make it on life's hurried tangled road, and who deliberately committed murder in order to find sanctuary in prison. A more impressionist song, "Oxford Town" (1963), concerned itself with black student, James Meredith, his registration at the University of Mississippi in 1962, and the violent aftermath that subsequently occurred. The song "Only a Pawn in Their Game" (1964), told the story of Medgar Evers, a black civil rights activist, shot dead in Jackson, Mississippi in 1963; while "Who Killed Davey Moore?" (1964) was a song about the black boxer, Davey Moore, killed in the boxing ring in 1963; also, the unreleased "Percy's Song" (1964) was a song telling the story of Percy Gioquintana, apparently a black waiter from Greenwich Village, who was sentenced to ninety-nine years in jail for the manslaughter of four people, in a drunk-driving accident in Illinois.[50] Such songs were not limited to Dylan's so-called protest period in the 1960s; there were later songs from the 1970s—for example, one might think of "Hurricane" (1976), Dylan's exuberant protest song about the black, middleweight boxer, Rubin "Hurricane" Carter, who was sentenced to sixty-seven years in jail for a murder he may or may not have committed. Another significant African

American man to be eulogized in song by Dylan was George Jackson, in the 1971 single release, called simply "George Jackson"—a double-sided single—with two different versions of the same song—it made a modest impression in the American charts, peaking at #33 in January 1972. The song represented Dylan's so-called return to social protest after a gap of several years, and was arguably one of the most revealing songs he was to write about a man. The song was apparently written spontaneously, on the news of the death in prison, of the famous black militant leader. It began with the bold and uninhibited statement:

> I woke up this mornin'
> There were tears in my bed
> They killed a man I really loved
> Shot him through the head[51]

Here Dylan was explicit in openly revealing his "love" for a man, expressing his feelings in a fashion he would rarely achieve when addressing a woman.[52] There was a sense in many of these songs, and especially in "George Jackson" and "Hurricane," of a secure masculine world, of a homosocial environment in which men were confident in their own company. Such a world could also be seen in the song "Joey" (1976), also from the *Desire* album. This could arguably be seen as one of the most contrived of Dylan's many songs about so-called heroes, and it was a song that caused a degree of discomfort among several of Dylan's critics,[53] not to mention Dylan's wider audience, who were aware of the actual reputation of Joey Gallo.[54] Nonetheless, within the canon of Dylan's work, the song remains a significant textual object, it was a song that unashamedly expressed an admiration for a man (albeit of Italian descent, not an African American) carrying out masculine acts, and demonstrating intense emotional feelings for other men.

Whether one describes this (Dylan's depiction of men of race) as a fetishistic fascination with the black male body, or whether one saw this merely as a response to a socio-cultural phenomena, was a point of interpretation. Such a setting obviously chimed within Fiedlerian concepts of sex and race, as discussed in Chapter 2; in addition, if one considers one distinct aspect of such an arena of speculation—Dylan's ambivalent attitude to the sport of boxing—then the picture may become clearer. In some songs Dylan has self-righteously protested against the brutality of the spectacle in which a black man can be killed, in the boxing ring, for the entertainment of a predominantly white audience.[55] While elsewhere he has celebrated and enthu-

4. Sexuality

siastically revered men who can take their opponents out with just one punch.[56] Insomuch, Dylan's preoccupation with boxing was of interest; that is, in the context in which boxing has been seen as a repressed homoerotic spectacle; a spectacle in which a predominantly white, male audience was sanctioned to take pleasure in the spectacle of two near naked men, dressed in a fetishistic way, often black, always young and muscular, attempted to commit often bloody violence on one another—with the audience often becoming intensely excited—albeit in a socially and culturally sanctioned environment. The homosocial and the latent homoerotic elements of such a spectacle being clearly apparent; although—as suggested—carefully concealed and vindicated within a specific social milieu; nonetheless, both in the cultural discourse of Bob Dylan's songs, and in the wider world in general, such a reading was available.[57]

* * *

As intimated in Chapter 1, if cultural theory has accomplished anything, it has demonstrated that any assumption—no matter how entrenched—can be challenged. Theory questions everything—and it has most certainly questioned the validity of religious belief. In this way, the influence of fundamentalist religion on Dylan's work: before, during and after the so-called "born again" songs of 1979–1981, would seem to be of some significance—and hence worthy of discussion here. If we strip away all extraneous social and cultural trappings—human beings would appear to have been ruled by two things: the need to be loved and the fear of death: love and death, Eros and Thanatos, in Freudian terms; the twin components of life and culture, and arguably the base cause of religion. The French philosopher and feminist theorist, Julia Kristeva, believed Christianity to be the ultimate home of the Law of the Father. Hence the conventional feminist response would be to argue that most of the great world religions have always, in fact, been political institutions; the world's great religions have always had one primary purpose: to control women and their sexuality.[58] This may seem almost a cliché, but in terms of Christianity and sexuality, proscription has always been the rule, as Rosalind Miles put it: "we are still stumbling through [a] Judeo-Christian minefield of sexual sin, guilt and repression."[59] Insomuch, religion has continually intimated that sex was wrong, when every human instinct said it was hugely desirable. This was especially the case in terms of homosexuality, both the Old and New Testaments had much to say on this[60]; and such a condemnation of homosexuality, especially in the New Testament, may have had more to do with the then current model of homosexuality in the Greco-Roman world, that of pederasty, the sexual use of young boys by adult males. In any case, by around 500CE Christianity had taken over Western civilization, Hellenistic ideas of rationality had been repressed, and for over the next one thousand years religious, and to some extent political discourse, would be ruled by Christianity. This being the context, albeit at a far remove, that might be seen as forming the basis of Dylan's quoted comments at the Hartford concert.

In the context of such Hellenistic ideas, one notes that the philosophical world has always tended to challenge the more dogmatic aspects of religion. For example, Socrates believed that the greatest danger "to both society and the individual" was "the suspension of critical thought." While Euripides posed the famous question: "Do we, holding that the gods exist, deceive ourselves with unsubstantial dreams and lies, while random careless chance and change alone control the world." Later philosophers were still more critical, David Hume, in somewhat anti–Semitic mood, asked, of the Virgin Mary: "What is more likely—that the whole natural order is suspended—or that a Jewish minx should tell a lie." While Hegel simply came to the overarching conclusion that God was a human construct. Martin Buber, the Jewish philosopher renowned for his concept of "I and Thou," posed the riddle: "To the Christian the Jew is the incomprehensibly obdurate man who declines to see what has happened, and to the Jew the Christian is the incomprehensibly daring man who confirms, in an unredeemed world, that its redemption has been accomplished." Havelock Ellis, albeit in a satiric mode, suggested that: "The whole religious complexion of the modern world is due to the absence in Jerusalem of a lunatic asylum." Finally, Bertrand Russell, in a characteristically even-handed way, commented: "My own view on religion is that of Lucretius. I regard it as a disease born of fear and as a source of untold misery to the human race. I cannot, however, deny that it has made some contributions to civilization."

Insomuch, a belief in a literal god, as the ultimate creator of the universe, together with a literal belief in the afterlife, cannot help but seem to border upon the irrational and the neurotic. As is well known, Freud dismissed religion as a universal neurosis; Freud's argument being that religious ideas were delusions and fulfillments of the oldest and strongest and most urgent wishes of mankind.[61] In addition, we know what Marx thought of religion and its corrosive effects on the human beings it encounters; religion was "the sigh of the oppressed creature, the sentiment of a heartless world and the soul of

4. Sexuality

soulless conditions," it was, in Marx's famous phrase, "the opium of the people." In essence, a logical and analytical account of religion would suggest that there is no evidence—and no reason—to presume any of its claims are justified. In addition, it is possible to contemplate the value of a moral existence, without recourse to the false and pious hopes of a life to come. We have a moral conscience because we have evolved as a species to realize it is often more advantageous to avoid amoral cruelties—to possess some degree of empathy—without a need for a belief in a so-called sky God—still less a literal belief in so-called holy scripture. Not so according to the lyrics of Dylan's song "Precious Angel" (1979), here there was either faith or there was unbelief—and there was no neutral ground—one either believed in the scripture or one did not.

In terms of Holy Scripture, Terry Eagleton has noted that "both Islamic and Christian versions of fundamentalism denounce idolatry, yet both make an idol of a sacred text."[62] In employing elemental poststructuralist thought, Eagleton went on to make the point that the term "sacred text" contains a self-contradiction, insomuch as all texts are "profaned by a plurality of meanings."[63] In other words, fundamentalist religions require believers to accept, on faith, an absolute belief in a prescribed list of written principles; the problem that then arises being that such literal mindedness cannot deal with the changing context of such sacred texts in terms of contemporary life. One might note here how other discourses; for example, philosophy, the arts in general, and certainly the sciences, are continually open to change—often revolutionary change—should better ways of thinking come along. As Eagleton has argued, the objection to religious fundamentalism is not that they "have principles, but that the have the wrong ones; that they base their principles on the foundation of a text" and that they are ultimately "ready to destroy the whole of creation for the purity of an idea."[64] In terms of Christianity, the religion most relevant in a discussion of Dylan's work, its sacred text is arguably the one text that has most influenced Western civilization; however, whether the influence of the Bible has been a cause for good or the opposite remains open to question.

All human societies have made attempts to come to terms with life and death, to attempt to gain an understanding of the world and to get at the truth of existence. One way of getting at this truth would be to turn to religion; however, if one responds to a question such as "How did DNA occur?" by saying "God made it," then this would not seem to push the argument very far, merely leading to a state of mind that requires no sense of further intellectual enquiry[65]; as Lawrence M. Krauss put it: "*God* seems to me to be a rather facile semantic solution to the deep question of creation."[66] In terms of creation myths: the core Christian belief is as follows: Jesus of Nazareth, who preached in Palestine some 2,000 years ago, was the son of God, he was born of a virgin and sent into the world by his father to redeem mankind of Adam's sin; he was crucified and rose from the dead and all those who believe in him will be granted eternal life.[67] Yet the idea that a creator of a hundred million stars in our galaxy alone—a galaxy some 13.8 billion years old—would have decided to redeem mankind by having his son crucified—at least raises the issue of the matter of scale.[68] From a neutral position, there would therefore seem to be questions to raise about Christianity, a religion that posits the idea of drinking the blood of a supposed supernatural being who was crucified nearly 2,000 years ago; and the lurid and sadomasochistic image of a near-naked man, hanging by spikes from a piece of wood; as a central icon, would appear hard to accept—unless you happen to be a Christian—as 2.2 billion people happen to be.[69]

There is, however, an alternative point-of-view. It is self-evident that all the main world religions—Christianity included—came about in much earlier stages of history. As David Lodge has noted, religion has had a different function at different times of human experience, when, as Lodge puts it: "the lives of a large proportion of the human race [were] made chronically wretched by poverty, ill health and violent oppression [and for whom religion was] the only thing that made life meaningful and worth living, by its promise of a better life to come."[70] The author and general detractor of all things relating to fundamentalist belief, Christopher Hitchens, made a similar point:

> One must state it plainly. Religion comes from the period of human prehistory where nobody—not even the mighty Democritus who concluded that all matter was made from atoms—had the smallest idea what was going on. It comes from the bawling and fearful infancy of our species, and is a babyish attempt to meet our inescapable demand for knowledge (as well as for comfort, reassurance and other infantile needs). Today the least educated of my children knows much more about the natural order than any of the founders of religion, and one would like to think—though the connection is not a fully demonstrable one—that this is why they seem so uninterested in sending fellow humans to hell.[71]

Hitchins offers a convincing explanation for the origins of religions—and yet the majority of them are still with us. Why should this be so? In a sense religion might be seen as comparable to the current interest in conspiracy theories; the way in which we wish to provide meaning to what were most likely meaningless events. As Rob Brotherton has noted: "conspiracy theories don't merely aim to *describe* something that has happened; they purport to *reveal* hitherto undiscovered plots in the hopes of persuading the as yet unalerted masses."72

In such a sense, religion could perhaps be seen as the greatest of all conspiracy theories, with Christianity being merely one version, but nonetheless representing what might be described as the greatest myth of western culture. However, it is a myth that Bob Dylan appears to have once accepted. As such, it remains something of a mystery why intelligent individuals, Dylan included, cognizant of at least some of the arguments as presented above, should have possessed such literal beliefs in supernatural events: that a man could perform miracles, that a man could raise himself from the dead; not to mention the concept of heaven and hell and the prospect of life after death for all living souls. Why Dylan should have bought into such a narrative is difficult to answer, but he was not alone, he was an American living in a somewhat credulous society, a society where polls have suggested "far more people believe in angels ... than believe in evolution."73 Since 1981, few of Dylan's songs have been as concerned with such eschatological issues, and Dylan has rarely performed any of his more extreme "born-again" songs in concert; hence it is tempting to speculate whether Dylan still holds to such fundamentalist views. In the song "Huck's Tune" (2007), Dylan may have offered a clue to his current thinking. In one of the song's more lucid couplets, Dylan sang that he had found hopeless love in the room above. The room above perhaps indicating the "upper room"—the Cenacle—this being the place traditionally held to be the site of the Last Supper. For Dylan to cryptically allude to this as "hopeless love" was perhaps a subtle attempt at defining the Christian message, the Christian myth. Yet the acerbic and bitter taste of Dylan's statements, in song and in live concerts from 1979 to 1981, remains: he was a born-again Christian—but a cynic might ask where were the born-again lions. Alternatively, a cynic might also think of James Joyce and his translation of the bible—as "buy-bull"—once again, a cynical response might conclude this was exactly what Dylan had bought into.74

* * *

Religion might therefore be said to have had a significant effect on Dylan's attitude to sex and human sexuality. Insomuch, a linkage to religion, within the context of a homosocial argument, might be seen in the case of one man, one masculine figure, one iconic male presence, a man who has, as yet, not been specifically seen in such a context: the man whom Dylan once famously called his "real hero."[75] Throughout his career Dylan's spiritual journeys have comprised of a wide and diverse range of areas: 1960s psychedelic drug-mysticism, Zen-Buddhism, Judaic philosophy, the Tarot—and others, but perhaps the most significant has always been Christianity; what John Herdman has described as: "a consistent apocalyptic world view and a fascination with the figure of Christ."[76] As such, it would seem self-evident that Dylan has, throughout his career, devoted a great deal of interest to the symbolic and literal figure of Christ, an interest that has, as Herdman put it, often been taken to the extent of a fascination, specifically in terms of Christ as a masculine figure, as an iconic figure of specific importance. One is not referring here merely to the so-called "born-again" songs of the late 1970s and early 1980s. A fascination with Christ can be seen before and (to some extent) after this time; a number of critics, for example, Craig Snow, have pointed out that a Christian ideology, with its love of a masculine God, with its love of the Father, with its love of Christ, was not unique to this time.[77] Dylan's embrace of a fundamentalist belief, at the end of the 1970s, merely made explicit what had always been prevalent in his work. The use of a Christian ideology as in such early evangelical songs as: "I'd Hate to Be You on That Dreadful Day," "Quit Your Low Down Ways," "Whatcha Gonna Do?" "Train A Travellin'," all emanating from the early 1960s, strongly suggested that a Christian way of thinking was apparent from the beginning of Dylan's career.[78]

In the 1966 *Playboy* interview Dylan was asked, by Nat Hentoff: "What do you have to look forward to?" To which Dylan responded: "Salvation. Just plain salvation." However, in the same interview Dylan also made a number of statements that now appear so liberal and so radical as to be almost pelagian in nature. These statements would provide a stark contrast to some of Dylan's later spiritual beliefs:

> I'm really not the right person to tramp around the country saving souls…. I'm not about to tell anybody to be a good boy or a good girl and they'll go to heaven…. People that use God as a weapon should be amputated upon…. My motto is, never follow anything…. I wouldn't advise anybody to do anything.[79]

By 1979, and as evidenced by stage comments such as the ones cited at the beginning of this chapter, Dylan would seem to have distanced himself from these liberal admonitions. The three so called "born-again" records: *Slow Train Coming* (1979), *Saved* (1980), *Shot of Love* (1981) and the prolific live performances that accompanied them, demonstrated a different view of the world. "There is a Master Creator, a Supreme Being in the Universe," so said

4. Sexuality

Dylan, talking to radio host, Bruce Heiman, in December 1979, in the only interview he gave at the height of this period. In the same interview, Dylan went on to say:

> Christ is no religion. We're not talking about religion. Jesus Christ is the way, the truth and the life.... I don't sing any song which hasn't been given to me by the Lord to sing.... Christ didn't preach religion. He preached the truth, the way and the life.[80]

The fundamentalist discourse of the songs on: *Slow Train Coming, Saved, Shot of Love*, together with the rigidly conservative nature of Dylan's comments in live concerts at the time, of which—as intimated above—the quote at the opening of this chapter was only one example, demonstrated, one could argue, a completely divergent approach to ways of thinking about the world. However, of specific interest was the clear emphasis on the masculine nature of God, note that Dylan referred, in the interview with Heiman, to a "Master Creator." In other words, the Deity was decidedly of a male gender, as made clear in Dylan's songs and public comments of the time, here was a clear construct of God in Christ, of God personified as a man. One might therefore speculate whether the preoccupation with a sense of salvation in Christ could be seen as having finally replaced the idea of redemption through a woman's love, and that the idea of an omniscient father figure, a figure that haunted so much of Dylan's work, had finally supplanted the primary area of romantic interest: the heterosexual love of women.

* * *

As has been intimated, it would seem fair to say that there was at least a degree of sexual ambiguity in the middle 1960s, both from the evidence of Dylan's work and from the perception of some of Dylan's critics. In the case of the latter, one might also cite, for example, Angela Carter, who, describing Dylan's stage persona at the Royal Albert Hall concert of 1966, thought of him as an "asexual being."[81] Greil Marcus, describing the same concert, commented that Dylan's diction was "almost effete.[82] In a wider context, Tim Riley observed that: "He [Dylan] never sounded like he was having any fun with the opposite sex."[83] While John Gordon wrote an entire essay musing on the possible transvestite nature of the *Bringing It All Back Home* record cover,[84] and Craig McGregor noted an unequivocally ambivalent slant to Dylan's work in the mid–1960s, McGregor went on to comment: "[A] strand to Dylan's music is its 'gay' component … there is a camp bitchiness, a penchant for the cheap put-down which limits the effectiveness of his songs, from 'Positively 4th Street' to some of the tracks on *Blonde on Blonde*."[85] It should be made clear here that there was no intention to suggest that Dylan's work contained an overtly homoerotic subtext; this would obviously be dependent upon the individual listener's response to that work. However, there is a sense that all individuals have an acceptance that there exists another side to one's sexuality, no matter how covert or dormant. For example, one might consider this comment by Norman Mailer, who might be seen as one of the bastions of heterosexual masculinity, at least as far as American literature was concerned: "There is probably no sensitive heterosexual man alive who is not preoccupied with his latent homosexuality."[86] Or as Marlon Brando once said: "Like the vast majority of men I've had several homosexual experiences and I'm not remotely ashamed of it."[87] In such a context one must obviously at least allow for such a component within the ideological structure of Dylan's work. At the same time, because of cultural conditioning, one must also allow for a prohibitive restraint in admitting to this, as Lynn Segal has argued:

> Homosexual men are feared and envied as sexually exotic, alien, unnatural, oral, anal, compulsive, violent, infectious, suicidal, and a threat to wife, children, home and phallus ... straight men are both terrified of, yet passionately attracted to, powerlessness and loss of control.[88]

In a similar vein, Roger Horrocks suggested:

> The gay man is a threat to the macho man, since he reveals explicitly that which the macho man must suppress as deeply as possible: his need for the love of other men, and the possibility of taking the feminine role.[89]

There was a sense here in which such elements could be seen in Dylan's work; albeit laden within a repressive and unexplored discourse. As alluded to earlier in this chapter, Allen Ginsberg was a poet who was not as repressive, but who was always close to Dylan, at least in an artistic sense; Ginsberg made the following comment, in 1996, just before his death, a comment that arguably encompassed the tensions in much of the heterosexist discourses within Dylan's work. Ginsberg was reflecting upon the 20th century and the issue of masculine violence; he stated that:

> The repression not only of the homoerotic, but just a tender aspect, the feminine aspect of men, is perhaps the cause of the greatest human misery of this present century. The vast concentration camps, the depredation of nature, the destruction of the environment, the lack of tenderness—and perhaps even maybe all this aggression and destructiveness—is a reaction to hide the impulse of tenderness, and to disguise it.[90]

4. Sexuality

This issue might be explored further via the more abstract connotations of a theoretical approach; specifically via the approaches found within queer theory, as it has come to be known. Queer theory emerged as a distinct field of criticism in the 1990s,[91] arising "from a coalition (at times an uneasy one) of feminist, post-structuralist and psychoanalytical theories,"[92] but it was not, as the name appeared to imply, merely to the exclusive interest of "gay" men and lesbian women—to people of alternative sexual orientations.[93] Instead, queer theory aimed to do for sexuality what feminism had accomplished for gender inequality. Different sexualities became the subject of analysis and understanding; with one of the main aims of queer theory being to deconstruct and to erode such binary oppositions as: man/woman, male/female, heterosexual/homosexual, active/passive and so on—demonstrating that such pairings were not absolute—but were instead part of a continuum. The idea of sexuality having a continuum was a key issue for queer theory, and at its core it was asking the following question: how do you get all these polymorphous, nominally bisexual beings to focus sexual attention and desire towards members of the opposite sex and to engage in penile/vaginal intercourse. As such, queer theory argued that sexuality was socially and culturally constructed, that it was beyond the bounds of biological determinacy; for example, it challenged attempts, by science, to find a "gay gene," denying the idea that sexuality was definable within a scientific discourse. Insomuch, queer theory has attempted to theorize both sex and gender as a socio-cultural condition, as a performance, rather than having an overarching biological basis.[94]

One of the key philosophers of queer theory was Michel Foucault[95]; for Foucault language was never innocent, it was always positioned within a discourse,[96] within a form of social and political control in which "truth" became relative and pragmatic. In this context there was no single determinate truth to any particular narrative or event, only a conflict of interpretations whose outcome was ultimately determined by power.[97] Foucault argued that what we perceive as truths were instead powerful cultural myths[98]; as such, Foucault argued that the classical order of political rule, based on sovereignty and rights, had been replaced with a new regime of power exercised through the stipulations of norms for human behavior.[99] In other words, it was Foucault's argument that sexuality was "nothing more than a means through which power has been organized in Western society."[100] Perhaps one of Foucault's key ideas was that there was no actual essence to sexual behavior, and that the modern concept of sexuality was a recent invention.[101] In an overarching sense, Foucault argued that sexuality was not an innate occurrence, but a his-

A Wanderer by Trade

torical construction, and that a history of sexuality was a history of various forms of repression that have taken place in order to control it.[102] As Tasmin Spargo put it: "A vital feature of Foucault's argument is that sexuality is not a natural feature of human life, but a constructed category of experience which has historical, social and cultural, rather than biological origin."[103]

Another influence on queer theory, although within a differing context to Foucault, was Sigmund Freud. Freud has not, as yet, been discussed in specific detail within this study; however, queer theory—in one sense at least—can be traced directly to Freud; to Freud's famous comment, that human beings were "polymorphously perverse." In this way, Freud appeared to assert that "normal" sexuality was not necessarily identified with heterosexuality; Freud holding to the idea that the sexual instinct was heterogeneous, that it sought pleasure in whatever diverse ways it could find.[104] As Jonathan Ned Katz put it: "Freud's idea that heterosexuals are made not born, is still one of his most provocative, his most subversive theories."[105] For Freud, all human beings were predominantly erotic, with a continual desire for pleasure, for what later theorists would call *jouissance*. Insomuch, Freud believed all human behavior could be explained via its need for gratification.[106] As Katz argued: "The built in goal of Freud's 'sexual instinct' is satisfaction not increase. 'Pleasure,' Freud emphasises, is the 'main purpose' of 'our mental apparatus'—a machine with satisfaction as its mission."[107] As such, through the Pleasure Principle, if nothing else, Freud's influence on queer theory would seem to be clearly apparent—as his influence can arguably be seen in other diverse arenas.

In terms of Freud's significance to intellectual thought as a whole, this has always been a debatable issue; however, it is difficult to ignore Freud, no matter how one might disagree with his ideas. Freud's influence would appear to have become so all embracing that, in a sense, it no longer matters whether or not his ideas were valid. For example, the Oedipal complex may be as preposterous as it is uncomfortable, but nonetheless it is difficult to ignore, so commonplace has it become within the cultural currency. In this way, whatever his critics might claim, Freud has had "a monumental impact on Western thought and philosophy."[108] Freud may have been disparaged by some, but philosophy and theory have mostly reacted positively to his ideas. As Copernicus demonstrated the world was not the center of the universe, as Darwin demonstrated man was not the center of the animal world; so Freud demonstrated the conscious mind was not the "master of its own house."[109] There is no actual evidence for much of Freud's work; however, as intimated, the

4. Sexuality

mere fact that his ideas have circulated so widely in the culture, have become so ingrained within the public consciousness, cannot help but add weight to his work. Psychoanalysis, like structuralism, was a grand attempt to apply logic to the human subject, and Freudian theory at least provides a paradigm for understanding the way human beings behave. As such, Freud must be seen as one of the most influential thinkers of the twentieth century. As Marjorie Garber commented:

> By turns brilliant and infuriating, self-doubling and self-assured, Freud is the intellectual forerunner of most modern and postmodern speculation on sexuality—and bisexuality. Popularised, quoted out of context, dehistoricized, and rewritten by followers often less brilliant and more dogmatic than he, Freud, like Shakespeare has become a cultural monolith.[110]

Garber refers to Freud as a cultural monolith, and Freud's methods have certainly been of interest to literary and cultural critics, insomuch as they seek the unconscious of the novel, film, play, poem, song, etc., in the same way Freud sought the unconscious of his patients. The classic method of the patient lying on the psychoanalyst's couch, free-associating in such a way as repressed fears and conflicts could be brought into the open, instead of remaining buried in the unconscious; such a method could be seen as an analogous technique to the one literary and cultural critics employ in order to interrogate cultural texts from a theoretical point-of-view.[111]

In terms of Bob Dylan's attitude to Freud, the only discernible reference in song would appear to be in "Talkin' World War III Blues" (1963), with its satiric rhyming of ouch and psychiatric couch.[112] Elsewhere, Dylan's appraisal of Freud would seem to have been scarcely appreciative; in *Chronicles*, during a discussion of his reading habits in the 1960s, he related this short encounter with Freud, or at least with Freud's work:

> There was a book by Sigmund Freud, the king of the subconscious, called *Beyond the Pleasure Principle*. I was thumbing through it when Ray [a friend in Greenwich Village with whom Dylan was staying] came in, saw the book and said, "The top guys in that field work for ad agencies. They deal in air." I put the book back and never picked it up again.[113]

While in an interview, with Scott Cohen in 1985, Dylan made the following reproachful comment:

> I never read Freud. I've never been attracted to anything he has said, and I think he's started a lot of nonsense with psychiatry and that business. I don't think psychiatry can help or has helped anybody. I think it's a big fraud (pun not intended) on the public.[114]

The fact that Dylan seemed so guarded around Freudian thought was perhaps suggestive of the wariness of what might be revealed via a Freudian reading of his work; this perhaps being akin to his reticence around human sexuality in his work as a whole—as has been discussed earlier in this chapter. Also of interest was the way in which Dylan referred to Freud as "the king of the subconscious"—if one considers just this one aspect of Freud's work, then Dylan's claim of Freud being a fraud (an old joke, anyway) might be undermined, at least to some degree. Freud put forward the idea that there was a part of the mind beyond the conscious, but which, nevertheless, has a profound influence on our lives and actions. In other words, Freud allowed us to accept the "role of the unconscious to our everyday discourse"[115]—that is, we now acknowledge the unconscious without question, with the corollary that we accept other motivations to those of our conscious mind. Such motivations, within a Freudian way of thinking, usually having a sexual derivation; in other words, we "are complex beings whose sexuality plays a major part in who we are," and that this is "entirely a result of Freud's thinking."[116]

* * *

In approaching a summary to the chapter, it would seem valid to suggest—in terms of issues pertaining to sexuality—that Bob Dylan remains a contradictory writer and performer; and, significantly, a knowingly contradictory writer and performer. In addition, Dylan remains a writer and performer who has often been prepared to assume a trickster's disposition; as he once commented: "I can't say I haven't done my share of playing the fool."[117] One might therefore think here of the poet as trickster, one who deliberately sets out to cause confusion, and thus it is important to at least have an awareness of elements of deliberate obfuscation, of a deliberate sense of what might be termed: a ludic ambiguity. In this light one song worthy of consideration in such a context might be said to be the song "Jokerman" (1983); insomuch as this was a text on which a number of critics have written at length, reading a wide variety of meanings into the term in the song's title. However, few critics would seem to have seen the song in the literal sense: to argue that the Jokerman in the song could be read simply as a joke on maleness, on masculinity itself, on what it means to be a man. In other words, the Jokerman was literally a joker-man, a caricature, a burlesque, a pastiche of masculinity. A man who was half this and half that, half god and half devil, half divine and half evil, a trickster; as intimated, literally a joker-man, not a genuine man; instead a joker-man/Jokerman, giving a performance of being a man.

4. Sexuality

Within a study that would put forward the aim of attempting to describe, explain and even define masculinity, as found within the work of Bob Dylan, such a reading of the aforementioned song, "Jokerman," if only within a consideration of its one-word title, could be seen as adding weight to the idea, to the concept, to the theoretical model, that masculinity could be seen as a mere performative measure. Thus adding weight, once again, to Judith Butler's sense of gender being a performance, with masculinity measured here as a comedy of itself, a performance, an act, an improvised space, a space wherein different sexual identities could be adopted and where different gendered roles could be played-out. As previously mentioned in Chapter 3, in one of his great songs of gender ambiguity, "Just Like a Woman" (1966), for Dylan to say someone fakes just like a woman could not help but bring up ideas of the performative quality of gender roles, suggesting a level of complexity and fluidity within this song, together with a number of other examples in Dylan's work. Hence, in a similar way, the song "Jokerman," fulfills the same role, "he" jokes just like a man. It was arguably one of Dylan's most revealing songs—and one of his most complex—hence no explanation would seem necessary here, to explain the lack of an interpretation beyond the single word title of the text.

As this chapter will hopefully have shown, a significant component of Bob Dylan's work could be seen as being concerned with the sexual relationships between men and women, although perhaps not with as great a significance as might generally be perceived within a general discussion of Dylan's work. In this sense it would appear that the overall question, relating to the songs of Bob Dylan, would seem to continually return and to revolve around the concept of what might be defined as personal identity; in other words, what does it mean to be a man, and how does this function when placed into the arena of interpersonal relationships. Furthermore, if identity, within Dylan's work, was framed in large part by possessing a sense of gender—by being masculine—then it would perhaps appear to be useful to look at the sense of self in Dylan's work, to focus and to look at identity, at masculine identity, and at how such an identity was constructed. Hence, in this way, the next chapter of this study will look at the issue of identity in the love lyrics of Bob Dylan. In a final summation, such a discussion will attempt to venture towards an explanation of what this term, identity, could be envisaged as embracing, what this term, in Dylan's work, may have actually signified.

5

Identity and Duality

> "I cannot say the word eye anymore."
> —Bob Dylan, liner notes to *Highway 61 Revisited*

In 1975, the American playwright Sam Shepard asked what might be seen as a pivotal question in terms of Bob Dylan and the notion of identity:

> The only protected space is up on stage. Dylan says it's the only time he feels alone. When he's up there. When he's free to work his magic. No one can touch him. No one can sidle up, pretending it's all just an accidental encounter, and pick his brains, his heart, his skin, his flesh and blood. All they can do is imagine what he's like. You can see them staring hard into his white mask, his gray-green eyes, trying to pick at the mystery. Who is he, anyway?[1]

The question: "Who is he, anyway?" was an intriguing one. It was a question that resonated throughout Shepard's book, throughout many other books on Dylan, throughout this present work, not to mention the way it resonated throughout a significant element of Dylan's own work. It was a question writers, critics and fans have been asking, whether consciously or unconsciously, for as long as "Bob Dylan" has been known to the world. To put this simply, we all want to know who he is; thus, while having an awareness of the potential hazards inherent in approaching such a question, it is nonetheless a question that will at least be approached during the course of this chapter.

In this sense, it would seem that an interrogation of this question, an exploration of who "Bob Dylan" is, could also be seen as part of an exploration of the attributes and characteristics of a specific masculine identity. Also, it would appear that an interpretation of Dylan's work in this context—the way in which the performative figure we witness as "Bob Dylan" acts upon an interpretation of the songs in question—may at least offer some kind of explanation to some of the questions raised in this study; that is: issues surrounding masculinity, femininity and sexuality. Thus far in this study some degree of care has been taken to separate the author of the texts under discussion, from

5. Identity and Duality

the texts themselves. However, as there is, self-evidently, a physical being existent in the world who is responsible for the creation of the texts under discussion, and, as it is now intended to look at the subject of identity as it appears in such work, then the question of how much the persona of "Bob Dylan" affects the way we deal with such texts would seem pertinent. In other words, the significance of the persona of "Bob Dylan" would now seem to require at least some degree of debate.

* * *

However, before embarking upon such an exploration, the subtle difference being made between Bob Dylan and "Bob Dylan" should perhaps be noted. This study has no interest in Bob Dylan; such an interest only applies to "Bob Dylan"—the persona within the songs. In this way there will be no intention to investigate how much Dylan's personal life intrudes into his work; as has been previously intimated, this would seem to be a reductive, not to say futile task.[2] However, notwithstanding the obvious and arguably convincing quality to such a proposition, it has to be accepted that this is a method many writers—writing about Dylan—have consistently adopted; for example, even a writer as well-regarded and as critically aware as Michael Gray has commented:

> It is exceptionally difficult, and not necessarily worth trying to distinguish the work from the man…. Dylan sings, "Honey I want you," or even, "Carry yourself back to me unspoiled," we link the "I" and the "me" first to Dylan himself. He projects his personal in his artistic self.[3]

One might argue against this and suggest that such a point of view limits the ways in which we might interpret Dylan's work—that there is no reason to accept that Dylan projects his personal self into his artistic self—or at least he may do so, but we, as readers of Dylan's work, have no way, and indeed, have no need to account for this. Furthermore, a reading of such work will be greatly enhanced if we simply avoid accepting such a proposition. If one considers a particularly apposite example, a song such as "Sara" (1976), as previously intimated in Chapter 3, here one found a song that has almost universally been interpreted as somehow being "about" Dylan's ex-wife. It was of no consequence that nowhere in the song was it specifically stated that this was a song about Dylan's marriage to a woman called Sara Dylan. Perhaps Dylan did write the song about his wife, perhaps he did not; we will never know and it would seem wholly pointless to speculate one way or the other. The specific point in question would appear to revolve around the proposition that potential autobiographical allusions should not prevent us from seeing this song (or any Dylan song) as a textual creation; a textual creation open to whatever interpretation we, the reader or listener, might wish to adopt.

Roland Barthes' essay, "Death of the Author," previously discussed in Chapter 1, obviously has a resonance in relation to the above argument. In *Alias Bob Dylan*, his first study of Dylan's work, Stephen Scobie wrote that:

> The theory of the "Death of the Author" is, however, much more sophisticated than any simplistic dismissal of biographical information. At its most radical it calls into question the way we view not only authors but all so-called "individuals." It depends upon a fundamental questioning of the notion of personality, of the self. In what sense can an author (or indeed anybody) be said to be an autonomous, coherent individual?[4]

Scobie's perceptive, if somewhat speculative interpretation of Barthes, opened up an interesting line of enquiry. The idea of questioning the notion of personality and identity was, one might argue, a significant factor in a consideration of Dylan's work; as Scobie put it, in Dylan's work "identity is never unproblematic"[5] Furthermore, the way in which Dylan constructs a sense of personal identity, and specifically the way he constructs a sense of a gendered identity was, one could suggest, more pertinent to a discerning and productive argument than mere biographical enquiry.

* * *

In such an arena there was a sense in which the whole idea of the concept of "Bob Dylan" could, in itself, be questioned and could be seen as a creative structure. In a certain sense one could envisage a discourse in which "Bob Dylan" had created himself. One of Dylan's numerous biographers, Clinton Heylin, began his biography of Dylan with this provocative, but nonetheless pertinent observation: "In 1986 Bob Dylan was twenty-six years old. His creator, Robert Allen Zimmerman was forty-five."[6] Thus, here there was an idea of seeing "Bob Dylan" as a manufactured production, a sense in which someone called Robert Allen Zimmerman had been performing the role of "Bob Dylan" for all this time, or at least for the time in which the world had been aware of "Bob Dylan." Dylan himself would seem to have had at least an awareness of the nuances of this argument, at a press conference, in Australia in 1986, he commented: "I'm only Bob Dylan when I have to be Bob Dylan, most of the time I can just be myself."[7] The obvious question that then arises

5. Identity and Duality

is who this "myself" might be, who is actually performing the role of "Bob Dylan." This was a question, one might imply, that a large part of Dylan's art explores, and one that will be explored in this chapter.[8]

* * *

At the same time, it must be admitted that the idea of "Bob Dylan," as a persona, has always been a significant element of Dylan's appeal, and one that would appear to at least partially answer the question: why Dylan's work has so often been viewed in an autobiographical light. In other words, the substance and power of Dylan's personality has gone some way in providing a potential solution to the following question: why have so large a percentage of Dylan's audience paid such close and unfluctuating attention to the author, at the expense of the creative textual potentiality of the work. Bob Dylan would appear to possess what might be described, for want of a better term, a charismatic personality. As one trawls through the many anecdotes told about Dylan, in the numerously available biographical sources, a powerful charismatic personality would seem to be one of the most common attributes ascribed to him. The following series of comments offer a mere impression of such material available; firstly, the journalist, Al Aronowitz:

> Bob is the most psychic person I know. You've got to be a heavyweight to play with Bob.[9]

Joan Baez:

> There aren't too many people who have as much charisma as Bobby has. I've never met anyone who has as much.[10]

The singer David Blue:

> His power, his mystique, just affected people in crazy ways, even from hearing him on records you have to say, this guy knows, this guy feels, and [you want] to be like him.[11]

The folk-singer Rambling Jack Elliot:

> There was something about Bob. He had the same kind of magnetism as James Dean. Dean was the first cat I ever met with that kind of thing, that magnetism, and Bob was the second I ever met.[12]

Dylan's first record producer, John Hammond:

> They were discovering the word for what he had, charisma, somehow when he stood alone to sing, eyes and ears were riveted on him.[13]

One of Dylan's later record producers, Jerry Wexler:

A Wanderer by Trade

> When Dylan walked into the control room at Cherokee, [the recording studios where the *Slow Train Coming* album was made] everyone backed-off, forming a *cordon sanitaire* around him. No one spoke until he did, so powerful was his aura.[14]

Filmmaker, Mel Howard:

> If he's displeased, if he's like down, or turned off, it's really hard to work with him because he's got such a heavy presence.[15]

Singer Sylvia Tyson:

> The thing that Dylan had was a real presence, you literally couldn't take your eyes off him.[16]

And finally, the singer David Crosby:

> He had a glow, like an aura. Everyone in the place was stunned. They'd never seen anything like that in their lives before.[17]

A wide selection of sources have been included here, merely to demonstrate how compelling is the available evidence. In other words, the concept that Dylan has at least been commonly perceived as a charismatic personality would not appear to be in doubt. Of course, charisma is a common, not to say clichéd description of performers and celebrities in the public eye, but in Dylan's case any sense of hyperbole would appear to be unwarranted, there being clear and strong evidence that there was a genuine argument in play. Even a critic as discerning, erudite and astute as Christopher Ricks, was able to state of Dylan: "But we're not supposed to fall in love with him, are we? We only think he is the most amazing phenomenon in our lifetime."[18] However, charisma remains a problematical concept to explain; a dictionary definition might offer an initial solution, as in, for example: "*Charisma*—a compelling attractiveness or charm that can inspire devotion in others."[19] Such a definition would seem to correspond with David Blue's comment about Dylan's power and mystique affecting people, merely from hearing his records, and hence would seem particularly pertinent and relevant to the argument. The sense of a compelling attractiveness could be seen here as extending from performer to listener via the recordings we, the audience, experience. Dylan's mystique, presence, personal magnetism, personal allure or simply, charisma, could therefore be perceived at a distance as well as in personal encounters. This issue therefore representing a subject area a critic of Dylan's work must be attentive to, at least to a certain degree.

A sense of the issue of a charismatic dimension to Dylan's personality could be perceived if one looks at the history of a publication like *The Tele-*

5. Identity and Duality

graph. This was ostensibly a fan magazine, published in the UK, and dedicated to all facets and to all things Bob Dylan. In its own way it was highly successful—if only in terms of its longevity: running from 1981 to 1996, totaling fifty-six quarterly issues, only ceasing publication with the death of its founder and editor, John Bauldie, in 1996. The foremost and paramount observation to make is that the magazine was primarily concerned with Dylan as a personality; the majority of the material within the magazine was more concerned with Dylan's life than with his work. The second observation to make is that the membership of the magazine (which numbered several thousand) was predominantly male.[20] The fifty-six issues contained a large number of quality color photographs of Dylan, a great deal of emphasis was given to how Dylan looked, and there was generally a preoccupation with Dylan as a physical figure, encouraged, of course, by Dylan's own sense of the significance of his image and appearance. One is not suggesting that the readership consisted of "closet male-tribadic admirers" of Bob Dylan, but nonetheless the attention to Dylan, as a man, by a large number of other men, raised a number of pertinent issues.[21] For example, it confirmed the idea of the pervasive nature of the Dylan mystique, it also confirmed ideas of homosociality, as discussed in Chapter 4 and throughout this book, and finally, it also offered, from a certain vantage point, the importance of the question that opened this chapter: Who is Bob Dylan?

* * *

The nature of identity in Dylan's work had a diverse range of other components, a much greater complexity than the nominal idea of hero-worship by way of overtly charismatic and homosocial factors. One might argue that the concept of identity, as presented within Dylan's work, had a more diverse structural integrity, and that there was, within a wide array of Dylan's songs, an almost narcissistic preoccupation with identity. One of the most significant facets of this preoccupation could be seen in the varied number of songs that dealt directly with identity in what might be described as a duality of voices. There was a sense in which such songs appeared to describe the common theme of a twinned self, a *doppelgänger*, an opposite, a duality of a different nature. For example, in the song "Love Is Just a Four Letter Word" (1965), such a duality of voices involved a seemingly vain exploration of the self, with the singer searching for his double, while at the same time looking for complete evaporation—to the core. In the song "Abandoned Love" (1975), there was a sense of betrayal felt by the narrator, wherein he appeared to believe he had been deceived by the clown—inside of himself. In "Every Grain of Sand" (1981), there was a sense of melancholy, in which the protagonist in the song once again professed to a sense of duality, of having another self within the self, of having a dying voice within. In the song "Jokerman" (1983), there was a similar sense of interior conflict, with the male protagonist shedding another layer of skin—while keeping one step ahead of a persecutor within. This was a sense of conflict repeated in the song "Where Are You Tonight (Journey Through Dark Heat)" (1978), wherein the male protagonist fought with his twin—such a twin being referred to as the enemy within.[22]

In an interview in March 1978, only two to three months before he recorded the final song cited above, "Where Are You Tonight (Journey Through Dark Heat)," Dylan had told the journalist, Barbara Kerr: "Each man struggles within himself. That is where the fight is. One part of man against the other. That's the real struggle. If you can deal with the enemy within then no enemy without can stand a chance."[23] The idea of searching for another identity at the core of one's being, the idea of the clown inside oneself, of the dying voice within, the idea of a persecutor within, together with an enemy within—could all be interpreted in a number of different ways. However, one plausible way of interpreting such a preoccupation, with a twinned or divided self, could be to discern of a male-female dichotomy within the individual psyche. Thus the struggle could conceivably be seen as that of the masculine side of the psyche, in conflict with the feminine side, and vice-versa. Antony Easthope, in his influential book of the 1980s, *What a Man's Gotta Do: The Masculine Myth in Popular Culture*, spoke of the "enemy within" in a similar context:

> The masculine ego has to defend itself from the enemy within, and this mainly takes the form of its own femininity ... his struggle to be masculine is the struggle to cope with his own femininity."[24]

The "enemy within" was clearly positioned here as being problematical in relation to the confident, unchallenged construct of masculinity. Hence one obvious conclusion to make would be to see the "enemy within," in the songs of Bob Dylan, as a feminizing influence in terms of a masculine construct of identity.[25]

In such a context, it is perhaps important to be cognizant that the idea of having two differing halves within one body has, in fact, had a long antecedence. Philosophers as diverse as Plato and Jung have spoken of a craving for unity within the human psyche, for a sense of completeness, of having

5. Identity and Duality

been split from one's twin, from one's missing piece. In the fourth century BCE, in *The Symposium*, Plato had posited the idea of a golden age wherein human beings had been hermaphrodite, but were then split into male and female, resulting in a continual longing to reunite, to find one's twin, something only glimpsed in the orgasmic climax of coitus. A consequence of the split was that each half began to crave for its other half. Thus, or so one might argue, the dualistic conflict inherent in some of Dylan's songs: the enemy within, the persecutor within, the dying voice within, all could be seen as indicative of the male and female sides of the psyche striving to reunite with themselves. These elements of dualism in Dylan's work could thus be read as feminine constructs enclosed within a masculine imagination, a masculine body, a masculine psyche—and so on. This being represented via the distant and remote memory of asexuality, culminating within a yearning to reconstruct what had been lost long ago.

If one looks more closely at Dylan's work, it becomes apparent that there were a further number of songs in which ideas of duality could be seen. For example, in the song "Simple Twist of Fate" (1975), Dylan constructed the argument of feeling almost a sense of transgression in knowing and feeling too much within, with the sense that the female presence, the love object within the song, had become his twin. From the perspective of the above argument, these lines might be interpreted as reflecting upon the resistance the masculine voice often adopted in Dylan's work, the resistance towards allowing a feminized emotional response to take place. Thus one can perceive of the masculine voice denying any idea of emotional depth, this being contrasted against the impulse to perceive of a feminizing influence that would make the circle complete. In another love song, in what might be seen as one of his most exaggerated and overstated love songs, "Wedding Song" (1974), Dylan had put forward a masculine narrator who claimed that his loved one, presumably female, was the other half of him, and that "she" was the missing piece. In one sense, these lines seemed to recall the biblical story of Genesis, of God making Eve from Adam's rib; however, in contrast to such a reading, the lines could also be seen as recalling Plato's ideas surrounding the origin of the sexes, the idea of humanity having the desire to recreate a wholeness that had been lost in the splitting apart of male and female.

This concern, what might even be described as an anxiety over (gender) identity, could be seen within further examples of Dylan's work, it being a repeated trope that was revisited over and over again. For example, in a song from the very beginning of his career, "Mixed Up Confusion" (1962); within the text of an under-appreciated but intriguing song, Dylan's male protagonist was looking for a woman whose head was mixed up in the same way his was—hence clearly delineating the idea that they were, in some way, paired or twinned. Thus there was a sense in which here, and throughout his work, Dylan had positioned a divided identity, a divided self. This could be seen, in a literal way, in the case of the desperate men and the desperate women who were divided in "Changing of the Guards" (1978), one of Dylan's most narratively beguiling songs. While in "Tangled Up in Blue" (1975), the masculine narrator may have proclaimed that he had to get to "her"—the female presence he was addressing throughout the song—he had to get to her somehow; however, in a sense, and from the perspective of one interpretative stance, this represented not merely a wish to be reunited with a woman, with a female archetype, but with a component part of his own self. As David Pichaske put it:

> If our personalities do, in fact, contain male and female halves, and the ritual marriages which end so many Renaissance dramas, fairy tales, legends and songs are really integrations of the male and female sides of the personality, and the male and female figures of literature and dreams are archetypes we unconsciously play and replay in our subconscious—then any song involving male and female archetypes is really an examination of component parts of our psyche and all of Dylan's women are part of his search for a female other.[26]

The idea of the human spirit—especially the masculine—being split into two has been explored in a wide range of literary texts; for example, in Robert Louis Stevenson's famous novel, *The Strange Case of Dr. Jekyll and Mr. Hyde*, in Edgar Allen Poe's short story, "William Wilson," and in Joseph Conrad's novella, "The Secret Sharer." In each of these texts men were haunted by another self, by a twin, by a *doppelgänger*. This was a theme that could, one might argue, be seen within a range of songs in which Dylan posited a duality of identity. Insomuch, the song "I and I" (1983), could be read in such a way; it was a text whose title has generally been interpreted as referring to a Rastafarian expression, meaning oneself and God; however, it could also be read as an example of a song about a differentiation of identity, the duality of identity, a self literally divided into I and I. The song began with a conversation between the self and the self, with the singer recalling how long it had been since a strange woman had slept in his bed; watching her sleeping and poetically imagining, within an oneiric discourse, how free her dreams must have been, before going on to envisage the woman in another lifetime—seemingly married to King David—while he wrote his psalms alongside moonlit

5. Identity and Duality

streams.[27] Later in the song, the masculine voice informed that someone else was speaking with his mouth, but he was listening only to his heart. As such, there were obvious questions as to whom was the "I" speaking and to whom was the "I" listening. Hence once again there was a sense of duality in the construct of an identity being expressed; the song offering the depiction of a conversation between the self and the self, the I and another I, and, in one reading at least, a dialogue between two gendered selves, twinned inside a single identity, could therefore be perceived.

* * *

In *True Dylan* (1987), the one-act play Sam Shepard wrote about his relationship with Dylan, there was the following exchange:

SAM: I've heard this theory that women are rhythmically different from men. By nature. That the female rhythm is a side-to-side, horizontal movement and the male rhythm is vertical, up and down. Do you feel those different kinds of rhythms in you?

BOB: Yeah, sure. We all do. There's that slinky, side-to-side thing and the vertical, up-and-down one. But they're a part of each other. One can't do without the other. Like God and the Devil.[28]

The comment that men and women were "a part of each other" would obviously seem to be a clear example of Dylan (albeit within the play's fictitious discourse) portraying men and women as opposing parts of each other.[29] In an interview conducted a few years before, in *Playboy* magazine, in 1978, Dylan had commented: "A soul mate—what do they mean by soul mate? There's a male and female in everyone, don't they say?"[30] Hence one could argue that these comments relating to the idea of a female twin, and of a striving towards a female double within the male psyche, could be seen, at least in part, as explaining some of the underlying tensions found within significant areas of Dylan's work. This was seen, for example, in the way the men in Dylan's work seemed to be in consistent retreat from the women they would feign to be involved with. As discussed in Chapter 2 of this study, such men were constantly striving to remove themselves from a feminine influence. In this way the issue of identity, a masculine identity, arguably represented a significant preoccupation within Dylan's work, a preoccupation that runs from the very start of Dylan's career in the early 1960s, up until the songs on *Time Out of Mind* (1997), and, to some extent at least, the songs that have subsequently been released up until the present day.

In this context, it would thus seem pertinent that a number of the monographs thus far written on Dylan from an analytical and critical perspective have focused on the issue of identity. One might think here of the books of Aidan Day, Stephen Scobie, John Herdman, and even, to a certain extent, Sam Shepard; all these books have concentrated, to a certain extent, on the idea of how the self identifies with itself in Dylan's work. For example, Aidan Day's book began with the statement:

> The issue of identity constitutes a primary imaginative focus to [his] body of work.[31]

While Stephen Scobie wrote of:

> [T]he definitive image of what I have called the mask of the divided self—the double, ghost, alias or shadow that always intervenes in the supposedly unified human subject.[32]

And likewise, John Herdman, posing the following question, appeared to have been exploring a similar topic:

> Without wishing to venture into psychology, I have the impression that he [Dylan] has never been too sure of who he is outside his art.[33]

And finally, Sam Shepard, who again appeared to be pursuing a similar theme:

> Dylan has invented himself. He's made himself up from scratch. Bob Dylan is an invention of his own mind.[34]

One might partially concur with the opinions of such authors; however, it would seem that the preoccupation with identity, the preoccupation with the concept of "Bob Dylan," the preoccupation with the lack of certainty in a supposedly unified human subject, might also have had a more specific explanation. One might again suggest that such preoccupations in Dylan's work, the way in which his work repeatedly returned to the association and the cohesion between identity and duality, had a resonance within a discourse surrounding the concept of a sexual and a gendered identity. Bob Dylan's work was not so much haunted by ghosts and doubles that intervened between a supposedly unified human subject; the primary focus was not so much constructed around the uncertainty of who he was inside or outside his art, but was primarily attentive to the ambiguities and dislocations within a gendered identity—at least this is the argument made herein, made within this study. In this sense, the artifice of identity, both in Dylan's work and in the way Dylan has created the persona we know as "Bob Dylan," suggests the idea of a continual performance; and, once again, could be framed as drawing upon Judith Butler's concept of gender (and hence identity) as a performance,

5. Identity and Duality

as an act. To put this in simple terms, this was the idea that one can simply make oneself up, a sense in which "Bob Dylan" did invent himself, in which he was able to "make himself up." Furthermore, if one can invent one's identity, then one might plausibly formulate the idea that one can also invent and perform one's gendered identity.

One of the more noteworthy ways in which Dylan invented himself, or made himself up (as Sam Shepard put it) was via the conceptual use of the mask, both real and metaphorical. At least this is the theory Greil Marcus puts forward; according to Marcus, Dylan has, throughout his career, consistently made use of a variety of masks to disguise the real constituent of identity, as Marcus put it: "Few performers have made their way onto the stage of the twentieth century with a greater collection of masks than Bob Dylan."[35]

Within this context, and in a literal sense, one might recall Dylan's famous and oft-quoted comment, at the so-called Halloween Concert of October 31, 1964, at the Philharmonic Hall in New York City: "It's Halloween," Dylan told his audience, "I've got my Bob Dylan mask on. I'm masquerading."[36] This was as explicit a statement as Dylan would make in suggesting "Bob Dylan" was a mask, a façade, behind which laid another constructed entity. It is of interest to note that eleven years to the day of the concert at the Philharmonic Hall, on October 31, 1975, on another Halloween night, on the opening night of the Rolling Thunder Revue, at the Plymouth War Memorial Auditorium in Plymouth, Massachusetts, Dylan wore what was literally a Bob Dylan mask. Sam Shepard was present to describe the event:

> Tonight Dylan appears in a rubber Dylan mask ... the crowd is stupefied. A kind of panic-stricken hush falls over the place ... is this some kind of mammoth hoax? An impostor! The voice sounds just the same. If this is a replacement, he's doing a good job. He goes through three or four songs with the thing on, then reaches for the harmonica. He tries to play it through the mask but it won't work, so he rips it off and throws it back into the footlights. There he is in flesh and blood! The real thing ... it's a frightening act even if it's not calculated for those reasons. The audience is totally bewildered and still wondering if this is actually him or not.[37]

There were a number of ideas at play here; for example, the concert in 1975, on the Rolling Thunder Revue tour, was a performance in more ways than the obvious one. Bob Dylan was on stage as "Bob Dylan," but he was also wearing a Bob Dylan mask, as if to almost suggest "Bob Dylan" was a hollow entity, and that behind the mask lay another mask, hiding a figure forever unnamed and unknown. "The real thing" here, as Shepard put it, could be read within the way in which gender, itself, could be envisaged as a mask. A mask one wears, a mask behind which the real self hides; the mask being an analogous concept to the Butlerian idea of gender as a performance, the surface upon which we disguise and forge and play out our concept of identity.

* * *

In terms of such a theoretical model, much of Butler's work interrogates the process "by which we become subjects when we assume sexed/gendered identities."[38] According to Butler, the body—using Julia Kristeva's concept of the abject—is "'a heterogeneous assemblage of drives and needs, a theorization that automatically explodes the notion that [the] body is a singular identity.'"[39] In addition, Butler describes the subject as continually being "in-process" and that it is "constructed in discourse by the acts it performs."[40] Insomuch the gendered body becomes an ongoing discursive practice, an ontological given, wherein "sex and gender are 'phantasmatic' cultural constructions which contour and define the body."[41] In such a way, as intimated previously in this study, Butler's work consistently affirms the instability and indeterminacy of all sexed and gendered identities; this dovetailing with her notion that "gendered and sexed identities are performative."[42] In other words, sex and gender, as Simone de Beauvoir famously intimated, is something we do, rather than something we are.[43] Hence, to summarize, gender is not "something one *is*, it is something one *does*," it is an act, or to put this more specifically, it is a sequence of acts, it is "a verb rather than a noun, a 'doing' rather than a 'being.'"[44]

* * *

In a further and differing context, one might perceive of how one of the most obvious ways in which we make use of masks resides in the names we are either given or give to ourselves. Names and masks thus become synonymous, literal and "princely" signifiers within a linguistic discourse. The use of names was important in Dylan's work, as they are in every other writer's work; however, in this case there was a sense in which Dylan's own name was, in itself, an artistic invention. As we know, Bob Dylan was not Bob Dylan's "real" name, whatever "real" in this context may have been thought to mean; behind the name "Bob Dylan," merely lay another name, another "princely" signifier: Robert Allen Zimmerman, and behind this another name, but one which was forever unknown and unspoken. Dylan has explored such a concept in his art; for example, in the song "Gotta Serve Somebody" (1979), he seemed to suggest the relative unimportance in the application of names: the outside world could call him Terry or Timmy, then—specifying more—the world could call him Bobby or Zimmy. All of this could not help but recall a similar sentiment expressed in an earlier song, in "Farewell Angelina" (1965), wherein Dylan had intimated the outside world could call "him" any name they liked, and that he would never deny it. In one of his early prose poems, "Advice for Geraldine on Her Miscellaneous Birthday" (1964), Dylan had written: "When asked t' give your real name— never give it."[45] This was reiterated in an interview with Jonathan Cott, in 1978, where Dylan commented that: "We never know our real names,"[46] All of which would appear to suggest a sense in which our real names are beyond mere simple signification, and that our real names are forever unknown and unspoken.[47]

However, we do have recognizable names, we have proper names; and proper names, as well as being rudimentary signifiers of gender identity, also have a certain relevance from within the discourse of a theoretical perspective. One is thinking here of Roland Barthes' comment that proper names were "the prince of signifiers," with connotations that were "rich, social and symbolic."[48] Barthes' comment can most readily be seen in extended narratives, such as those found in novels and in films. To cite just a small number of examples: one might think of Pip in *Great Expectations*, Peter Quint in *The Turn of the Screw*, Mr. Utterson in *Dr. Jekyll and Mr. Hyde*, Jane Eyre in *Jane Eyre*, Rick Deckard in *Blade Runner*, David Bowman in *2001: A Space Odyssey*, Betty Blue in *Betty Blue* and so on. All of these names have connotations that were rich, social and symbolic; that is: Pip would be the small seed who would grow to have greater and greater significance in the world. Peter Quint possessed a perverse name for a perverse character, Peter being slang for a penis, while Quint chimed with the Chaucerian word "queynte" a precursor of the so-called "c" word. Mr. Utterson was the character who told us most about the story being told, hence he literally "utters on." Jane Eyre was simply plain Jane, with her initials, JE, pointing towards the French *"je"* for "I"—in a novel very much concerned with the issue of "I." Deckard's name had obvious phallic connotations, taking into account he was a detective and had an ever-present big gun, he was "dick hard." David Bowman responded to Homeric traditions in his warrior name. Betty was Betty Blue because she was "blue" in terms of her depression and because her name could also be read as an indicator of the film's erotic content. As to Dylan's own name and its appropriation from Dylan Thomas, and there can be no other derivation, Robert Zimmerman could not have known the name and spelling from any other source. As to the rich, social and symbolic connotations of this name, it is perhaps best left as an open question; although one issue might be mentioned: Robert Zimmerman's middle name was Allen, hence the appropriation of Dylan—with the same number of syllables and the same rhyming qualities—all of this might be read as an echo of the original name, as if preserving some of the old identity in the new.

In terms of his proper name, as far as can be ascertained, Dylan only referred to himself once, by name, in his art; but that instance had a resonance that was both "rich and symbolic."[49] In his only "novel," *Tarantula*, Dylan explicitly externalized the idea of "Bob Dylan" in this self-composed epitaph:

> here lies bob dylan
> demolished by Vienna politeness—
> which will now claim to have invented him
> the cool people can
> now write Fugues about him
> & Cupid can now kick over his kerosene lamp—[50]

The intertextual provenance of this extract most probably derived from Francois Villon's poem, "The Testament," and, if this was the case—and the textual coincidences would tend to suggest this was so—then this was of some interest:

> Herein this upper room
> Is lain poor Francois Villon,
> Deep at rest.
> A little scholar who was slain
> By Cupid's fatal arbalest.[51]

This was of interest insomuch as it would seem that such an artistically maneuvered intertextual allusion further highlighted, and put into question, the concept of "Bob Dylan." There was a sense in which Dylan had purposefully assumed the identity of a poet from several centuries before—Villon was born in Paris, in 1431 and died in 1463. From Villon's text, Dylan took the same self-referential use of one's full name, the same artistic conceit of placing oneself into a fictitious discourse, the same idea of writing one's own (fictitious) epitaph and the same ironic use of Cupid's arrow. However, the idea of being demolished by Vienna politeness brought Dylan's epitaph very much into the twentieth century. Here Dylan would obviously seem to have been reflecting upon psychoanalysis, an interpretation supported in the way the "epitaph" continued:

5. Identity and Duality

> boy dylan-killed by a discarded Oedipus
> who turned
> around
> to investigate a ghost
> & discovered that
> the ghost too
> was more than one person.[52]

The idea of being demolished by Vienna politeness, and being killed by a discarded Oedipus, obviously pointed, albeit somewhat disparagingly, towards Freud. As intimated in Chapter 4, it would not seem appropriate to speculate upon Dylan's awareness of Freudian theory; however, the fact that Dylan writes: "the ghost was more than one person" would seem to be a pertinent idea in the context of the argument alluded to in this chapter. It would seem to at least offer an affirmation of the idea of a twin, of another self, of a double identity in Dylan's work. In other words, there was the implication that the ghost would simply reveal yet another ghost, a "discarded Oedipus," and that "boy dylan"[53] would remain an indefinable concept, an artifice, a performative construct.

* * *

The issue of the duality of identity in Dylan's work was obviously relevant within a Freudian context; in other words, correlating with Freud's underlying notion of the conscious and the unconscious elements as found within our make-up. Similarly, Jacques Lacan's reinterpretation of Freud would also seem relevant; the way in which Lacanian psychoanalysis deconstructed the idea of the subject as a stable amalgam of conscious thought; how it thus became more difficult to uphold the notion of an individual having a definitive identity, how this must be held in abeyance, and how we must ultimately see ourselves as a mere assemblage of signifiers clustered around a proper name.[54] According to Lacan, the very young child (what he called, in one of his lost-in-translation puns, the *hommelette*)[55] was not, at this stage, a human subject, merely a mass of polymorphous desires moving in various directions, and only gradually developing into a human subject by means of an illusory sense of identity, created through an identification with an external image or reflection. This being revealed in Lacan's concept of the "mirror stage," wherein the young child gained an illusory sense of control over what it perceived as reality; not yet able to speak, the child nonetheless identified with the image it saw reflected in the mirror. However, there was a split between the "I" who was watching and the

"I" who was watched; and the child, observing with satisfaction that it could control the image, did not perceive of a disruption, or a split between the two. It was only later, when the child left the comfort of what Lacan called the "imaginary stage," to confront what he termed the "symbolic order," the world of law, institution and, most importantly of all, language, that difficulties began to arise. We can never again regain the sense of wholeness perceived in the imaginary stage, and, as socialized adults, we were thus consumed in an endless process of deferred desire. Thus within the symbolic stage, within the world of language, we move from one signifier to another in an endless attempt to retrieve what has been lost; and there was therefore the idea that desire arose from this sense of a lack that yearned for completion, a longing that could not be fulfilled.

There was a desire, in the human subject, to become whole, but to Lacan this was an absurd undertaking, given that the notion of "lack" was at the core of human experience, the very idea of being human was intrinsically linked with alienation and loss. Lacan proposed the concept of being born into such a condition and then spending the rest of our lives attempting to overcome it. The original union with the mother being seen as perfect, a time when there was no clear distinction between subject and object. What followed was fragmentation, severed from the mother's body, outside of the satisfaction of the womb and the breast; we spend the rest of our lives attempting to rediscover this blissful state. However, this cannot succeed, there is no possibility of ever recreating a union with the mother, instead we console ourselves within a diverse range of displacement strategies. In this way it would appear possible to link the Lacanian idea of "lack," with the theme of a lost twin in Dylan's work. In other words, comparing Lacan's sense that the imaginary is forever lost, forever lost in an endless, fruitless search to regain it—with the repeated and seemingly endless and fruitless searches to regain a lost twin—as found within a number of Dylan's songs. As can be seen, within such songs, these searches would involve such human diversions as: sex, religion, culture and even artistic endeavor. Of course, according to Lacan this will always be a fruitless search, insomuch as the concept of being an "I," of having a sense of identity, was, in itself, founded upon a sense of loss and separation. To attempt to put this more plainly, one could say that to be a human being was to experience a sense of fracture. There was "no direction home" in a Lacanian universe, there was no place for the "I" to find a home in a Lacanian universe.

This argument was summed up succinctly by the academic and psychotherapist, Roger Horrocks:

5. Identity and Duality

> Lacan argues that the human being is fundamentally split, that being an "I" itself constitutes a cleavage in being.... It is not that the I is permanently dissatisfied, but that the I is constituted by, and as, dissatisfaction.[56]

Horrocks went on to argue that:

> Being born is the beginning of a long separation, which lasts until death, but sex seems to provide a temporary escape from self-hood and isolation.[57]

One of the primary ways we, as human beings, have attempted to retrieve a union with the self, with what might be described as the lost and magic kingdom of the self, has been, as Horrocks suggests, via sexual union. At the core of every individual there is a continual longing for an other; hence a sexual partner with whom to share the ecstasy of orgasm is sought—and the orgasmic experience is valued so highly, not merely for the intense feelings of physical pleasure, but for the illusory sense of a blending and blurring of identities, for the loss of the self in the other. In other words, the fleeting moments of *jouissance* allow for an albeit illusory sense of wholeness, and in the short moments of orgasm, when the individual can evade the prison-house of the self, when there can be a blending and blurring of identity, the loss of the self into another, all of this allows a return to such a lost kingdom. However, this is only transitory, we can only experience such a feeling momentarily, and such a union therefore comes to be seen as ultimately hollow.[58] In a colloquial sense, this might be referred to as, *la petite mort*, the little death, the momentary extinction from existence, the sense in which the erotic becomes a daemonic force, a voluptuous yearning for extinction, for the end of consciousness, for death itself. Such an interpretation of "Love Is Just a Four Letter Word" (1965), wherein the individual could achieve, complete evaporation to the core, could be made here, a sense in which the self wished for a kind of extinction; albeit, in reality, only a hollow and transitory union. As such, the repeated idea of a lost twin, as found so ubiquitously in Dylan's work, could be seen as pointing to this sense of hollowness—to this sense of transitory union.

* * *

As such, identity could therefore be seen as a fiction of itself, a mere misrepresentation, a mere effect of the discourse, a mere outcome of the instability of the sign. In Western philosophy the conscious mind has long been regarded as the essence of self-hood, a view encapsulated by Descartes' famous phrase, "I think therefore I am." However, within Lacanian and poststructuralist thought, the self, in itself, has been deconstructed, shown to be merely a linguistic effect of the discourse, not an essential identity.

In a similar context, Terry Eagleton has spoken of the dilemma of such an individual, placed within a post–Freudian universe: "We are severed from the mother's body: after the Oedipal crisis, we will never again be able to attain this precious object, even though we will spend all our lives hunting for it."[59] All of this would seem to offer at least one explanation for Dylan's idea of a "discarded Oedipus," that is, of the mother's body as a lost object, one to which we can never return. This could be seen via the sense of yearning in such songs as "Love Is Just a Four Letter Word" and others cited in this chapter; that is: the impossibility of ever finding the magic door to a lost world, of ever finding a way of returning to a lost paradise. Furthermore, one could read into this search—a search that was most probably just as fruitless—the impossibility of ever fully embracing a gendered identity, at least of ever finding one outside of the performative context of such a concept.

At its most rudimentary hermeneutic level, such a yearning, such a longing, could be read as a metaphorical desire, a metaphorical compulsion, to pursue a return to the mother's womb. At the end of the song "Billy" (1973), Billy the Kid was positioned as figuring a way to get back home, and there was a sense—again within a certain specific reading—in which this alluded not merely to a material home, or even to Billy's physical demise, but a return to the mother, a return to the womb. However, the more such protagonists attempted to do this, the more they seemed doomed to failure, the more they were doomed to see only their own beginnings. The sense of attempting to rediscover and to recreate our origins, the endeavor to discover our "invisible selves," to paraphrase the way Dylan seemed to articulate this dilemma in "Where Are You Tonight (Journey Through Dark Heat)" (1978), was, or so one could argue, re-enacted at a cultural as well as a personal level. In other words, in the ways in which we attempt to interpret textual creations; that is, within the act of reading cultural texts, of encoding and decoding cultural texts, as—for example—the way in which we attempt to read the songs of Bob Dylan.

One might recall here an episode in David Lodge's novel, *Small World*. An albeit overtly parodic episode, wherein Morris Zapp, an American professor of English Literature, lectured his audience on the impossibility of ever fully interpreting any text. Zapp discussed the "hermeneutic fallacy" in "terpsichorean terms," as follows:

5. Identity and Duality

> The dancer teases the audience, as the text teases its readers, with the promise of an ultimate revelation that is infinitely postponed. Veil after veil, garment after garment, is removed, but it is the *delay* in the stripping that makes it exciting, not the stripping itself; because no sooner has one secret been revealed than we lose interest in it and crave another. When we have seen the girl's underwear we want to see her body, when we have seen her breasts we want to see her buttocks, and when we have seen her buttocks we want to see her pubis, and when we see her pubis, the dance ends—but is our curiosity and desire satisfied? Of course not. The vagina remains hidden within the girl's body, shaded by her pubic hair, and even if she were to spread her legs before us ... it would still not satisfy the curiosity and desire set in motion by the stripping. Staring into that orifice we find that we have somehow overshot the goal of our quest, gone beyond the pleasure in contemplated beauty; gazing into the womb we are returned to the mystery of our own origins. Just so in reading. The attempt to peer into the very core of a text, to possess once and for all its meaning, is vain—it is only ourselves that we find there, not the work itself.[60]

While Lodge was obviously adopting a deliberately risible tone in this part of his novel, there was, nonetheless, a serious intent at play. To be specific, Lodge was putting forward the proposition that the search for a sense of identity, together with the search for textual certainty, would be continually dislocated and ultimately rendered unattainable. A similar idea, albeit in a less erudite forum, was expressed in Dylan's song, "Denise" (1964); as discussed in Chapter 3, this was an unused and often overlooked song, but nonetheless a revealing work deriving from the time of Dylan's fourth record, *Another Side of Bob Dylan*. The song ended with the masculine narrator looking deep into the eyes of his loved one, presumably the eponymous Denise, but then admitting that all he could see was himself. Hidden away, at the end of this discarded song, was arguably one of Dylan's most interesting observations as to the enigma of identity; the male protagonist looked deep within the object of his desire, into Denise, but could see only himself. The male gaze, looking deep into Denise's eyes, or perhaps, in a metaphorical sense, the unconscious wish to gaze within her vaginal orifice, presented a dichotomy; for it could only see itself. In the same way as Morris Zapp's striptease observer seemed to go far too far, here there was once again the danger of overshooting the goal and seeing nothing apart from the mystery of one's own origins.

All of this would not be to suggest that this was necessarily Dylan's conscious intent when he drafted this song. However, this would be to miss the point; as previously discussed, in terms of reader response theory authorial intent has little significance, and a cultural text will say whatever it has to say; regardless of the author, it will respond to the creative interpretation of each individual reader and listener.[61] In any case, this was not an isolated instance; for example, in the song "Seeing the Real You at Last" (1985), there was a suggestion of the same predicament, with the "you" in the song seeming to be both the self *and* the object of desire: in the song, the male protagonist had sailed through the storm, strapped to the mast, in his attempt at seeing the real you at last. The male self, like a latter-day Odysseus, was tied to the mast, which could be interpreted (albeit somewhat crudely) as referring to his own sense of symbolic maleness, as if he was strapped to the burden of his own phallus. Yet at the same time, the masculine voice within the song appeared to experience the liberating sense of seeing the other self, the other side of the gender divide, his contrary gendered twin. This being one way, it might be argued, of interpreting the text within such a contextual setting. In a slightly later song, "Born in Time" (1990), this was demonstrated even more explicitly; wherein the masculine voice within the song admitted how he contemplated his love object from deep inside of himself, when we (and the plural pronoun "we" was all important), when the two protagonists in the song, male and female, were born in time, from deep inside of one another. Hence once again there was a sense of the protagonist in the song talking both to the female presence he was involved with, but also talking to himself, to a dichotomous presence within his own psyche, a presence that could be seen as having a feminine side to its sense of identity.

The allure of the female subject in Dylan's work, amalgamated with anxieties about its point of origin, was the specific issue of interest here. In other words, if the dark portal of a woman's vaginal orifice represented the beginnings of life, then by definition it also pertained to the end of life. In this way, and within a pre–Oedipal landscape, the vaginal opening becomes a reprehensible object, as Lynn Segal put it: "a condensed symbol of all that is secret, shameful and unspeakable in our culture."[62] The vagina thus becomes an almost unspeakable object, represented by our most prohibited and illicit word, our most tabooed signifier,[63] what Norman Mailer described as, "the unmentionable womb, that spongy pool, that time machine with a curse, a dam for an ongoing river of blood."[64] Julia Kristeva's model of the abject perhaps being of relevance here; Kristeva has argued that any secretion or discharge that leaks from the body—especially the feminine body—defiles and becomes abject. Women's blood was particularly abject within a patriarchal discourse, insomuch as women's blood pointed towards the fertile nature of the female body and hence bore witness to woman's alliance to the natural world. At its most extreme, the most abject example would be the menstruating woman, blood flowing from a vagina unconsciously reminding men of

5. Identity and Duality

their base fears of castration. As such, the vagina remains an enigma, a supposedly abject object, full of moisture and fluidity, a pre–Oedipal space, often associated with unclean and improper associations, but ultimately pointing towards the beginnings of life.

One might perceive here of a potential explanation, albeit positioned within a psychoanalytical reading, as to why so many of the male subjects in Dylan's songs were constantly running from the feminine world they so paradoxically craved. As Roger Horrocks put it:

> The vagina is the gateway to the womb, which men can periodically re-enter. Men yearn to get inside this body again, to feed from it again, to go back to their point of origin.[65]

However, there was a risk involved here, the risk of losing oneself, as Julia Kristeva put it:

> [I]n the rapture of love the limits of one's identity vanish, at the same time as the precision of reference and meaning become blurred in love's discourse.[66]

At a more prosaic level, one might read a motive here for Dylan's insistence to preserve and maintain an identity as a man, for his consistent exploration of this theme in his work, and how this may at least partially explain the profound ambivalence towards women within his songs; in other words, both the desire for women and the need to escape from a feminine domain. In this way, such an interpretative scenario offered one potential explanation for what often appeared to be a misogynistic discourse in much of Dylan's work, and it also offered at least one explanation for the barely concealed concern—and even fascination—with the ubiquitous homosocial discourses occurring within Dylan's work. At times this almost appeared to have homoerotic dimensions, albeit rigorously disguised and buried deep within an array of repressed desires. In this sense, it would seem possible to conclude that there was a homoerotic cathexis[67] within some of Dylan's songs, at least within the psychoanalytical reading as presented here.

* * *

In his song, "You're Gonna Make Me Lonesome When You Go" (1975), Dylan had referred to the French poets: Paul Verlaine and Arthur Rimbaud; and Rimbaud would certainly seem to be a poet to whom Dylan has often been compared.[68] In this sense, Rimbaud's famous and now almost hackneyed phrase in studies of Dylan: *"Je suis un autre"*—or "I is another"—might come to mind when attempting to sum up Dylan's attitude to identity. Such a statement attended to a sense of duality when attempting to construct a sense of the self, when attempting to construct a sense of identity.[69] In this sense "Bob Dylan" might be seen as an entity created and expressed by a self forever unknown to us, a self forever implied but never reached. In this sense, "I" literally becomes another. However, if "Bob Dylan" was not Bob Dylan, this would seem to beg a question, a question that began this chapter: "Who is he, anyway?" When one considers the work of Bob Dylan this would appear to be a constant implication. There was, and is, a sense in which we can never solve the enigma. We can only pick at the mystery, as Sam Shepard put it; or as Shakespeare put it in *Hamlet*, we can only pluck at his mystery.[70]

Dylan, true to the complexity and satiric sophistication of his art, was, of course, aware of the potential absurdist nature of identity, and has caricatured the impossibility of ever being able to talk about it with any degree of certainty. In 1965, he wrote that: "I cannot say the word eye any more—when I speak this word, it is as if I am speaking of somebody's eye that I faintly remember—there is no eye—there is only a series of mouths."[71] The play on the homophones "eye" and "I" demonstrated how aware, how subtle and, at times, how disdainful Dylan could be on the subject of identity. However, in approaching a conclusion to this argument, one could contend that the concept of identity in Dylan's work was, nonetheless, a major preoccupation. In part, this preoccupation with identity might be seen as offering an explanation for the overtly biographical interpretations that have so often been made of Dylan's songs, interpretations that, one might argue, have reduced the possibilities and potentialities of hermeneutic readings of Dylan's work.[72] One of the arguments made throughout this study has been to question this approach, and that it is only when we disregard "Bob Dylan," as the author of these songs, that we can fully appreciate the significant areas of discourse with which his work deals. One of the most significant areas argued herein, concerned such a continual preoccupation with identity, specifically with the idea of the twinned self, the sense of an "I" and an "I," the idea of a male to female dichotomy locked within the discursive practices of the songs, in both a textual and subtextual way.

As part of a final summation to this chapter, one might put forward the suggestion that an exploration of Dylan's art, an exploration of the way in which his songs have journeyed around a range of ideas concerned with personal identity, reveals at least a part of the essence of what lays at the "heart of his mystery," as Sam Shepard put it. This could be argued insomuch as in the one instance in which "Bob Dylan" actually appeared as a protagonist in

5. Identity and Duality

his art; in other words, the one instance when the persona of "Bob Dylan" appeared by name; when, for just one time, there was no room for speculation as to who he was talking about, here there was a sense of a deliverance from the relentless sense of semiotic deferral, the continual movement of one signifier to another. Here, in this rare exception, when any sense of an "I" was stripped away, when the mask was removed, we were told that "Bob Dylan" was killed by a discarded Oedipus—and that his ghost was more than one person. As such, and within the context of a psychoanalytical way of thinking, this could be interpreted as suggesting such a persona—as discussed throughout this chapter—was left merely looking into his own self; perhaps even into the aperture of his own origins. Hence the question that began this chapter, Sam Shepard's speculation: "Who is he, anyway?" changes into a slightly different question, a child-like, but nonetheless universal and all embracing question: "Who are we, anyway?" This, one might finally argue, was the question Dylan's art was consistently asking of us. Perhaps it is an unanswerable question, but nonetheless it is a question Dylan's work appears to continually and deliberately provoke: Who are we, anyway?

Closing Remarks

This study has dealt with a specific range of issues in its discussion of the work of Bob Dylan. These issues have concerned themselves primarily with the performative aspects of gender—and the ways in which such theoretical concepts can be seen as functioning within a diverse range of Dylan's lyrics. The discussion has consisted of five main subject areas, which may be categorized in the following way. Firstly, in Chapter 1, an overview was made into a number of theoretical issues, and how they might be used in relation to a discussion of Dylan's work, specifically from the perspective of gender studies; in other words, the various approaches and arguments that might be considered within the analysis herein. Following on, Chapter 2 considered the construction of masculinity within a number of Dylan's texts; notably the preoccupation of masculinity with movement in a significant number of songs, and the way movement, or travel, might thus be seen as a gendering experience within Dylan's work. In Chapter 3 a detailed discussion was made into the way in which Dylan's texts have approached the female presence, with the strong implication of there being a misogynistic discourse in a diversity of Dylan's songs. In Chapter 4 an analysis was made into the way sexual relationships were dealt with (or, perhaps more pertinently, not dealt with) within Dylan's work; the ambiguities and sometimes contradictory attitudes Dylan's songs adopted in dealing with a disparate range of human sexualities. Finally, in Chapter 5, a discussion was offered into the ways in which the above issues culminated in terms of the construction of identity within Dylan's work, an identity in which notions of duality continually appeared to present themselves.

The theoretical approaches primarily chosen for this study, namely feminism, gender studies and queer theory, might be seen as having at least some relevance with the so-called "real world." For example, feminism and current ideas surrounding issues of gender would appear to have something to say, from both within and without the academy. As Terry Eagleton has argued:

> Of all such theoretical currents, it [feminist theory] was the one which connected most deeply and urgently with the political needs and experience of well over half of those actually studying literature. [One presumes Eagleton was referring here to the consistently skewed ratio of female students who study humanities at university level.] Feminist theory provided that precious link between academia and the real world ... it is possible to ignore phenomenology or semiotics or reception theory—indeed the vast majority of human kind have proved singularly successful in doing so—but not consumerism, the mass media, aestheticized politics and sexual difference.[1]

In this sense it has to be acknowledged that some aspects of literary (or cultural) theory would seem to have been too arduous, too problematic to a general readership. In a way, this could be seen as evidence that the significance of some aspects of theory would seem to be undermined; in other words, if phenomenology and semiotics and reception theory (and to this one could add a number of other examples: poststructuralism/deconstruction theory, postcolonialism, new historicism, cultural materialism) have failed to find any function within the wider culture, then might their substance, their significance as ideological and theoretical bodies of work be questioned. Feminism and gender studies, together with Marxism and psychoanalytical theory—and even some elements of postmodernism—have entered into the general discourse of intellectual thought, but this has not been the case with other theoretical approaches that have so concerned the academic world for the last several decades. However, disregarding such potentially troublesome questions, the aforementioned idea that literary theory can handle Bob Dylan would seem to remain a valid one. Therefore, equipped with an awareness of the problems of dealing with the complex make-up of Dylan's art,[2] and with the relevant theoretical approaches and components to hand, one might restate the following question: what do the lyrics of Bob Dylan tell us about constructions of gender and sexuality, masculinity and femininity, identity and duality—and how can theoretical approaches to this issue assist in pursuing an answer?

In the second chapter of this book, an attempt to do just this was begun, to begin to apply theory to aspects of Dylan's work. Here the argument was put forward that masculinity was, at times, defined by travel, by movement, by not stopping, by categorically refusing, as Dylan colloquially put it in "I and I" (1984), to stay put. As has been argued this idea of "not stopping" would appear to have been one of the primary ways in which the men, in a significant number of Dylan's songs, have attempted to respond to the restrictions of the socio-cultural environments they found themselves inhabiting. To get "on the road" thus became a way of repudiating responsibility, of metaphorically shedding the chains of a social and cultural life. A 1960s contemporary of Dylan, Jimi Hendrix, once claimed: "If I'm free, it's 'cos I'm always running."[3] It would appear there was a sense that the men in Dylan's work were always running; always running in an attempt, not merely to stay free, but also, and perhaps most significantly, to resist enclosure within a feminized, domesticated world. This was seen most clearly in the discussion of one of Dylan's (with the assistance of co-writer, Jacques Levy) most intriguing songs, "Isis." Here the conceptualized notion of "the West" acted as an invitation, as an invocation, to journey into the metaphorical body of a New Eden, a landscape unstained and unsullied, a "new frontier" in which a search for identity and a romanticized expression of masculinity might be constructed.

However, one has to be aware that masculinity within Dylan's work could also be viewed from a wide range of differing perspectives. In Dylan's work masculinity was not a single, unchanging entity; in contrast, it was a diverse and continually changing structure. For example: from the 1960s to the present, the experience of the American male, or any man in the western world for that matter, has undergone a wide number of changes. In the late 1960s and into the 1970s, the burgeoning feminist movement compelled men to at least begin to confront the issue of sexual politics, and one might argue that this subsequently brought about a sense of quasi-crisis within masculinity in general. A sense in which it was no longer inevitable that boys should be brought up to be warriors, a world in which men could no longer be secure as breadwinners. In a previous time men had been supposed to be aggressive, competitive, hard and rough, as against women who were supposed to be nurturing, co-operative, soft and smooth. Man was the hunter—active, dominant and rational, while woman was the homemaker—passive, submissive and emotional. Such a change in society could readily be seen within Dylan's work, herein there would appear to have prevailed a narrative in which these previous models and ideals of masculinity could be seen to be fragmenting, and to be no longer holding to the same sense of credibility. It was in such an environment, containing such an array of conflicting ideas, that Dylan's edifice of masculinity could be seen as being constructed.

While Dylan's portrayal of man as a sexual exile was perhaps something of a universal trope; nonetheless, it was a trope that was afforded an exaggerated importance in Dylan's work, and, significantly, it was consistently linked to the sense of a gendered identity. In this way it could be said that Dylan's positioning of the men in his songs, within such a role, succeeded in

Closing Remarks

raising a number of relevant questions for discussion. For example, what implications could be said to have arisen from such a romanticized vision of masculinity; why could Dylan's work so rarely fully describe the complex relationships between men and women, and what, in essence, were men running from? It was argued, in the second chapter of this study, that there was something about the make-up of masculinity, within Dylan's work, that caused a retreat from the feminine sphere of influence. It would perhaps seem too simplistic to suggest that men consistently travelled, within the discursive practices of Dylan's work, merely to escape from a feminine world, from what appeared to be both a fear and a desire for women. However, there was a sense in which there may have been at least an element of validity to this argument. In other words, men were constantly running, constantly moving, constantly travelling, because they feared (albeit unconsciously) the abject nature of women, and by inference the symbolic zero of their own origins, which connoted both life and death, and which, if they were ever to stop running and moving and travelling, would thus threaten to reveal the illusory nature of the masculine sense of identity so inscribed within many of Dylan's songs.[4]

As to the way in which women were positioned in Dylan's work, as discussed in Chapter 3, this was a more diverse and a more subtle subject area to attempt to fully encompass. It would seem accurate to say that Dylan has always been a writer of notable love songs, although possibly not in the way this term might generally be understood; insomuch as many of Dylan's so-called love songs had darkly satirical undertones, thus perhaps positioning Dylan as more accurately a notable writer of anti-love songs. As intimated, it was manifest that many of the men in Dylan's work possessed feelings of anxiety and apprehension towards women, however why this should have been so was not always wholly understandable. One potential explanation might be seen within Michel Foucault's dictum that what is "true" depends on who rules the discourse.[5] In this sense, one might argue that men have always ruled the discourse, and that, within the confines of an androcentric hegemony, the female voice has always been trapped inside a male "truth." In Foucauldian terms "truth" merely becomes an ideological maneuver of the discourse; "truth" being dependent on who had the most power to confirm it. Insomuch, the implications of a feminist argument have forced men to at least think about femininity and hence about masculinity itself. Bob Dylan's work, over the last fifty years, coinciding with the multiple and complex changes in society, (including the current wave of feminism), can thus be seen as imbued with doubts and fears and anxieties over what it meant to be a man, especially what it meant to be a man striving to come to terms with women and with the influence they possess.

All of this could be seen as pertinent to the argument, made throughout this study, the argument that there was a sense in which Dylan's work demonstrated a fracture, an inconsistency, a flaw within masculinity; or to put it another way, the idea of a deficiency, a failing, or even an absence, within such a masculine construct of identity. Thus one perceives of a sense, albeit in what was most probably an unconscious way, in which the men in Dylan's songs were required to convince themselves they were strong and powerful, even when this was not required, even when they perhaps appeared to protest too much. The fact that so many of the men in Dylan's work appeared to have an apprehension of women, even to fear women, to fear the power women possessed: their reproductive abilities of mothering, their emotional awareness, their powerful if abstruse sexualities; all these facets of femininity served to remind men of their own inadequate sense of identity. At least this was one reading of the ideological maneuvers at play within Dylan's work, within much of the gender dynamics present within many of Bob Dylan's songs.

The discussion of sexuality, in Chapter 4, pointed towards what was perhaps one of the most significant issues raised within this discussion of Dylan's work. This was, one might argue, the way in which Dylan's songs have consistently resisted the sense of secularization in society—specifically the reduction of a patriarchal influence via organized religion. Such a lessening of the influence of organized religion was perhaps less apparent in America, than it was in the rest of the Western world, but nonetheless religion—specifically Christianity—would appear to have been challenged to a greater extent in the post-war world, a period roughly coinciding with Dylan's own lifespan, than in any other time. In contrast to such social and cultural changes within society, one might contend that Dylan's work has always demonstrated a preoccupation, perhaps what might even be described as a fascination, with an all powerful, patriarchal and *masculine* God. This need not be limited to Dylan's so-called "Born-Again" period, it has been apparent within Dylan's work throughout his career. In reading against the grain of these songs, the preoccupation with men, and the fixation upon the figure of Christ, would seem to have been one of the key issues surrounding Dylan's attitude towards masculinity, femininity and the sexual relationships between the two. The ways in which the lyrics continually seemed to orbit around Christ, or at least an emblematic figure of Christ, suggests how the spiritual embrace of an ultimate masculine figure, to some extent at least, compromised the erotic embrace of women—and, potentially, men as well.

* * *

As intimated in the opening chapter of this study, the Foucauldian argument, that the terms "heterosexual" and "homosexual" were relatively recent concepts, had a certain significance in this context. Foucault pointed out how other cultures, at other periods in time, had been less preoccupied with dichotomous binary categories and more tolerant of ambiguities within gender role-play. Thus one might argue the following premise, albeit within a somewhat generalized Foucauldian reading of history: that there was a correlation between the rise of capitalism, in the nineteenth century, and the proscription of same-sex eroticism and other sexual behaviors, at approximately the same time. In other words, alternate sexual behaviors, that might have been seen as threatening to the patriarchal dominion of the family, could not be accepted. Thus one can perceive a sense in which sexuality, and especially, male sexuality, had to be continually regulated into the production— not merely of material gain—but of children and the establishment of a secure domestic environment. As such, within such a rigidly enforced patriarchal structure, and within the subsequent proscription of sexual behaviors, men thus tended to find themselves entrapped within the confines of marriage, family and procreation; such a predicament creating a number of tensions and anxieties within the male psyche. As has been argued, such a predicament would also appear to have at least contributed to an explanation for the repeated tensions and anxieties within much of Bob Dylan's work. Thus the homosocial desires, so consistently redolent in so many of Dylan's songs, could be seen as confirming a capitalistic structure in which a monogamous heterosexuality was essential. In other words, within a capitalist society, concerned with reproduction, lineage, ownership and property, certain behaviors were therefore essential—this being readily apparent in Dylan's work—even if repressive anxieties were also readily apparent. To put this specifically: within much of the canon of Dylan's work there were consistent indicators of homosociality, together with the idea of gender as a performative construct, that could not help but reveal social and cultural pressures, pressures that were readily apparent across a diverse range of Dylan's songs.

* * *

In Chapter 5 of this study, the issue of identity was considered and—to some degree—interrogated. Insomuch, it would appear that the issues raised herein pointed to the ways in which Dylan's texts consistently gestured towards the fracture of identity; this occurring within what might be described as the postmodern environment. It would seem possible to argue that Bob Dylan's songs, once again spanning a similar time frame, were responding to the postmodern era, albeit in what was likely an instinctive and even naïve way. This postmodern era, which according to some began with the end of the Second World War, to others in the 1950s, or even the 1960s, has been seen as an era in which a fundamental shift occurred in the human psyche, in which there was a lessening of belief and confidence in traditional values; a time when tales of truth and progress became harder to uphold; when the so called "grand narratives"—the idea that history was the story of man's evolution towards enlightenment—began to have less and less relevance. The postmodern era was a time when the concept of truth, in itself, became relative; there were differing kinds of truth within differing discourses and within different power structures. In a postmodernist discourse truth was thus reduced to being the product of interpretation, dependent on whomsoever happened to hold the most power. Hence, in terms of the human subject, this would become, as Terry Eagleton would argue:

> [A]s much a fiction as the reality he or she contemplates, a diffuse, self-divided entity without any fixed nature or essence."[6]

In a similar sense, Mark Simpson suggested that postmodernism was a cultural movement that had been:

> rapidly stripping everyone of their consoling determinacies, fragmenting identities, as more and more people were exposed to market forces and the maelstrom of consumerism.[7]

The idea of the postmodern movement provoking self-divided and fragmenting identities could be seen as being one way of understanding the ambiguities apparent within the concept of identity, as presented in Bob Dylan's work. The marketplace, what Simpson calls the maelstrom of consumerism, affecting far more than the arrangement of erotic proclivities, the postmodern environment affecting the very way in which we perceive of ourselves as individuals.

Jean François Lyotard may have famously defined postmodernism as representing an "incredulity towards meta-narratives."[8] However, it was nonetheless self-evident that, within the discursive practices of Dylan's textual creations, there was one clear example of complete credulity towards one very specific "meta-narrative." The meta-narrative in question being Christianity; Dylan's embrace of born-again Christianity—and here the reference would be to the overtly fundamentalist content of Dylan's work in the late 1970s and early 1980s.[9] This element of Dylan's career could be interpreted in a number of ways; however, it would seem clear that, in one way at least, this could be seen primarily as a means of making sense of a nihilistic environment, a way of regaining some kind of meaning within a seemingly meaningless world, a way of surviving in a ruthless world. In other words, a means of regaining at least a sense of the grand or meta-narratives of human progress, a way of making tenable the idea of there being some "point to it all." As such, the Christian notion of redemption became a way of negating the postmodern predicament of an irrelevant and meaningless world. It would seem tenable to argue that Dylan's work has always pointed to the anxieties of living in such a world, and, unable to cope with such a premise, it was eventually forced to retreat towards an all powerful masculine God, a construct that enabled the forging of a meaning to life and existence, in spite of dwelling within a postmodern world of chaos and confusion—mixed up or not. The significant point made here being the idea that Dylan's flight to Christ was not merely a retreat from women and feminist concepts, as intimated elsewhere in this book, but also a flight from the postmodern condition, from the bleak and disheartening reality of life in the late twentieth century.

In beginning to draw towards a final summary, one might begin by inferring the following: Bob Dylan is an individual who has both inhabited, and influenced, American society and culture through the second half of the twentieth and into the twenty-first century. As such, Dylan remains an artist who has consistently attempted to make sense of the conflicting messages such an environment has given him. In his work, he has at least attempted to explore such an inherently problematical issue as the search for a valid identity, no matter its "postmodernist" limitations. In terms of an identity, and specifically a masculine identity, one finds a consistent striving for freedom on behalf of the men in Dylan's work, with the notion that a masculine identity was inherently bound up with the idea of movement. However, simultaneous to this, the songs have presented both a desiring for, and a fearing of, the feminine; and this, one could argue, represents one of the primary and essential paradoxes in Dylan's work. To some extent this explains the sense of the implied misogyny often found within such work. The obvious corollary being the idea that while travel provided an escape from the world of women, from the world of domesticity, from the world of responsibility, it also suggested an innate wish to encounter men, usually located in a carefully constructed and inherently innocent wilderness. Moreover, the evidence of an only tenuously concealed ambivalence towards sexual relationships, together with the evidence of an ambiguous but consistently present homosocial and even homoerotic subtext in Dylan's work, served to further augment such an argument.

As intimated above, it would seem clear that Dylan's work was fully aware and fully attentive to the fact that Christianity has dominated Western thought for much of the last two thousand years. In this way, it would appear self-evident that Dylan also had the ability to understand that Christian ideologies had, to a certain extent at least, influenced his own work. A conventional feminist perspective might conceive of Christianity simply as the means by which men have sought to control women's bodies; in other words, the idea that the control of women's sexuality was vital to the maintenance of patriarchy, and that one of the main ways in which this has been maintained has been via religion. However, in addition to this, one could also put forward the idea that Christianity has also acted to control male sexuality. The proscriptions inherent within a Christian ideology, together with the proscriptions inherent in a capitalist system (which, to some extent, Dylan's work has always subscribed to), might arguably be seen as attempting to proscribe the unconscious desires the men in Dylan's work possessed. To put this more specifically, both Christian and capitalist ideologies have always moved to proscribe any sense of homoerotic desire between men. Men being defined, within the hegemony of Western socio-cultural forces, as fathers, husbands and workers, not as masculine wanderers, not as outlaws in a landscape liberated from the restrictions of society and culture. Thus, to some extent, the ideal of masculine freedom, as exemplified via travel and movement in Dylan's work, could be seen as being compromised. To restate the core argument of this study: one reading of Dylan's work in such a light thus reveals a dilemma for the male protagonists in a significant number of Dylan's songs; such men can escape the domestic dominion of women, but cannot find any meaningful relationships with the men they encounter in the wilderness: a consummation of this desire being proscribed by both church and state. Thus such masculine wanderers were forever cast in an imbalance, caught between two opposing poles: unable to live with women, unable to live without them, with the continual, un-resolvable tension between such a dilemma seeming to represent a way of defining the masculine voice in much of Dylan's work.

Closing Remarks

One of the dominant ideas this study has explored, in order to illuminate these conflicting discourses, has been the idea that identity was forged, in large part, via the concepts of gender and sexuality. Who we are being dependent, in some significant part, on whether we were male or female, masculine or feminine, heterosexual or homosexual. However, the study has also been attentive to the concept that there was an underlying falsity, a mistaken assumption, an illusory quality to these often taken for granted oppositions. As such, and within the framework of Judith Butler's ideas of gender and performativity, this study has sought to demonstrate the existence of an underlying sense of anxiety towards gender identity in Dylan's work. Furthermore, the way in which such a sense of anxiety could ultimately be envisaged as being representative of social and cultural constructs, thus would seem to offer the opportunity for a wider area of debate. For if one's identity did not reside within one's gender, or even in the nature of one's sexual desires, then where exactly did it reside? If one were to relate this to a wider view of masculinity, then Bob Dylan, like many men living in the contemporary world, becomes merely a product of such social and cultural conditioning; and hence his songs only succeeded in demonstrating the intriguing depiction of what it might mean to be a man, living at this time, attempting to reconcile the conflicting messages as to what a sense of personal identity (gendered or otherwise) might actually represent within such an environment.

* * *

In approaching the closing pages of this book, an overall consideration of Dylan's cultural significance might be seen to be warranted. Christopher Ricks famously stated that he regarded Dylan to be the greatest living user of the English language; a claim backed-up—to some extent at least—by Dylan being awarded the Nobel Prize for Literature in 2016.[10] However, there are those who would disagree; for example, cultural historian, James Park, who stated that Dylan's work was "self-indulgent, repetitive, naive, confused and second-hand."[11] In looking at Dylan's body of work, without bias, it would seem that at least some of it often falls into all five of the categories Park cites, especially the latter. As has been seen, elsewhere in this book, see the discussion in the introduction, it is readily apparent that Dylan's work often appeared to have a second-hand quality, the charges of plagiarism all too often being difficult to dismiss.[12] As to a more precise appraisal of the work: in a syntactical sense the songs often showed an overarching lack of precision; for instance, the casual use of spelling—the constant elision and the colloquial dropping of "g's," the use of such contractions as "ain't," "gotta," "gonna," and so on. In a similar sense, the use of punctuation would hardly seem to be that of the greatest living user of English; to cite just one example, in "Tangled Up in Blue," Dylan was somehow able to speak of "carpenter's wives," a phrase that would seem to make no grammatical sense at all. Dylan was also able to entitle an entire album, *Self Portrait*—when dictionary citations routinely insert a hyphen between the two words. To this one might add other examples: the title of Dylan's 2001 release, *"Love and Theft"* was both italicized and given seemingly redundant quotation marks[13]; while the film *Dont Look Back* has always, somewhat curiously, lacked an apostrophe. In the case of *Dont Look Back*, there is no such word as "dont" in the English language, hence the ambiguity as to how to pronounce it—logically it should perhaps rhyme with "font" but the word has routinely been pronounce as if it were "don't"—whether Dylan or D.A. Pennebaker (the film's maker) was responsible for this anomaly is not known.

In a stylistic sense there were other issues to consider; for example, there was the use of pleonasms—the use of tautology, prolixity and logorrhea—that is, the use of more words than necessary to convey meaning. One might think of such instances as: the basement down the stairs in "Tangled Up in Blue," the unknown hour that no one knew in "When He Returns," the fatal doom in "I Am a Lonesome Hobo," the visions in the final end in "I Pity the Poor Immigrant," the phony false alarms in "Sad-Eyed Lady of the Lowlands," even the black crows in the meadow in "Black Crow Blues," are not all crows generally perceived to be black? In addition, there was also the issue of cliché; it has been said that Dylan plays with clichés, subverts clichés, deliberately uses the cliché for aesthetic purpose[14]; however, he also often uses clichés simply as clichés; the truth of the matter (to use a cliché) is that Dylan's work is often scattered with the presence of indolent and gauche cliché usage. Finally, Dylan's skill with rhyme has often been commented upon, but for most of the time—to cite one of his many clichés—such rhymes seldom surprise. There is insufficient space here to construct a detailed criticism of the quality of Dylan's writing, but in a limited appraisal, in terms of the technicalities of writing, it would seem fair to say that there are valid criticisms to be made of the Nobel laureate and the supposed greatest living user of English.

In addition, there were also a number of individual works, individual songs, that were of questionable and doubtful quality; songs that a songwriter portrayed as the greatest living user of the English language might have found

Closing Remarks

difficult to defend. For example, such a song as, "Roll on John" (2012), a paean to John Lennon, albeit thirty years out of date, was performed so risibly and had lines so inane that some reviewers wondered if Dylan should simply give up. In addition, to select a random sample, there were such songs as: "Is your Love in Vain?" (1978)—thought by some to be a genuine contender for the worst ever Bob Dylan song; or there was the entirely innocuous "To Be Alone with You" (1969)—replete with its absurdly incongruous title; and also, "Ballad in Plain D" (1964), a song many people (Dylan included) judged would have been better had it remained unwritten, or at least unreleased.[15] As to an overall estimate of Dylan's cultural reputation, it would therefore seem overly ambitious to make the claim he was the greatest living user of the English language. It would seem that Dylan's artistic status totals more than the sum of its parts: his facility for singing is well known, as a guitarist or pianist he is usually unremarkable,[16] the vintage whine of the harmonica is, as often as not, far from coming from a good year; likewise, his other artistic ventures as painter, sculptor, actor, film-maker, memoirist and even disc-jockey, seldom wholly impress. Perhaps Dylan's real reputation lies in a small cross-section of the songs he wrote—primarily in the 1960s. However, even here there is a sense that he has yet to paint his masterpiece. If one thinks, for example, of a work, of an artistic creation, such as Stanley Kubrick's film, *2001: A Space Odyssey*; by any measure this *was* a masterpiece, it was indubitably one of the most original films ever made, a film with a complete sense of itself, a film with a complete sense of otherness, a film influenced by no one else, a film that effortlessly rewards with each successive viewing, a film that does not date, a film whose reputation seems to grow exponentially with the passage of time. Bob Dylan's career has certainly had a longevity; he seems to have also had the ability to place himself in the right place at the right time, but it is difficult to think of anything in Dylan's canon that compares with the artistic and cultural significance and legacy of Kubrick's film. In essence, it is perhaps the nagging doubt that so much of Dylan's work was so derivative, that hence precludes appraising his work in such an extravagant way as Ricks and others have done. Bob Dylan, in one opinion at least, has as yet to attach a signature to his masterpiece; as Leonard Cohen put it—his masterpiece remains unsigned—and most likely it forever will.

* * *

In looking towards the sense of a final ending, to allude to another of Dylan's many pleonasms, one might do well to leave the last words to Dylan himself, to end with the final words of one of Dylan's most significant songs of recent times; his final song released in the twentieth century, his century. To end with a series of lines that would seem to sum up many of the issues this study has been attempting to encompass; a series of lines that would seem to point not merely to the central questions of this study, but also to such universal, if unanswerable and even clichéd questions, such as how did we get here, where are we going, and what happens to us after we die? Bob Dylan's journey, the journey of the many men in his songs, the journey all men and women undertake, and, in a sense, the journey of this study itself, are all responses to the same question. These are questions that may never be answered but are nevertheless worth asking. One should not be reticent in asking such questions, for, as Roland Barthes tells us, writing is the art of asking questions, not of answering or resolving them. Thus these are questions left unanswered; they remain as issues for further discussion. I finish with these lines from the 1997 song "Highlands."

> Well, my heart's in the Highlands at the break of day
> Over the hills and far away
> There's a way to get there, and I'll figure it out somehow
> But I'm already there in my mind
> And that's good enough for now[17]

Chapter Notes

Introduction

1. In addition, there was also the fact that these dates were the same as those covered by one of the first major publications of Dylan's work: *Lyrics 1962–1985*.

2. Those albums being: *Knocked Out Loaded* (1986), *Oh Mercy* (1989), *Under the Red Sky* (1990), *Time Out of Mind* (1997), *"Love and Theft"* (2001), *Modern Times* (2006) and *Tempest* (2012)—with a further album, *Together Through Life* (2009), consisting of songs co-written (with one exception) with Robert Hunter.

3. In addition to this, there have also been a series of limited edition, vinyl only albums; albums that appear to have been released for copyright purposes alone: *The 50th Anniversary Collection* (2012), *The 50th Anniversary Collection 1963* (2013) and *The 50th Anniversary Collection 1964* (2014).

4. In terms of the overarching artistic legacy of Bob Dylan's work, the *Bootleg Series* could be seen as having a specific significance. As of the time of writing, the series has reached number thirteen: *Trouble No More—The Bootleg Series Vol. 13 1979–1981*, released on November 3, 2017. As a whole, the series has possessed something of an inconsistency in terms of artistic quality, with the nadir of the series perhaps being the 2010 release *The Bootleg Series Vol. 9: The Witmark Demos: 1962–1964*, a lackluster collection of merely functional performances, often having a less than professional level of sound quality. Of the forty-seven songs on the album only a very few tracks had any merit at all; for example, the song "Gypsy Lou," with Dylan at least attempting an actual performance; otherwise the collection was an uninspiring assortment of tawdry performances, replete with slip-ups and mistakes. On one track, "Let Me Die in My Footsteps," Dylan actually stopped the performance midway through, complaining he had sung the song too many times. To release such material would therefore hardly seem to demonstrate a great deal of respect for the aesthetic facilities of the audience.

5. It is interesting to note how modest Dylan's record sales have been; as Ian Bell commented: "To this day people are sometimes astonished by how few records Dylan has sold in the course of five decades ... publishing rights have brought him great wealth ... but the billion whatever sales attributed to the Beatles or Presley have never been in his grasp ... Bob Dylan may have sold perhaps 80 million albums: it isn't much to show for 50 years" (Ian Bell, *Once Upon a Time: The Lives of Bob Dylan*, Edinburgh: Mainstream, 2013, pp. 225 and 458). The actual certifiable number of units sold may have been even lower, only 45.3 million; if one compares this to a contemporary artist; as, for example, Taylor Swift, from 2006 to the present she has sold 175 million units—nearly four times as many sales as Dylan has managed, and in about one fifth of the time.

6. If one was to be honest, it would seem that much of this material would have been better left undisturbed, and that to release such material only succeeded in diluting the quality of Dylan's creative output, only serving to reduce the reputation of the original recordings. An apt comparison might be to consider the work of Stanley Kubrick: as far as can be ascertained not a single frame of out-take footage has ever emerged from any Kubrick film. The reason being that Kubrick purposefully destroyed all the unused footage he shot on each of his films. Hence Kubrick's work will always remain undiluted, his finished body of work is all we will ever have—not so with Bob Dylan.

7. Clinton Heylin, *Dylan: Behind the Shades*, Harmondsworth: Penguin, 1991, p. 220.

8. For example, one might note such subtle revisions as the replacement of the word "leave"

instead of "put" in the line: "Should I leave them by your gate"—or the substituting of "Child of a hoodlum" instead of "Child of the hoodlum" and so on.

9. Clinton Heylin, *Behind Closed Doors: The Recording Sessions, 1960-1995*, Harmondsworth: Penguin, 1995, p. 142. In addition, one might note Stephen Scobie's prescient comment: "*Lyrics* ... bears many signs of carelessness and incompletion, as if Dylan lacked interest in publishing a complete, properly edited and definitive text" (Stephen Scobie, *Alias Bob Dylan Revisited,* Red Deer, Calgary, Alberta: Red Deer College Press, 2004, p. 112).

10. It should be noted that this almost risible error, from "Precious Angel," has subsequently been corrected on Dylan's website, www.bobdylan.com.

11. One potential solution here would be to refer to manuscript copies of Dylan's work. However, with the exception of the newly established Bob Dylan Archive at the University of Tulsa, the relative paucity of such materials would appear to render this a somewhat unproductive exercise.

12. Neil Corcoran, "Going Barefoot: Thinking About Bob Dylan's Lyrics," *The Telegraph 27*, Summer, 1987, p. 97.

13. Simon Frith, *Music for Pleasure* Cambridge: Polity, 1988, p. 120. Frith goes on to make the same general point, the idea that song writing is ultimately an oral and not a literary form.

14. See listings in the bibliography for details of the several books Williams has written on Dylan as a performing artist.

15. John Herdman, *Voice Without Restraint: A Study of Bob Dylan's Lyrics and Their Background,* Edinburgh: Paul Harris, 1982, pp. 142–143.

16. Stephen Scobie, *Alias Bob Dylan,* Red Deer, Calgary, Alberta: Red Deer College Press, 1991, p. 40.

17. See Clinton Heylin, *Stolen Moments: The Ultimate Bob Dylan Reference Book,* Romford: Wanted Man, 1988.

18. In addition, there are also legal, ethical and moral considerations in dealing with pirated or so-called bootlegged recordings, recordings made without the consent of the artist. Insomuch, one might question how much critical attention should be given to such illicitly recorded texts, texts that the artist did not intend for consumption, other than in the live arena of the concert hall in which it was originally performed.

There are ideas here of a live performance acquiring a vital part of its potential via the fact it was such an ephemeral creation; together with the incumbency, upon a critic, to pay primary attention to the work the artist or writer *has* selected for publication and public consumption.

19. For example, the website www.setlist.fm composites an estimate, as of August 28, 2018, that Dylan has thus far performed a total of 3,641 concerts, from the beginning of his career, in the early 1960s, to the present day. As the majority of these concerts would seem to be available in recorded form it would take some 377 days of continuous listening—over a year of Dylan performances without restraint. The idea of embracing such a cornucopia of concerts would seem to be simply not tenable. According to the same website, the top ten songs performed in such concerts were as follows:

All Along the Watchtower
Like a Rolling Stone
Highway 61 Revisited
Tangled up in Blue
Blowin' in the Wind
Ballad of a Thin Man
Maggie's Farm
Don't Think Twice, It's All Right
Mr. Tambourine Man
It Ain't Me Babe

The prospect of listening to "All Along the Watchtower," apparently Dylan's most performed song, in over 2,000 separate performances, would not seem a particularly inviting one. In a further context, it is of interest that nine out of these ten most performed songs derived from the 1960s, the only exception being "Tangled Up in Blue"—from 1975—perhaps adding weight to the idea that Dylan's most significant work derived from the 1960s. (See https://www.setlist.fm/stats/bob-dylan-1bd6adb8.html, accessed on the same date as cited above.)

20. The question of how much account should be given to later variations of earlier texts is open to debate. If we do allocate a primary textual authority to the recording itself, then the possibility arises of Dylan, having made an error in the recorded performance, then having the opportunity to correct this, either in print or performance.

21. Other critics would appear to concur; for example, Ian Bell: "No one should rely on bob-dylan.com as the last word (or even the first) where the songs are concerned" (Bell 2013, p. 469).

Notes—Introduction

22. In this context, it might be well to remember that Plato claimed that speech was more reliable than writing, insomuch as the presence of the speaker made it less likely that his or her words would be misinterpreted.

23. Such accusations are too numerous to consider in detail, but two comments, from two recently published monographs, might offer some sense of the issue: "Dylan is lauded as one of the most original artists of the age and accused, simultaneously, of relentless plagiarism" (Bell 2013, p. 241). "The songs on this album [*Love and Theft*] consistently run a fine line between postmodern intextextuality and old-fashioned plagiarism" (Scobie 2004, p. 79).

24. Joni Mitchell used this term, of Dylan, in an interview with the *Los Angeles Times* on April 22, 2010.

25. The Book of Ecclesiastes 1.9 says: "There is nothing new under the sun"—and Dylan has made ubiquitous use of the Bible throughout his career. In fact, whole books have been devoted to cataloguing such a usage; however, the following list represents some of the most obvious examples of songs that have made use of biblical scripture:

    The Times They Are A-Changin'
    All Along the Watchtower
    Dear Landlord
    I Pity the Poor Immigrant
    One More Cup of Coffee
    When He Returns
    Watered Down Love
    Every Grain of Sand
    I and I
    Sweetheart Like You

26. The folk tradition is an enduring one, and Dylan, especially at the beginning of his career, often made use of existing folk songs, usually in terms of melody, but sometimes as an inspiration for lyrical invention. Once again the list is a long one, but some of the most significant examples are as follows:

    Ballad of Donald White: Peter Amberley
    The Death of Emmett Till: Colorado Highway
    Walls of Redwing: The Road and the Miles to Dundee
    Ramblin' Gamblin' Willie: Bremen on the Moor
    Blowin' in the Wind: No More Auction Blocks
    Girl from the North Country: Scarborough Fair
    Masters of War: Nottamun Town
    A Hard Rain's A Gonna Fall: Lord Randall
    Don't Think Twice …: Who'll Buy Your Ribbons
    Bob Dylan's Dream: Lord Franklin
    Oxford Town: Ida Red
    Seven Curses: Anathea
    Percy's Song: The Wind and the Rain
    Ballad of Hollis Brown: Pretty Polly
    With God on Our Side: The Patriot Game
    Restless Farewell: The Parting Glass

As far as the folk tradition goes, it might seem overly acerbic, but disregarding the esteem felt by some for the tradition, it is difficult not to speculate how much better folk songs might have been, had they been written by songwriters—rather than "the folk."

27. Publilius Syrus, "Lovers know what they want, but not what they need" (*Moral Sayings: A Roman Slave*).

28. Euripides: "The same man cannot be well skilled in everything, each has his own special excellence" (*Rhesus*).

29. Clinton Heylin, *It's One for the Money: The Song Snatchers Who Carved Up a Century of Pop and Sparked a Musical Revolution*, London: Constable, 2016, p.368.

30. Cited in Heylin 2016, pp. 368–369.

31. Heylin, 2016, p. 184.

32. Heylin, 2016, p. 186.

33. Cited in Heylin 2016, p. 368.

34. Heylin 2016, p. 369.

35. Attributed to Max Beerbohm.

36. Attributed to William R. Inge.

37. Attributed to both T.S. Eliot and Lionel Trilling.

38. Paraphrased from Edward Quinn, *Collins Dictionary of Literary Terms*, Glasgow: HarperCollins, 2004.

39. Paraphrased from Michael Kelly (ed.), *French Culture and Society*, London: Arnold, 2001.

40. Terry Eagleton, *Literary Theory: An Introduction*, Oxford: Basil Blackwell, 1983, p. 205. Stephen Scobie has more recently made a similar observation, talking of the issue of identity, and the way in which our own sense of self is the product of a network of discursive practices. Scobie commented: "In this sense, far from being opposed to critical theory, Dylan's work thematizes one of its central questions" (Scobie 2004, p. 85).

Chapter 1

1. As to the history of theory outside of the twentieth century, literary theory has often been traced as far back as Aristotle's *Poetics*; insomuch, theory might be said to have begun almost as early as the first cultural productions we can trace.

2. Terry Eagleton, *Literary Theory: An Introduction*, Oxford: Basil Blackwell, 1983, p. vii.

3. Terry Eagleton, *After Theory*, London: Penguin, 2004, p. 27.

4. Paraphrased from Peter Barry, *Beginning Theory: An Introduction to Literary and Cultural Theory*, Manchester: Manchester University Press, 1995.

5. See Peter Barry, *Beginning Theory: An Introduction to Literary and Cultural Theory* (Third Edition), Manchester: Manchester University Press, 2009, p. 262.

6. Terry Eagleton in *The Guardian*, October 27, 1992.

7. Eagleton 2004, p. 29.

8. Terry Eagleton, *Literary Theory: An Introduction* (Second Edition), Oxford: Basil Blackwell, 1996, p. 206.

9. Terry Eagleton's book, *Literary Theory: An Introduction*, first published in 1983, was arguably the catalyst for such teaching, especially in the UK. As Peter Barry put it: "Most of the primary texts of literary theory had been written in French, with a few in German or Russian, and by no means all of them had yet been translated … an introductory overview of literary theory was a necessity, and the first book to meet this need was Terry Eagleton's *Literary Theory: An Introduction*, [giving] tutors confidence that it might be possible to teach it [literary theory] in a systematic way" (Barry 2009, p. 271 and p. 273).

10. Barry 1995.

11. Antony Easthope, *Literary into Cultural Studies*, London: Routledge, 1991, p. 65.

12. Barry 2009, p. 269. Among MacCabe's supporters were Raymond Williams and Frank Kermode, the former appreciating the Marxist aspects of MacCabe's work, and the latter the structuralist elements.

13. Barry 2009, p. 276.

14. David Lehman, *Sign of the Times: Deconstruction and the Fall of Paul de Man*, London: Andre Deutsch, 1991, p. 175.

15. Barry 2009, pp. 279–280.

16. Barry 2009, p. 281.

17. Lehman 1991, p. 259.

18. Lehman 1991, pp. 259–260.

19. Barry 2009, p. 282.

20. Barry 2009, p. 284.

21. Barry 2009, p. 284.

22. Barry 2009, p. 286.

23. Jonathan Culler, *Literary Theory: A Very Short Introduction*, Oxford: Oxford University Press, 1997, p. 4.

24. Culler 1997, p. 121.

25. Culler 1997, p. 122.

26. The general points raised here are paraphrased from Barry 1995, pp. 34–36.

27. Jonathan Ned Katz, *The Invention of Heterosexuality*, New York: Dutton, 1995, p. 184.

28. Katz 1995, p. 86.

29. Cited in Robert Goldenson & Kenneth Anderson, *The Wordsworth Dictionary of Sex*, Ware, Hertfordshire: Wordsworth, 1994, p. 113.

30. Lynne Segal, *Straight Sex: The Politics of Pleasure*, London: Virago, 1994, p. 72.

31. Cited in Katz 1995, p. 99. Originally included in: Gore Vidal, *At Home: Essays, 1982–1988*, New York: Random House, 1988, p. 48.

32. Guy Hocquenghem, *Homosexual Desire*, Durham: Duke University Press, 1993, p. 49.

33. Eagleton 1983, p. 132.

34. As Gore Vidal was famous for commenting: the most frequently performed sexual act is neither hetero- or homo- but onanistic.

35. Kinsey reported that 37 percent of men in America had achieved orgasm through homosexual contact. In 1993, Shere Hite would report that nearly 50 percent of men used some kind of anal stimulation when masturbating. While Mark Simpson, the journalist and originator of the term "metrosexual," noted: "In the hellish world of the homosexual, penis-bearers not only offered their bottoms to each other, but they also trivialised the phallus, its powers and its responsibilities (to impregnate and subjugate women), by turning this God-given answer to the otherwise overwhelming curse of feminine power, into just a plaything" (Mark Simpson, *It's a Queer World*, London: Vintage, 1996, p. 5).

36. Peter Watson, *A Terrible Beauty: A History of the Ideas That Shaped the Modern Mind*, London: Weidenfeld & Nicholson, 2000.

37. Watson 2000.

38. Culler 1997, p. 14.

39. Mark Simpson, *Male Impersonators*, London: Cassell, 1994, p, xi.

40. Marjorie Garber, *Vice-Versa: Bisexuality*

Notes—Chapter 1

and the Eroticism of Everyday Life, Harmondsworth: Penguin, 1995, p. 14.

41. In one of her most famous, if most outspoken comments, Sedgwick claimed that "the ultimate function of women is to be a conduit of homosexual desire" (cited in Gregory Castle, *The Blackwell Guide to Literary Theory*, Oxford: Blackwell, 2007, p. 106). Leslie Fiedler, writing twenty-five years before Sedgwick's ideas on homosociality, had made a similar point, talking of an: "unnatural triangle," through which "two men are bound to each other through the woman they jointly possess" (cited in Leslie Fiedler, *Love and Death in the American Novel*, New York: Stein and Day, 1966, p. 363). All of this might be enhanced via a homosocial joke, one of the very few homosocial jokes. It may, in fact, be the only one; but it goes as follows: "My wife left me for another man, I'll never forget him."

42. See Chapter 4 for a discussion of the way boxing was presented in Dylan's work, and the subsequent homosocial implications present therein.

43. Eve Kosofsky Sedgwick, *Between Men: English Literature and Male Homosocial Desire*, New York: Columbia University Press, 1985. A summation of the basic argument expressed here is made by Joseph Bristow in *Sexuality*, London: Routledge, 1997, pp. 204–209.

44. Judith Butler, *Gender Trouble: Feminism and the Subversion of Identity*, London: Routledge, 1990, p. 8.

45. Roger Horrocks, *Masculinity in Crisis*, London: Macmillan, 1994, p. 13, and Roger Horrocks, *Male Myths and Icons: Masculinity in Popular Culture*, London: Macmillan, 1995, p. 16.

46. Butler 1990, p. 6.

47. Castle 2007, p. 102.

48. Butler 1990, p. 122

49. Sara Salih, *Judith Butler: Routledge Critical Thinkers*, London: Routledge, 2002, p. 12.

50. Cited in Salih 2002, p. 12.

51. Salih 2002, p. 13.

52. Salih 2002, p. 14.

53. As Sara Salih put it: "it is impossible to overestimate the influence of the nineteenth century German philosopher G. W. F. Hegel on Butler's work" (Salih 2002, p. 1). Butler follows Hegel's notion of the dialectic, through which a thesis is proposed, negated by an antithesis and finally resolved into a synthesis; however, Butler argues that such a "synthesis or resolution is not final but provides the basis for the next thesis, which once again leads to antithesis and synthesis before the process starts all over" (Salih 2002, p. 3). Such a conjecture could be seen in terms of sex and gender; in other words, within the "formation of the subject within sexed and gendered power structures" (Salih 2002, p. 8).

54. Salih 2002, p. 7. It might be noted that when Butler discussed issues of gender within a scientific and medical framework she was not as secure of such a sense of acclamation. For example, Butler has claimed, albeit in a somewhat unspecific way, that "a good ten per cent of the population has chromosomal variations that do not fit neatly into the XX-female and XY-male categories" (Judith Butler, *Gender Trouble: Feminism and the Subversion of Identity*, London: Routledge, 1990, p. 109). As Salih notes, this "fact" leads Butler to suggest "that existing sex/gender binaries are inadequate for the task of describing and categorising indeterminate bodies" (Salih 2002, p. 61).

55. Katz 1995, p. 13.

56. Eagleton 1983, p. 112. Eagleton also noted that: "Meanings are not stable and determinate ... even authorial ones—and the reason they are not is because ... they are products of language, which always has something slippery about it" (Eagleton 1983, p. 69).

57. One thinks here of the hundreds of interviews Dylan has given over the last fifty-plus years; with comments that often seemed to be either deliberately absurd or deliberately deceptive—although at times very amusing—hence much of this can simply be dismissed—as having little or no relevance. However, this is not to say that some of the interviews Dylan has given, over his career, are not useful—a good example being the *Playboy* interview of 1966—hence, material from the published library of interviews will be used in this volume.

58. Edward Quinn, *Collins Dictionary of Literary Terms*, Glasgow: Harper Collins, 2004, p. 152.

59. Cited in David Lodge and Nigel Wood (eds.)., *Modern Criticism and Theory: A Reader*, London: Longman, 1992, p. 172.

60. Quinn 2004.

61. Stephen Trombley, *Fifty Thinkers Who Shaped the Modern World*, London: Atlantic, 2012, p. 335.

62. Trombley 2012, p. 335.

63. Cited in Barry 2009, p. 266. Here Derrida

was actually referring to a game of football—but the same metaphor might be applied to the act (or game) of reading.

64. Jeremy Tambling, *What Is Literary Language?* Milton Keynes: Open University Press, 1988, p. 72.

65. Barry 1995.

66. Barry 2009, p. 310.

67. Barry 2009, p. 310.

68. Storey, John, *Cultural Theory and Popular Culture: An Introduction,* Harlow: Pearson, 2001, p. 71.

69. Storey 2001, p. 73.

70. Stephen Scobie's book, *Alias Bob Dylan,* being the only other monograph to attempt to do this—at least as far as can be ascertained.

71. See Chapter 5 for a discussion—in relation to David Lodge's novel *Small World*—of how decidedly "dead-end" such dead-end interpretations might be.

72. Terry Eagleton, *Against the Grain: Essays, 1975–1985,* London: Verso, 1985, p. 78.

Chapter 2

1. The Playboy interview, as conducted by Nat Hentoff, reprinted in Craig McGregor, *Bob Dylan: A Retrospective,* New York: William Morrow, 1972, pp. 124–145, p. 143.

2. Robert Shelton, *No Direction Home: The Life and Music of Bob Dylan,* London: New English Library, 1986, p. 358.

3. See, for example, Steve Estes, *I Am a Man: Manhood and the Civil Rights Movement,* Chapel Hill: University of North Carolina Press, 2005. It has been suggested that the purpose of the phrase "I Am a Man" (which was used mostly in the United States but also in South Africa), was to refute the racially slurred term, "boy," as commonly used towards men of color in those countries.

4. David Pichaske, "Bob Dylan and the Search for the Past," in John Bauldie and Michael Gray (eds.), *All Across the Telegraph: A Bob Dylan Handbook,* London: Sidgwick and Jackson, 1987, p. 101.

5. The word performative is used here—in Butlerian terms—to describe how the body supplies a surface upon which various acts and gestures accumulate gendered meanings; this theoretical model will be discussed in more depth in Chapter 5.

6. Janet Wolff, *Resident Alien: Feminist Cultural Criticism,* Cambridge: Polity, 1995, pp. 115 and 122.

7. For example, consider the diverse range of women travellers delineated in *The Virago Book of Women Travellers,* ed. Mary Morris, London: Virago, 1996.

8. Cited in Wolff 1995, p. 123.

9. Cited in Gerda Siann, *Gender, Sex and Sexuality: Contemporary Psychological Perspectives,* London: Taylor and Francis, 1994, p. 29.

10. Cited in Peter Schwenger, *Phallic Critiques: Masculinity and Twentieth-Century Literature,* London: Routledge, 1984, p. 2.

11. It is possible that the song was based, to some extent at least, upon the story of Wild Bill Hickok, incidentally another rambling gambling man with a vaguely phallic name. Hickok was a gunfighter and a gambler; the subject of a number of outlandish stories, he was eventually shot to death, aged just thirty-nine, during a poker game in the appropriately named town of Deadwood, Dakota Territory. The cards Hickok was holding at the time, a pair of aces and a pair of eights, became known as the "dead man's hand," a detail with which Dylan's song concluded.

12. Transcribed from an audio recording of an interview with Studs Terkel, WFMT FM Radio, Chicago, May 1, 1963.

13. The phrase "keep on keeping on," was not, in fact, original to Dylan. It has been traced back to as early as the 1910s, according to Eric Partridge's *A Dictionary of Slang,* it was a common phrase at this time.

14. Paraphrased from the song "Ballad of Donald White."

15. Paraphrased from the song "Tangled Up in Blue."

16. Paraphrased from the song "Goin' Goin' Gone."

17. Paraphrased from the song "I and I."

18. There were a number of other songs extolling the virtues of masculine travel; for example, an early song from 1961, "Big City Blues," contained the following lines:

I've been thinkin' a[b]out you darlin'
You been on my mind
But I can't stay long in this here town
I ain't the settlin' kind.

The song does not appear to have been copyrighted—it is not included on Dylan's website—but nonetheless it represents an early example of the trope of masculine travel in Dylan's work. In addition, there were such songs as: "Bound to Lose, Bound to Win" (1963), a song detailing a male protagonist who was bound for walking the road again; "Farewell" (1963), a song that found a male protagonist repeatedly bidding farewell to a woman—his own true love; and finally, "Farewell Angelina" (1965), a seemingly Salvador Dali inspired song, wherein each verse ended with the male protagonist declaring he must go, he must leave, he must be gone.

19. As intimated above, in "11 Outlined Epitaphs" Dylan referred to Guthrie as his first and last idol; see *Lyrics*, p. 111.

20. See Shelton 1986, pp. 74–75.

21. Wayne Hampton, *Guerrilla Minstrels: John Lennon, Joe Hill, Woody Guthrie, Bob Dylan*, Knoxville: University of Tennessee Press, 1986, p. 179.

22. Jack Kerouac may have been a significant influence on Dylan's vision of masculine travel; however, it is perhaps pertinent to note that the "great prince of the road," who incidentally had never learned how to drive, eventually returned home, to his mother, finishing his life an alcoholic apostate to the life he had once espoused. Not so with Bob Dylan, he remains "on the road" up to the present day.

23. www.bobdylan.com. See also, *Lyrics*, p. 61.

24. www.bobdylan.com. See also, *Lyrics*, p. 271.

25. Michael Gray, *Song and Dance Man: The Art of Bob Dylan*, London: Hart-Davis MacGibbon, 1972, p. 290.

26. The fact that Chaynee County would seem to have had no part in John Wesley Harding's story, or, in fact, to have existed at all, might be seen to imply a further lack of credibility as to the scenario presented within the song.

27. It has been suggested that Dylan may have deliberately spelt the name of John Wesley Hardin(g) incorrectly, adding a "g" when no "g" was required, as if to amend for the elision of many "g"s" elsewhere in his songs, especially early in his career. Incidentally, John Wesley Hardin(g) was far from being a friend to the poor, he seems to have been a wholly amoral character who claimed to have killed forty-two men. As has been often commented, the Christ-like attributes bestowed on him within the song's narrative may have had more to do with the initials JWH (as in Yaweh) than with the supposed version of the outlaw as depicted in the song.

28. The song was subsequently officially released in 2010, on the compilation *The Bootleg Series Vol. 9: The Witmark Demos: 1962-1964*.

29. Michael Wood, *America in the Movies or, Santa Maria, It Had Slipped My Mind*, London: Secker and Warburg, 1975, p. 43.

30. Wood 1975, p. 43.

31. It should be stated here that the song was, in fact, co-written by Dylan with Jacques Levy, as were most of the songs on the *Desire* collection, and hence there were a number of potential considerations concerning authorship. However, I would concur with Betsy Bowden, who has pointed out: "since separating Levy's contribution to 'Isis' from Dylan's would be a task as formidable as seeking the communal origins of a Child ballad, I must refer to the song as if Dylan wrote it." (Betsy Bowden, *Performed Literature: Words and Music by Bob Dylan*, Bloomington: Indiana University Press, 1982, p. 47). On the one hand, this raised further intriguing ideas to explore—the idea of the song being written by two men responding to the idea of the two men journeying together in the song itself, thus adding a certain resonance to an appreciation of the text. However, on the other hand, placing this idea aside, I would request the understanding of co-author Levy if I refer to Dylan as author for the sake of clarity and convenience, and omit "and Levy" when referring to the authorship of the lyric.

32. *Writings and Drawings* was the precursor of *Lyrics*, first published in 1973, and was the first major collection of Bob Dylan lyrics. In a sense the book represents the very best of Bob Dylan, insomuch as it represented his complete oeuvre at that time, dating from 1962 to 1971. As such, and lacking the arguably inferior material that would come throughout the 1970s, 1980s, 1990s, and beyond, it hence might be said to represent Dylan's most impressive volume of work.

33. If one supposes, just for a moment, an autobiographical context, then the wild west Dylan was rambling out of could have been seen as Minnesota, Dylan's home state, a state around a thousand miles west of New York; however, hardly representative of the wild west as it would commonly be envisaged.

34. The song was later released in a revised form, in 1986, as "Brownsville Girl."

35. Jane Tompkins, *West of Everything: The Inner Life of Westerns*, New York: Oxford University Press, 1992, p. 11.

36. Tompkins, 1992, p. 4.

37. Tompkins, 1992, p. 220.

Notes—Chapter 2

38. Contemporary events have overtaken Dylan's 1970s appropriation of the name, Isis. In the present day the name now represents, in mnemonic form, something very different to an ancient Egyptian goddess. This was to prove a somewhat unfortunate coincidence for the daughters of the Bob Dylan fans who had named their female offspring in such a fashion, such a name now possessing a somewhat unfortunate connotation. See the article in *The Guardian*, by Chitra Ramaswamy, September 20, 2016: https://www.theguardian.com/world/2016/sep/20/isis-terrorism-jokes-woman-named-egyptian-goddess (accessed September 3, 2017).

39. www.bobdylan.com. See also, *Lyrics*, p. 378.

40. Transcribed from an audio recording of a concert performance in Montreal on December 4, 1975; a performance included in the film, *Renaldo and Clara* (1978).

41. Leslie A. Fiedler, *Love and Death in the American Novel*, New York: Stein and Day, 1966, p. 350–351.

42. Aidan Day, *Jokerman: Reading the Lyrics of Bob Dylan*, Oxford: Basil Blackwell, 1988, p. 38.

43. Stephen Scobie, *Alias Bob Dylan* Red Deer, Calgary, Alberta: Red Deer College Press, 1991, p. 161.

44. Wilfrid Mellers, *A Darker Shade of Pale: A Backdrop to Bob Dylan*, London: Faber and Faber, 1984, p. 189.

45. John Herdman, *Voice Without Restraint: A Study of Bob Dylan's Lyrics and Their Background*, Edinburgh: Paul Harris, 1982, p. 74.

46. In other words, right is also "right," insomuch as it stands as much for the opposite of wrong as it stands for the opposite of left. This being seen in heraldic terms, from the Latin: dexter and sinister; or in other languages; for example, as in French with *adroit* and *gauche*.

47. Paul Hodson, "Bob Dylan's Stories about Men," in Elizabeth Thomson and David Gutman (eds.), *The Dylan Companion*, London: Macmillan, 1990, p. 185.

48. Tompkins, p. 39. In the context of Tompkins' comment, one might also cite Leslie Fiedler's observation: "The hero did not go out alone to encounter the spirit of the wilderness—but travelled always with a companion and guide" (Leslie Fiedler, *Love and Death in the American Novel*, Normal, IL: Dalkey Archive, 1997, p. 360).

49. Paraphrased from Tompkins, 1992, p. 12.

50. Tompkins, 1992, p. 37.

51. Allen Ginsberg, in a typically creative and original discussion of the song, in his untitled liner notes to the *Desire* album, spoke of: "To Isis, Moon Lady Language Creator Birth Goddess, Mother of Ra, Saraswati & Kali-Matoo, Hecate, Ea, Astarte, Sophia & Aphrodite, Divine Mother."

52. Note that Paul Williams makes a similar point to this: Paul Williams, *Bob Dylan Performing Artist: 1974–1986: The Middle Years*, London: Omnibus, 1992, p. 67.

53. It has been suggested that this part of the song may have been influenced by D.H. Lawrence's short novel, *The Man Who Died*, also known as *The Escaped Cock* (1929), a retelling of Christ's resurrection, wherein the Christ-like protagonist reawakened to explore a redemptive sexual relationship with the Egyptian goddess Isis.

54. Roger Horrocks, *Male Myths and Icons: Masculinity in Popular Culture*, London: Macmillan, 1995, pp. 80–81.

55. The use of the word "cursed" in this line was of interest; insomuch as it has been suggested that to many listeners the word might have sounded more like the word "kissed." As discussed in the introduction, such a level of sophisticated homophonic ambiguity should not be overlooked in relation to Dylan's songwriting.

56. Tompkins, 1992, p. 84.

57. This connection to ancient Egyptian mythology has been discussed by a number of other Dylan commentators; for example, see Scobie 1991, p. 161, and Bowden, 1982, p. 48.

58. As in the colloquial phrase: "the family jewels."

59. Kenneth Branagh, in his 1996 film of *Hamlet*, arguably one of the most thought-provoking of the play's many cinematic adaptations, carefully enunciated the word in this fashion, deliberately pronouncing the word, "nothing" as "no thing." See Chapter 3 for a further discussion of this, and for specific details regarding the significance of the quotation in the play.

60. The issue is further clouded insomuch as in the song's earliest publication, in the *Desire* song-folio of 1976, the text followed the performed version, word for word.

61. James Joyce, *Ulysses*, Oxford: Oxford University Press, 1993, p. 732. It is clear that

Dylan was undoubtedly aware of Joyce's work, to some extent at least. For example, in the song, "I Feel a Change Comin' On" (2009), there was a passing reference to Joyce. While in *Chronicles Volume 1* (2004) Dylan wrote: "James Joyce seemed like the most arrogant man who ever lived, had both his eyes wide open and great faculty of speech, but what he say, I knew not what." It is likely that Dylan may have been indicating, here, his bafflement over *Finnegans Wake*; however, given the narrative construction of "Isis," it is possible that he was more familiar with *Ulysses*—a demanding, but far more readable novel.

62. Herdman, p. 76. See also the following corresponding comment by Leslie Fiedler: "The lover is not in love with the woman at all, but with suffering itself—ultimately with death" (Fiedler 1997, p. 50).

63. Day, 1988, p. 41.

64. It might be noted that both Allen Ginsberg and Dylan, himself, connected Isis with the moon in their liner notes to *Desire*; Ginsberg referring to Isis as a "Moon Lady" and Dylan referring to Isis's moonshine shining upon him.

65. It might be remembered that the narrator of the song was reassured by his male companion, who had told him (in verse four): "we'd be back by the fourth"—presumably this being the fourth of May—one day short of the fifth of May—when the adventure had begun.

66. Joseph A. Boone, "Male Independence and the American Quest Genre: Hidden Sexual Politics in the All-Male Worlds of Melville, Twain and London" in Robyn R. Warhol and Diane Price Herndl (eds.). *Feminisms: An Anthology of Literary Theory and Criticism*, New Brunswick: Rutgers University Press, 1991, p. 961.

67. Boone, 1991, p. 961.

68. Boone, 1991, p. 962.

69. Boone, 1991, p. 964.

70. Fiedler, 1997, p. 211.

71. It is difficult not to notice, in the case of Ishmael, how his name deconstructed in such a way as to add a further sense of gender ambivalence.

72. Boone, 1991, p. 969. Note that Dylan has explored the relationships within Melville's novel in a much more literal way, in "Bob Dylan's 115th Dream" (1965), although pitched here at an exaggeratedly parodic and satirical level.

73. Fiedler, 1997, p. 344.

74. Camille Paglia, *Sex and Violence, or Nature and Art*, London: Penguin, 1995, p. 14. Such an idea was also expressed by American poet and writer Phyllis McGinley: "Women are the fulfilled sex. Through our children we are able to produce our own immortality, so we lack that divine restlessness which sends men charging off in pursuit of fortune or fame or an imagined Utopia. That is why we number so few geniuses among us" (Phyllis McGinley, *The Province of the Heart* New York: Viking, 1969).

75. Horrocks 1994, p. 154.

76. Tompkins p. 1992.

77. Toni Morrison, *Playing in the Dark: Whiteness and the Literary Imagination*, London: Picador, 1992, p. 72.

78. Fiedler 1997, p. 12.

79. Fiedler 1997, p. 365.

80. James Park (ed.), *Cultural Icons: Cultural Figures Who Made the 20th Century What It Is*, London: Bloomsbury, 1991, p. 133. To some Fiedler's views leaned towards the racist; however, this was mainly because of the archaic nomenclature of race used by Fiedler—writing in the late 1950s and into the 1960s, in a style that was something of an anathema to modern, politically correct critics.

81. Fiedler 1997, p. vi.

82. Fiedler 1997, p. 25.

83. Fiedler 1997, p. 26. Elsewhere in the book, Fiedler returned to this subject, in what might almost have suggested a previously unwritten verse of Dylan's song, "Wanted Man," he argued: "They are on the run ... from Aunt Polly and Aunt Sally and Widow Douglas and Miss Watson, from golden-haired Becky Thatcher" (Fiedler 1997, p. 271).

84. Fiedler 1997, p. 347.

85. Fiedler's "chevalier of the city streets" might remind one of Raymond Chandler's famous phrase: "Down these mean streets a man must go." Whether anyone has questioned quite why a man must go down such means streets would seem uncertain; it being a similarly unanswered question as to the one that asks: why so many men, in so many of Dylan's songs are depicted as walking down so many roads.

86. Fiedler 1997, p. 404.

87. Morrison, 1992, pp. 49–50.

88. The song has never been officially released or seemingly even published. However, a performance of it is included in the film of Dylan's 1966 tour of Britain, *Eat the Document*.

89. www.bobdylan.com. See also, *Lyrics*, p. 61.

90. Such an idea would appear to be continuing late into Dylan's career; the most recent album of new songs, *Tempest* (2012), released when the singer was into his seventies, included a number of songs detailing a similar theme. Of especial interest was the title track, one of Dylan's more interesting songs of the twenty-first century, a characteristically perverse retelling of the sinking of the Titanic. A song intent of telling a tale of disembark—wherein the male narrative voice still seemed absorbed with what appeared to be an ultimately hopeless quest.

91. www.bobdylan.com. See also, *Lyrics*, p. 61.

92. This idea continues as a theme later in Dylan's work; for example, in one of Dylan's most interesting songs of the 1980s, "New Danville Girl" (1985), co-written with the late Sam Shepard and later redrafted and released as "Brownsville Girl" (1986). This was a large, sprawling, cinematic Western that opened with a man riding alone across a desert—and closed with repeated images of death, with the stars being torn down.

93. In the film *Dangerous Minds* (1995), Michelle Pfeiffer—as a high school teacher working in a school in an economically deprived part of California—compared Dylan Thomas's line to this particular line in Bob Dylan's song. This perhaps demonstrating something of the resonance the line in Dylan's song possessed—at least in the sense of its intertextual relationship to Thomas's poem.

94. It is perhaps significant that Dylan opened his famous "comeback" tour of 1974 with a summation of this idea. Dylan began the first concert of the tour, in Chicago on January 3, 1974, with a rewrite of an obscure song, "Hero Blues" (1964). The redrafted version of the song included a line that seems particularly pertinent here: "One foot on the highway, one foot in the grave."

95. Tompkins' argument here was reminiscent of the following comment by Leslie Fiedler: "Those cowboys, for instance, who ride off into the sunset leaving the girls they have rescued behind [can thus] be imagined as representing the innocence of the West" (Fiedler 1997, p. 347).

96. Paraphrased from Tompkins, 1992, p. 24.

97. Wood, 1975, p. 42.

98. It might be noted that although there was a lot of walking in Dylan's work, predominantly men walking, there was, however, little sense of the *flâneur*, and still less of the *flâneuse*. *Flâneur* being a French term suggestive of the urban explorer, a man of leisure, an idler, a connoisseur of the street, an emblematic figure of the modern urban experience. In the discursive practices of Dylan's lyrics walking seems to have been a much more important and much more gender orientated affair.

99. Jack Kerouac, *On the Road* New York: NAL, 1957, p. 196.

Chapter 3

1. Peter Watson, *A Terrible Beauty: A History of the Ideas that Shaped the Modern Mind*, London: Weidenfeld & Nicholson, 2000.

2. Paraphrased from Raman Selden, *A Reader's Guide to Contemporary Literary Theory*, Hemel Hempstead: Harvester Wheatsheaf, 1993, p. 203.

3. Lynne Segal, *Straight Sex: The Politics of Pleasure*, London: Virago, 1994, p. xiii.

4. Cited in Gerda Siann, *Gender, Sex and Sexuality: Contemporary Psychological Perspectives*, London: Taylor and Francis, 1994, p. 125.

5. For example, note the thinly veiled reference to abortion in the song "Lenny Bruce" (1981). Dylan claiming that Bruce did not cut off any babies' heads, seeming to chime with Pat Robertson's claim that feminists were "killing" their children.

6. "You're No Good" was not, in fact, written by Dylan; as intimated, it was an adaptation of an earlier song by Jesse Fuller. Nonetheless, Dylan's ownership of the song in performance was so comprehensive as to render it his own, and thus to give it a sense of being a part of the general body of his work.

7. It is arguable as to what time the current feminist movement came to prominence; some would argue that feminism did not begin to make a real impact on Western culture and society until the early 1970s. However, the reference here being to the burgeoning feminist movement, which was already apparent in the 1960s, the time Dylan was writing some of his most significant work.

8. Note that while Dylan unquestionably wrote a number of songs, in the 1960s, protesting against the evils of war in a generic way—for example, "Masters of War" and "With God on Our Side"—he was decidedly reticent about

Notes—Chapter 3

Vietnam. As John Orman commented: "To many of his followers, Dylan was betrayed by his own silence in relation to the Indochina war and America's involvement in it" (John Orman, *The Politics of Rock,* Chicago: Nelson Hall, 1986, p. 86). Dylan's audience had to wait as late as 1985 and the song "Clean Cut Kid" until they had a Bob Dylan song specifically concerned with the American experience in Vietnam, a surprising fact given that Dylan was often ascribed as being " the voice of protest" in the 1960s. Dylan's seeming disavowal of such contemporary events, in the 1960s, sometimes gave his work an incongruous quality, especially in the case of the war in Vietnam. As Stephen Scobie put it: "*Nashville Skyline* was not the album you wanted to listen to as you were shipped out to Vietnam" (Stephen Scobie, *Alias Bob Dylan Revisited,* Red Deer, Calgary, Alberta: Red Deer College Press, 2004, p. 66).

9. Transcribed from an audio tape recording of an Australian radio broadcast by Ricks, *Bob Dylan Revisited,* c. 1980, no other citation details are known.

10. See, for example, "[O]nly now did he approach his anguish with sufficient perspective to write two of his greatest love songs 'Tomorrow Is a Long Time' and 'Don't Think Twice, It's All Right'" (Clinton Heylin, *Dylan: Behind the Shades,* Harmondsworth: Penguin, 1991, p. 56)

11. www.bobdylan.com. See also, *Lyrics,* p. 61.

12. Christopher Ricks famously, and, in a certain specific sense, correctly, declared this to be the case on *Kaleidoscope,* a BBC Radio 4 broadcast, on 2 January 1986: "What I think is newly established by this [the release of *Biograph*] is his greatness as a love singer, I think this has been largely designed to bring that home to us" (private audio recording of the broadcast).

13. Craig Robert Snow, *Folk-Singer and Beat Poet: The Prophetic Vision of Dylan,* Unpublished Doctoral Thesis, Purdue University, 1987, p. 148.

14. As far as can be ascertained, it is not even known if Dylan, himself, ever recorded the song. A number of versions of the song do exist by other artists, Joan Baez having recorded the most well known version; however, it would appear that no version by Dylan has ever been referenced. Note that this claim may perhaps be a hazardous one to make, and hindsight may prove it to be unfounded; this being so as so much of Dylan's back catalogue of unreleased material, especially from the 1960s, has now been made available and released in official form—it is possible that a version of the song, most probably a studio outtake, will be made available. For example, for many years it was thought that Dylan had not recorded the song "Farewell Angelina"; however, in 1991 a previously unknown performance, from 1965, was released on the compilation *The Bootleg Series Volumes 1-3.* Nonetheless, for the moment, one merely has to presume that "Love Is Just a Four Letter Word" was a song unique in being left both unrecorded and unperformed.

15. See Tim Parrish, *Walking Blues: Making Americans from Emerson to Elvis,* Amherst: University of Massachusetts Press, 2001, for a cogent and thoughtful discussion of the issues of race in the song.

16. It has been said that Dylan was thinking of Prince when he wrote the song; however, Robert Johnson may have been more of a direct influence. In his song "Terraplane Blues," Johnson used a similar variety of salaciously scripted sexual metaphors: the song spoke of: heisting his mama's hood, of checking her oil, of mashing down on her little starter, and so on.

17. www.bobdylan.com. See also, *Lyrics,* p. 272.

18. www.bobdylan.com. See also, *Lyrics,* p. 276.

19. The scene in question occurred in *Hamlet* during the play within the play; wherein Hamlet attempted to entrap Claudius by re-enacting the murder of Old Hamlet; shortly before this, there was a brief exchange between Hamlet and Ophelia:

Hamlet: Lady, shall I lie in your lap?
Ophelia: No, my Lord.
Hamlet: I mean, my head upon your lap?
Ophelia: Ay, my Lord.
Hamlet: Do you think I meant country matters?
Ophelia: I think nothing my Lord.
Hamlet: That's a fair thought to lie between a maid's legs.
Ophelia: What is, my Lord?
Hamlet: Nothing. (*Hamlet* III.2.110–119.)

Incidentally, the word, "nothing"—and the wordplay to signify literally "no thing"—no phallus—would find its way into a number of Dylan songs—as discussed in the previous chapter of this book.

20. The text discussed here is taken from the original, still officially unreleased recording of the song. In one of the many vagaries in the editing of *Lyrics,* this "joke" was removed in

Notes—Chapter 3

the published version. Instead of the subtle wordplay of the performed version of the song, we were offered a more prosaic text, with the masculine voice merely asking of Denise if she was concealed on the shelf. As with other examples, discussed elsewhere in this study, a later revision of a lyric could arguably be said to have been deliberately sanitized and hence possessed a lesser impact than the originally performed version.

21. The only example that comes to mind arises in the case of "House of the Risin' Sun," the traditional song performed on Dylan's first album, *Bob Dylan*. It was usual, when the song was performed by a male performer, for the gender of the first person voice to be changed from a "poor girl" to a "poor boy," ruining her/his life in the brothel called the Rising Sun. However, in Dylan's version he performed the song (as in "North Country Blues") in a female voice—retaining the original female first person narrative.

22. Dylan is thought to have only performed this song once, at the Berkeley Community Theatre, on December 4, 1965; one review succinctly described it as "a wrong number" and it subsequently did not reappear in live performance—on the rest of the tour, through the end of 1965 and into 1966.

23. www.bobdylan.com. See also, *Lyrics*, p. 250. The archaic and arguably sexist language, in which the song was expressed, was perhaps partially explained via its folk-song origins; it would seem to have been based, at least in part, on the traditional English folk song "John Riley," which opened in a similar way to Dylan's song:
> As I walked out one morning early,
> To breathe the sweet and pleasant air.
> Who should I spy but a fair young maiden,
> Whose cheeks were like the lily fair.

In this way, one must again be aware of the level of subtlety and nuance in Dylan's work, the sense in which he may have put to use a wide manner of artistic devices to create the various dialogues he wished to explore. In this way, the seemingly sexist language of "As I Went Out One Morning" may not have been quite as sexist as it seemed.

24. www.bobdylan.com. See also, *Lyrics*, p. 409.

25. John Herdman, *Voice Without Restraint: A Study of Bob Dylan's Lyrics and Their Background*, Edinburgh: Paul Harris, 1982, p. 44.

26. *Toronto Sun*, February 28, 1978.

27. David Griffiths, "Talking about License to Kill," in Elizabeth Thomson and David Gutman (eds.), *The Dylan Companion*, London: Macmillan, 1990, p. 264.

28. www.bobdylan.com. See also, *Lyrics*, p. 474. The last two lines quoted here were different to those actually sung on the recording, they were also different to the transcription on the lyric sheet included with the compact disc, and also different to the lines as published in the song folio in 1983. However, as intimated previously, the version of the lyrics, as published on Dylan's website, are now seen as the authoritative source of the published work.

29. It is likely that this was a deliberate intent, insomuch as Conrad was pictured on the cover of *Desire*, the album on which the song originally appeared. It might also be noted that Conrad's influence was apparent elsewhere on the *Desire* album; the song "Black Diamond Bay" would appear to have been significantly based on plot elements from Conrad's novel *Victory*; whether such an intertextual allusion derived from Dylan, or from his co-writer of the song, Jacques Levy, is open to question, but Conrad was undoubtedly a significant influence on the album.

30. "Sara" has uniformly been read as a song "about" Dylan's then wife, who was also called Sara. However, this would be to make the mistaken assumption that the male voice in the song was Bob Dylan, himself. There was no reason to assume this and hence the song may have been "about" any woman called Sara, any idea of an autobiographical intent had little textual validity and was purely the interpretation of those listeners who drew this particular conclusion.

31. www.bobdylan.com. See also, *Lyrics*, p. 473.

32. *Rolling Stone*, June 21, 1984. Two years later, at a concert in Sydney, Australia, Dylan performed a rare live rendition of "License to Kill." It was February 12, 1986, only a few days after the Challenger Space Shuttle disaster. The song was introduced by Dylan as: "'A song about the space programme,' and he went on to refer to 'America's tragedy' but then added the rejoinder, 'They had no business being up there in the first place, as if we haven't got enough problems down here on earth'" (cited in Clinton Heylin, *A Life in Stolen Moments: Bob Dylan Day by Day, 1941-1995*, London: Music Sales, 1996, p. 269).

33. Griffiths in Elizabeth Thomson and David Gutman 1990, p. 264.

34. Note that the moon has always had decidedly romantic associations in Dylan's work: the moon was something for a Jokerman to dance to; for Sweet Melinda's clients to howl at; it was a Spanish moon rising on the hill; the midnight moon on the riverside; the moonlight swimming in a sad eyed lady's eyes and a moonlit stream for King David to write psalms about. The songs in question being respectively: "Jokerman," "Just Like Tom Thumb's Blues," "Abandoned Love," "Dark Eyes," "Sad Eyed Lady of the Lowlands" and "I and I."

35. Note, for example, the use of the word 'hill' in: "It Takes a Lot to Laugh, It Takes a Train to Cry," "Idiot Wind," "Shelter from the Storm," "Foot of Pride," "Tombstone Blues" and so on in a number of other songs—in each instance the reference could be seen as signifying Calvary, albeit within only one of many hermeneutic discourses.

36. The line "Sitting there in a cold chill" offered greater detail, insomuch as Dylan has often used the word "cold" to be suggestive of death. In this context, one might note the use of the word in such songs as: "Joey," "Ballad of Hollis Brown," "Lily, Rosemary and the Jack of Hearts" and so on throughout a number of other examples.

37. Valerie Solanas, author of the infamous radical feminist text *SCUM Manifesto*, may have had something to say about this aspect of the song. Solanas's book argued that man's violence was destroying the world and that women should "do away" with the masculine gender (this perhaps contributing to a mistaken rumor that SCUM was an acronym for "Society for Cutting Up Men") and should set up a new society without men. The manifesto only received widespread publicity after Solanas's failed attempt to assassinate Andy Warhol, in 1968. Whether Solanas ever commented on "License to Kill" is not on record, she died in 1988, five years after the release of *Infidels*.

38. Germaine Greer, from *The Female Eunuch*, cited in Craig McGregor (ed.), *Bob Dylan: A Retrospective*, New York: Morrow, 1972, p. 397. This was a similar way of picturing women as the one Joseph Bristow noted: "During the 19th century, European and American cultures insisted on dividing femininity into angelic and demonic, virtuous and vicious types—implying, at all times, that these apparently opposite poles of good and bad women were in some respect interdependent" (cited in Joseph Bristow, *Sexuality*, London: Routledge, 1997, p. 42).

39. Ursula K. Le Guin, *Dancing at the Edge of the World*, London: HarperCollins, 1989, no page number.

40. Betsy Bowden, *Performed Literature: Words and Music by Bob Dylan*, Bloomington: Indiana University Press, 1982, p. 56.

41. Bowden 1982, p. 27.

42. www.bobdylan.com. See also "Highlands," in Bob Dylan, *Time Out of Mind* (New York: Special Rider Music, 1997), p. 45. Stephen Scobie points out how the scene in the restaurant in "Highlands" had a "remarkable close parallel" to a scene in Erica Jong's 1990 novel, *Any Woman's Blues*. Scobie cites the following passage from the novel: "I am looking now at one the paintings I painted to his design—he had scribbled a rough sketch on a napkin; I, of course, had painted it—and there's no denying that it's an abortion, not in my style at all" (cited in Scobie 2004, p. 337).

43. As Ian Bell succinctly put it: "[Dylan's] habitual treatment of women ... exposed a deficiency in human sympathy. His understanding of one half of the species was limited" (Ian Bell, *Once Upon a Time: The Lives of Bob Dylan*, Edinburgh: Mainstream, 2013, p. 385).

Chapter 4

1. Robert Shelton, *No Direction Home: The Life and Music of Bob Dylan*, London: New English Library, 1986, pp. 353–354.

2. Transcribed from an unofficial recording of the concert at the Bushnell Memorial Hall, Hartford, Connecticut, on May 8, 1980. As far as can be ascertained, these stage comments have not previously been cited in published form, although, as along with seemingly everything else, such transcripts are available on the internet.

3. Note that Dylan had first used the phrase "the holy slow train" in 1965, on the liner notes to the album *Highway 61 Revisited*.

4. See, for example: Craig Robert Snow, *Folk-Singer and Beat Poet: The Prophetic Vision of Dylan*, Unpublished Doctoral Thesis, Purdue University, 1987, p. 37. In his dissertation Snow made a convincing case for Dylan as a latter-day Beat poet and made a number of pertinent comparisons between Dylan's work and Ginsberg's.

5. As will be discussed later, an obvious point to make here would be to acknowledge the differing constraints between a poet on the page, as with Allen Ginsberg; and with a songwriter, as with Bob Dylan. In other words, poetry on the page allowed for much greater freedoms of explicit expression than was the case in commercial popular music.

6. The phrase "self confessional," as used here, would intend to compare Dylan's reticence to Ginsberg's openness in matters of sexual expression; Ginsberg had a candour in his work that was nowhere to be found in Dylan's. This being seen, to excellent effect, in Ginsberg's reading of his poem "Kaddish" in Dylan's film *Renaldo and Clara* (1978). "Kaddish" was Ginsberg's great poem detailing the life of his mother, Naomi Ginsberg, and the following line: "O mother farewell/with a long black shoe ... with your old dress and a long black beard around the vagina" was used by Dylan to great effect in the film, but it would have been impossible to imagine Dylan ever writing such a line.

7. Incidentally, as is well-known, the phrase "love is just a four letter word," did not originate with Dylan. It had been previously used in Tennessee Williams' play *Cat on a Hot Tin Roof* (1955), which is where Dylan most probably first heard it.

8. In "Hurricane" Dylan offered a further echo of the invective signifier in question, in the song's seventh verse, via a presumed knowledge of rudimentary French, Dylan's pronunciation of "murder" as "merd-ur" was most probably a deliberate echo of the French, *merde*, hence obviously chiming with the faecal expletive elsewhere in the song. In addition, there was a further reference insomuch as Dylan rhymed "murder" with "ass in stir"—hence contributing an additional scatological inference.

9. "I'm Not There" is listed on Dylan's website, www.bobdylan.com, but perhaps wisely it offered no attempt at a transcription; when attempts have been made to transcribe the song (as in those commonly available on the internet) the results have hardly been useful. Although the song has achieved a degree of fame—Todd Haynes's film of 2007 was named after it—it seems to have been a song that Dylan never actually finished, when seen on the page it generally appears as grammatically incoherent, at times a mere babble of linguistic inconsistency.

10. As Greil Marcus noted: "The performances were originally made for the performer's own ears alone; this was art not meant for consumption" (Greil Marcus, *Invisible Republic: Bob Dylan's Basement Tapes*, London: Picador, 1997, p. xiv).

11. *The Basement Tapes*, originally recorded in 1967, were first officially released in 1975, but then, for a significant period much of the collection remained unreleased, with only twenty of the one-hundred plus performances being available within a public forum. The subsequent release, in 2014, of the so-called "complete" compilation, provided some 138 home recordings of greater and lesser interest and of greater and lesser audio quality on *The Bootleg Series, Vol. 11: The Basement Tapes Complete*. Whether or not any further material remains unreleased—too bawdy or otherwise—is open to question.

12. In terms of the influence of D.H. Lawrence, one might think here of the famous scene in *Women in Love*, wherein a fig was graphically compared to the anatomy of the female pudenda. In the 1969 film version of the novel, Ken Russell would make use of Lawrence's poem "How to Eat a Fig" to graphically exemplify and enhance this point.

13. See Betsy Bowden, *Performed Literature: Words and Music by Bob Dylan*, Bloomington: Indiana University Press, 1982, p. 30.

14. Craig McGregor (ed.), *Bob Dylan: A Retrospective*, New York. Morrow, 1972, p. 13.

15. Steven Goldberg, "Bob Dylan and the Poetry of Salvation." Reprinted in McGregor, pp. 371–372.

16. Michael Gross, *Bob Dylan An Illustrated History*, London: Elm Tree, p. 56.

17. Michael Gray, *Song and Dance Man: The Art of Bob Dylan*, London: Hart-Davis, MacGibbon, 1972, p. 229.

18. John Herdman, *Voice Without Restraint: A Study of Bob Dylan's Lyrics and Their Background*, Edinburgh: Paul Harris, 1982, p. 23.

19. Sy Ribakove and Barbara Ribakove, *Folk Rock: the Bob Dylan Story*, New York: Dell, 1965, p. 116.

20. Robert Shelton, "Pop Singers and Song Writers Racing Down Dylan's Road," *New York Times*, August 27, 1965, reprinted in McGregor 1972, p. 79.

21. *New Musical Express*, May 22, 1965.

22. *Playboy*, March 1966; available in McGregor 1972, pp. 124–145, p. 144.

23. Terry Eagleton, *Literary Theory: An Introduction*, Oxford: Basil Blackwell, 1983, p. 197.

24. Incidentally, it should be noted that while

Notes—Chapter 4

researching this study no such similar example of a lyric being discussed within a heterosexual arena, in such detail, has been found.

25. Although the song does not seem to have ever developed from more than an initial sketch: one verse and a chorus line, it is worth noting that Dylan considered it worthy enough to at least attempt to produce a finished recording; according to the precise archivist Michael Krogsgaard, the song was recorded on October 5, 1965, between 7 p.m. and 10 p.m., with seven takes being attempted (cited in "Bob Dylan The Recording Sessions: Part One," *The Telegraph* 52, Summer 1995, p. 122)

26. Gray 1972, p. 91.

27. We can assume here that the narrator was a "him" for the obvious reason that the voice narrating the story was masculine.

28. www.bobdylan.com. See also, *Lyrics*, p. 264.

29. In a sense such an interpretation followed, not only the work of Judith Butler, but the earlier argument expressed in Leslie A. Fiedler's *Love and Death in the American Novel*. As previously intimated, in Chapter 2 of this study, this was Fiedler's innovative and pioneering book that anticipated the emergence of so-called queer theory in the 1990s, a book that cogently argued that there was a considerable degree of homoerotic imagery in so-called straight culture, specifically within the American novel, but also within a diverse range of other textual bodies.

30. As a protagonist in the song, Achilles was already cloaked within a discourse suggestive of homoeroticism; it is generally accepted that Achilles, the great hero of the Trojan War, had a same sex relationship with his friend, and brother-in-arms, Patroclus. Hence for Dylan to choose this nomenclature, to choose this particular proper name, seemed to be already positioned within a discourse of intentional ambiguity.

31. This song was of further interest insomuch as it seemed to be a song with a deliberately transgressional theme: it opened with a woman wearing masculine clothes and continued with such scenes as, for example, in verse five—wherein a tiny man was biting the ear of a soldier, while—at the same time—contemplating an act of forbidden love.

32. Gerda Siann, *Gender, Sex and Sexuality: Contemporary Psychological Perspectives*, London: Taylor and Francis, 1994.

33. Roger Horrocks, *Masculinity in Crisis*, London: Macmillan, 1994.

34. The song has not been commercially published and Dylan's website does not list it; the transcription above derives from the performance of the song in the film *Eat the Document*. In a (non-commercial) publisher's manuscript sheet (circulated in the 1980s) the line was slightly amended to read: "What kind of *friend* is this, who loves me behind my back?" However, Dylan at least appears to sing the cited version of the lyric on the film's soundtrack.

35. To put this explicitly: *Blood on the Tracks* had nothing at all to do with the break-up of Dylan's marriage—this may conceivably have been the original inspiration for the songs Dylan composed—but to therefore presume such rich and polysemantic texts were only concerned with such narrow issues was almost absurdly reductive.

36. Herdman 1982, p. 14.

37. Herdman 1982, p. 14.

38. See Ricks' comment, cited in Chapter 3, extolling the idea of Dylan's "greatness as a love singer."

39. Herdman 1982, p. 14.

40. Herdman 1982, p. 44.

41. Shelton 1986, p. 282. Shelton's implied choice of New Orleans as the location of "Desolation Row" was an interesting one. This might be inferred if one presumes of a deliberate intent on Dylan's part; in other words, in his placing "Desolation Row" at the end of *Highway 61 Revisited*. In a geographical sense, Highway 61 "began" near Dylan's birthplace of Duluth, Minnesota, and "ended" in New Orleans, but whether this was a deliberate intent on Dylan's part remains open to question.

42. Ellen Willis, "Dylan," *Cheetah*, 1967. Reprinted in McGregor 1972, pp. 218–239, p. 229.

43. The song was copyrighted in 1983; just two years before, on May 13, 1981, a gunman, Mehmet Ali Agca, had attempted to assassinate Pope John Paul II in the grounds of the Vatican; in other words, in the palace of the Pope, as Dylan would put it.

44. www.bobdylan.com. See also, *Lyrics*, p. 483. For the most part "Don't Fall Apart on Me Tonight" was arguably a somewhat banal and self-pitying song, rescued only by occasional flashes of wit or humour; for example, the lines:
"Who are these people who are walking towards you?
Do you know them or will there be a fight?"

Notes—Chapter 4

Here the agoraphobic protagonist sounded uncannily like the cowardly Donny (played by Steve Buscemi) as he would appear in the Coen brothers' film *The Big Lebowski* (1998), with the line being almost as amusing here, in the song, as it would later prove to be in the film.

45. It should be made clear here that there is no intention to suggest that this was necessarily Bob Dylan's implied meaning. As discussed in Chapter 1, Dylan's implied meaning will always be both uncertain and relatively unimportant— or at least of no inherent interest within a theoretical discussion of his songs.

46. A casual listener might have heard the line as: "and a Colt revolver clicked." However, the published version offered was that of a cold revolver clicking; as if Dylan was pedantically set on making a specific textual point. In fact, it is difficult to ascertain exactly what Dylan was singing on the original recordings of the song, his enunciation lacking sufficient precision to enable an accurate transcription, but cold revolver was (and remains) the extant published version.

47. This period has been deliberately selected, this being because, as discussed elsewhere in this study, Dylan's output since this time, albeit with some exceptions, would not seem to have merited as much critical attention.

48. See Jean-Charles Khalifa, "A Semantic and Syntactic Journey Through the Dylan Corpus," *Oral Tradition*, 22/1 2007, pp. 162–174.

49. One is aware that Dylan also wrote songs about the plight of black women, "The Lonesome Death of Hattie Carroll" (1964) being the obvious example. Yet it is apparent that this was the exception to the rule, Dylan's primary concern was consistently with black men, as the *résumé* of examples has aimed to make clear.

50. In addition, one might also cite other early songs such as: "The Death of Robert Johnson," "Ballad for a Friend," "Ballad of the Ox Bow Incident," "Poor Boy Blues," "Man on the Street" all from the early 1960s and all seemingly concerning African American men who had met with a series of violent fates.

51. www.bobdylan.com. See also, *Lyrics*, p. 302. Sean Wilentz makes a similar argument in his discussion of "George Jackson" (see Wilentz 2010, p. 153).

52. The other four of the five verses of the song did not compare well to the quality and to the direct sense of honesty of the opening verse; the rest of the song was somewhat pedestrian in its hagiographic depiction of Jackson. For example, the second verse mixed apologetic factual inaccuracy with bland cliché:
"Sent him off to prison
For a seventy-dollar robbery
Closed the door behind him
And they threw away the key"
The seventy dollar robbery was an armed robbery, a deliberate crime of violence, and to use a phrase as clichéd as "and they threw away the key" was hardly inspirational writing. The third verse, with its scatological use of prison argot, was simply trite in its rhyming of kneel and real:
"He wouldn't take shit from no one
He wouldn't bow down or kneel
Authorities, they hated him
Because he was just too real"
While the fifth and final verse was wholly facile with a closing metaphor that seemed insipid and ultimately meaningless:
"Sometimes I think this whole world
Is one big prison yard
Some of us are prisoners
The rest of us are guards"

53. See, for example, Lester Bangs, "Dylan's Dalliance with Mafia Chic," *Creem*, March 1976, pp. 33–44. In his article, Bangs succeeded in demonstrating Dylan's hypocrisy in portraying Joey Gallo as a hero. Bangs called the song: "one of the most mindlessly amoral pieces of repellently romanticist bullshit ever recorded."

54. The song was false from the beginning— it opened with an attempt at providing Joey Gallo's beginnings. He was born in Red Hook, Brooklyn, this was correct, but the comment that his birth occurred in the year of who knows when, was false; Joey Gallo was born on April 7, 1929—and would die, coincidentally, on the same date in 1972. One way of redeeming the amoral content of the song would be to see a deliberate intent on Dylan's part—in other words, this piece of misinformation acted to intimate that all else, from this first line on down, would be false and skewed from the reality of Gallo's life.

55. The obvious example intimated here being the aforementioned, "Who Killed Davey Moore?" (1964).

56. The example here being the aforementioned song "Hurricane" (1976).

57. See Joyce Carol Oates' book *On Boxing* for a further discussion on the issue of homoeroticism in the sport. To move for a moment

into a biographical discourse, it would seem as if Dylan was not averse to the art of boxing himself. It is known that Dylan employed the famous boxer Boom Boom Mancini sometime in the 1990s, presumably as a sparring partner. On his 1987 album, *Sentimental Hygiene*, Warren Zevon had included a song about Mancini, called simply "Boom Boom Mancini," and in 2002, shortly before Zevon's death, Dylan would attempt a performance of the song. A sound file of this performance, which occurred on October 4, 2002, in Seattle, is available on *You Tube*.

58. One could cite a number of scriptural passages to support this, but to note just one: "Submit yourselves unto your husbands as unto the Lord. For the husband is the head of the wife, even as Christ is the head of the church" (Ephesians 5:22–23).

59. Rosalind Miles, *The Rites of Man: Life and Death in the Making of the Male*, London: Grafton, 1991, p. 22.

60. Jesus himself said relatively little about sexuality and almost nothing about same-sex relationships; Jesus lived with twelve other men, he had a (male) disciple whom he loved. In addition, other than Jesus and the beloved disciple, there are several biblical affirmations of the deep love between same sex adults; for example, David and Jonathan, Ruth and Naomi, even if sexual relationships were not explicitly implied.

61. Roger Horrocks, *An Introduction to the Study of Sexuality*, London: Macmillan, 1997.

62. Terry Eagleton, *After Theory*, London: Penguin, 2004, p. 203.

63. Eagleton 2004, p. 203.

64. Cited in David Lodge, *Lives in Writing*, London: Vintage, 2015, p. 144.

65. Peter Watson, *A Terrible Beauty: A History of the Ideas that Shaped the Modern Mind*, London: Weidenfeld & Nicholson, 2000.

66. Lawrence M. Krauss, *A Universe from Nothing: Why There is Something Rather than Nothing*, London: Simon and Schuster, 2012, p. 171.

67. Arthur Goldwag, *Isms and Ologies: 453 Difficult Doctrines You've Always Pretended to Understand*, London: Quercus, 2007.

68. In addition, there is the question of why God would wait for so long. Humanity has existed for perhaps 100,000 years, so why would an all omniscient and all loving God allow so many generations of humanity to remain unredeemed.

69. As has been noted elsewhere, if Christ was the Son of God, if he had access to all knowledge, if he had really wanted to convince mankind of this, then he could easily have related, for example, some very basic but at that point in time unknown astronomical information, such as Jupiter has four moons, there are rings around Saturn, Mars has a giant volcano and so on.

70. Lodge 2014, p. 151.

71. Christopher Hitchens, *God is Not Great: How Religion Poisons Everything*, New York: Atlantic, 2007, p. 64.

72. Rob Brotherton, *Suspicious Minds: Why We Believe Conspiracy Theories*, London: Bloomsbury Sigma, 2015, p. 66.

73. Krauss 2012, p. 145.

74. Lou Reed perhaps put it best in his song "Strawman" from his album *New York* (1989). Amidst the unflinching polemic of all things wrong with America, Reed offered this satirical, if albeit anti-Semitic riposte to the baser aspect of Dylan's so-called born again period: does anyone need another self-righteous rock singer, Reed sardonically asked, whose nose had led him straight to God.

75. The comment derives from *Hard to Handle*, the concert video of Dylan's 1986 tour of Australia.

76. Herdman 1982, p. 82.

77. See Snow 1987, p. 4.

78. The point to be accentuated here is the fact that Dylan's work has consistently possessed a Christian ideology, but that around the dates 1979–1981 and, to a certain extent since then, the work has possessed an obsession with the figure of Christ as a masculine icon.

79. Nat Hentoff, "The Playboy Interview: A Candid Conversation with the Iconoclastic Idol of the Folk Rock Set," *Playboy*, March 1966, reprinted in McGregor 1972, pp. 124–145.

80. The interview was broadcast on KMEX radio, Tucson, on December 7, 1979, and a partial transcription was subsequently published in *The Telegraph* 29, Spring 1988, p. 49.

81. Angela Carter, "Bob Dylan on Tour," *London Magazine*, August 1966.

82. Marcus 1997, p. 34.

83. Tim Riley, *Hard Rain: A Dylan Commentary*, London: Plexus, 1992, p. 9.

84. John Gordon, "Dylan: A Few Years Older Than Israel," *Fusion*, June 25, 1971. Reprinted in McGregor 1972, pp. 164–166.

85. McGregor 1972, p. 12–13.

86. Norman Mailer, *Advertisements for Myself*, New York: Berkley, 1970.

Notes—Chapter 4

87. Interview in *Cine-Revue*, 1975. Susan Bordo has suggested that the actress Sally Quinn, who according to Bordo, "had dated both Brando and Bob Dylan in the mid-sixties," claimed that Dylan "adored, idolised [and] was terribly attracted to Marlon" (Susan Bordo, *The Male Body: A New Look at Men in Public and Private*, New York: Farrar, Strauss and Giroux, 1999, p. 133).

88. Lynn Segal, *Straight Sex*, London: Virago, 1994, p. 294.

89. Roger Horrocks, *Masculinity in Crisis*, London: Macmillan, 1994, p. 91.

90. Transcribed from a home recording of an interview with Allen Ginsberg, broadcast on BBC Radio, June 10, 1996.

91. Some commentators would place the emergence of queer theory as occurring slightly earlier; for example, Jane Gallop stated that "around 1985, feminism began to give way to what has come to be called gender studies" (Jane Gallop, *Around 1981: Academic Feminist Literary Theory*, New York: Rougledge, 1992, p. 275). Gallop perhaps choosing this year insomuch as 1985 saw the publication of Eve Kosofsky Sedgwick's influential book on queer theory, *Between Men: English Literature and Male Homosocial Desire*.

92. Sara Salih, *Judith Butler: Routledge Critical Thinkers*, London: Routledge, 2002, p. 8.

93. In much the same way the term "queer" did not necessarily signify homosexuality—instead signifying whatever was "queer" to conventional and conformist society. Michel Foucault's work would offer the opportunity of delineating one's identity in ways other than a gendered process; that is, one might express one's identity via the pleasure derived from; for example, a sadomasochistic lifestyle, rather than the fixed binary of hetero or homosexual activity. A useful discussion of this can be found in Tasmin Spargo, *Foucault and Queer Theory*, Cambridge: Icon, 1999.

94. Nick Lacy, *Introduction to Film*, Basingstoke: Palgrave Macmillan, 2005, p. 185.

95. Foucault died in 1984, some years before the advent of queer theory as a significant school of thought, but his work had a significant effect on other theorists beyond this date.

96. The word "discourse" being a significant concept in theory as a whole; but it was associated specifically with Foucault, who used the term to describe the way in which systems of power operated within culture, ideology and language.

97. Terry Eagleton, *Literary Theory: An Introduction* (Second Edition), Oxford: Basil Blackwell, 1996. As Foucault himself put it, perhaps summarizing a large part of his primary argument: "We are subject to the production of truth through power" (cited in Watson 2000, p. 628).

98. Spargo 1999.

99. Watson 2000.

100. Joseph Bristow, *Sexuality*, London: Routledge, 1997, p. 9.

101. Segal 1994.

102. Edward Quinn, *Collins Dictionary of Literary Terms*, Glasgow: HarperCollins, 2004.

103. Spargo 1999, p. 12.

104. Horrocks 1997.

105. Jonathan Ned Katz, *The Invention of Heterosexuality*, New York: Dutton, 1995, p. 184.

106. Judith Butler, *Gender Trouble: Feminism and the Subversion of Identity*. London: Routledge, 1990.

107. Katz 1995, p. 60.

108. Philip Stokes, *Philosophy: 100 Essential Thinkers*, London: Arcturus, 2003, p. 139.

109. Stokes 2003.

110. Marjorie Garber, *Vice-Versa: Bisexuality and the Eroticism of Everyday Life*, Harmondsworth: Penguin, 1995, p. 184.

111. Peter Barry, *Beginning Theory: An Introduction to Literary and Cultural Theory*, Manchester: Manchester University Press, 1995.

112. This would be to exclude the indirect reference to Freud in *Tarantula*, Dylan's self-composed epitaph to Vienna politeness—to be discussed in Chapter 5. Also, in the final verse of "Gates of Eden" the masculine narrator seemed to go out of his way to avoid any kind of Freudian analysis, making no attempt to interpret, to shovel a glimpse into his lover's dreams—which, in one reading at least, would seem to have been the basis of the phantasmagorical imagery found throughout the rest of this song.

113. Bob Dylan, *Chronicles*, London: Simon & Schuster, 2004, pp. 37–38.

114. *Spin Magazine*, December 1985. Dylan appears to confuse psychoanalysis with psychiatry, as he did in "Talkin' World War III Blues," but the point was made nonetheless.

115. Stephen Trombley, *Fifty Thinkers Who Shaped the Modern World*, London: Atlantic, 2012, p. 131.

116. Trombley 2012, p. 131.

117. This comment derives from the liner

notes to the *Biograph* compilation, released in November 1985.

Chapter 5

1. Sam Shepard, *Rolling Thunder Logbook,* Harmondsworth: Penguin, 1978, p. 79.

2. As Stephen Scobie put it: "The purpose of criticism is not to pander to the curiosity of gossip but to respond to the complexity of the texts themselves" (Stephen Scobie, *Alias Bob Dylan Revisited,* Red Deer, Calgary, Alberta: Red Deer College Press, 2004, p. 88).

3. Michael Gray, *Song and Dance Man: The Art of Bob Dylan,* London: Hart-Davis, MacGibbon, 1972, p. 90.

4. Stephen Scobie, *Alias Bob Dylan* Red Deer, Calgary, Alberta: Red Deer College Press, 1991, p. 18.

5. Scobie 2004, p. 35.

6. Clinton Heylin, *Dylan: Behind the Shades,* Harmondsworth: Penguin, 1991, p. 3.

7. Transcribed from a video/audio recording of a press conference, held in Sydney, Australia, on February 10, 1986; available on *YouTube.*

8. Note that this applies to the whole of Dylan's work, not merely to his song lyrics. For example, the film *Renaldo and Clara,* released in 1978, was in large part about what it meant to be "Bob Dylan," and who "Bob Dylan" might be, with "Bob Dylan" decidedly placed within quotation marks. See Chapter 6, "Renaldo and Bob," of Stephen Scobie's book, *Alias Bob Dylan,* for a fuller discussion of this issue in relation to *Renaldo and Clara.*

9. Al Aronowitz, "Dylan: He's Only Just Begun," *Melody Maker,* December 12, 1973, p. 19.

10. Cited in Anthony Scaduto, *Bob Dylan An Intimate Biography,* London: W.H. Allen, 1972, p. 34.

11. Cited in Scaduto 1972, p. 224.

12. Cited in Scaduto 1972, p. 59.

13. John Hammond, *John Hammond on Record: An Autobiography,* New York: NAL, 1977, p. 122.

14. Jerry Wexler and David Ritz, *Rhythm and the Blues: A Life in American Music,* London: Jonathan Cape, 1994, p. 291.

15. Cited in Larry Sloman, *On the Road with Bob Dylan,* New York: Bantam, 1978, p. 302.

16. Transcribed from an audio recording of a Canadian Broadcasting Corporation show, *As it Happens,* broadcast on April 4, 1979.

17. *The Telegraph 45,* Spring 1993, p. 20.

18. Ricks quoted on http://www.taxhelp.com/ndex-r.html. Accessed October 15, 1999.

19. Cited in *The New Oxford Dictionary of English,* Oxford: Clarendon, 1998, p. 307.

20. I do not have access to the precise figures of how the readership split into male/female ratios; I base this supposition on such factors as the gender of the contributors to the letter pages, on the gender of the authors of the various articles and essays in the magazine, on the general *milieu* of the magazine as a whole, and on remarks made in a number of the magazine's editorials.

21. One might consider the possibility (albeit a somewhat improbable one) that there may have been a certain sense of playfulness, on the part of Bauldie and the other contributing editors, in relation to issues of homosociality, especially as the overarching organization that published *The Telegraph* was called Wanted Man.

22. In terms of the duality of identity, it is perhaps of interest to note that a number of album covers featured reverse images of Dylan. Notably his first album, *Bob Dylan,* careful observation revealing the guitar strings running from treble to bass instead of bass to treble; similarly, the *New Morning* cover, the front cover was reversed—the song-folio having the correct representation; finally, the cover of *Blood on the Tracks,* this derived from a blown-up image of a photograph taken from the audience by Paul Till at the Maple Leaf Gardens in Toronto, on January 9, 1974—observation of the original photograph revealing that the image had been reversed, left was right and right was left. These instances may have been oversights, but they may have been deliberate, and—as such—they succeeded in showing Dylan's "wrong" face to his audience—a detail of which few members of Dylan's audience would probably have been aware, but a detail that may well have been a conscious design on Dylan's part—especially as other—undetected covers—may also have had reversed images.

23. *Toronto Sun,* March 1, 1978, p. 22.

24. Anthony Easthope, *What a Man's Gotta Do: The Masculine Myth in Popular Culture,* Boston: Unwin Hyman, 1986, p. 104.

25. One makes this point with an awareness of a potential contradiction inherent in the overarching argument being espoused in this study; in other words, that gender was a performative

structure. However, this would not seem too much of a contradiction; insomuch as it could be argued that it is possible to ascribe a performativity to the two differing genders being propagated within the one identity.

26. David Pichaske, "The Prophet and the Prisoner: Bob Dylan and the American Dream," *Telegraph 26*, Spring 1987, p. 77. Pichaske spoke of dreams being archetypes we unconsciously play and replay in our subconscious—and while dreams have not been discussed in detail within this study, dreams were, of course, a significant facet of Dylan's work. Dreams, Freud believed, were the residue of the day's anxieties; but Freud also believed dreams were "the royal road to the unconscious." Within Dylan's work there were a number of dreams: an initial dream: "Bob Dylan's Dream," then a "115th Dream," and then a "Series of Dreams"—the latter being a phrase Dylan may have come across (whatever his claims to have scarcely read Freud) in one of Freud's most influential works, *The Interpretation of Dreams*.

27. "I and I" has been compared to Leonard Cohen's song, "Hallelujah"—for example, both songs allude to King David and the music he made. In addition, it is said that Dylan and Cohen once discussed the two songs and compared the differences in their methods of composition. Cohen, in an interview with Paul Zollo, for the book: *Songwriters On Songwriting*, commented: "'Hallelujah' was a song that took me a long time to write. Dylan and I were having coffee the day after his concert in Paris, a few years ago, and he was doing that song in concert. And he asked me how long it took to write it. And I told him a couple of years. I lied actually. It was more than a couple of years. Then I praised a song of his, "I and I," and asked him how long it had taken and he said, 'Fifteen minutes.'" Available at: https://cohencentric.com/2015/11/04/bob-dylans-i-and-i-is-on-leonard-cohens-jukebox/ (accessed October 5, 2017). It might be noted, however, that Cohen's song has entered the culture, becoming a much covered and well known piece, while Dylan's song most probably remains known only to a lesser audience of people.

28. *True Dylan*, by Sam Shepard, cited in Don Shewey, *Sam Shepard* (New York: Da Capo, 1997), p. 232. This was a short, one-act play, Shepard wrote in 1987, constructed from a series of conversations between himself and Dylan—it was published in the July 1987 edition of *Esquire* magazine, but it would seem that the play itself was never staged. By way of an additional detail, it was of interest that the character of "Bob" seemed to compare women to the devil—linking back to the song, "You're No Good," as discussed at the start of Chapter 3 of this book.

29. In a similar context, this exchange at the end of the 1978 *Playboy* interview, conducted by Ron Rosenbaum, seems relevant to this argument:

> *Playboy*: You were quoted recently as having said something about having a Gemini nature.
>
> Dylan: Well, maybe there are certain characteristics of people who are born under certain signs. But I don't know, I'm not sure how relevant it is.
>
> *Playboy*: Could it be there's an undiscovered twin or a double to Bob Dylan?
>
> Dylan: Someplace on the planet, there's a double of me walking around. Could very possibly be.
>
> *Playboy*: Any messages for your double?
>
> Dylan: Love will conquer everything, I suppose.

http://www.interferenza.com/bcs/interw/play78.htm (aAccessed October 5, 2017).

30. Cited by Pichaske in *The Telegraph 26*, p. 78.

31. Aidan Day, *Jokerman: Reading the Lyrics of Bob Dylan*, Oxford: Basil Blackwell, 1988, p. 1.

32. Scobie 1991, p. 131.

33. John Herdman, *Voice Without Restraint: A Study of Bob Dylan's Lyrics and Their Background*, Edinburgh: Paul Harris, 1982, p. 136.

34. Shepard 1978, p. 100.

35. Greil Marcus, *Invisible Republic: Bob Dylan's Basement Tapes*, London: Picador, 1997, p. 220.

36. Transcribed from an audio recording of the concert at the Philharmonic Hall, New York City, October 31, 1964, subsequently released, in 2004, as: *The Bootleg Series, Vol. 6: Bob Dylan Live 1964, Concert at Philharmonic Hall*.

37. Shepard 1978, p. 114. It is possibly a reflection of the importance of this performance that Dylan chose to begin his film *Renaldo and Clara* (1978) with it; the film opened with the song "When I Paint My Masterpiece," sung by a character called "Renaldo," played by someone called "Bob Dylan" wearing a "Bob Dylan" mask; all of which added a further level of ambiguity to the sense of masquerade, to the use of masks, to the complexity of identities being performed.

38. Sara Salih, *Judith Butler: Routledge Critical Thinkers*, London: Routledge, 2002, p. 2.
39. Salih 2002, p. 40.
40. Salih 2002, p. 44.
41. Salih 2002, p. 49.
42. Salih 2002, p. 10.
43. Salih 2002. De Beauvoir famously stated, in her book *The Second Sex*, "one is not born, but rather becomes a woman."
44. Salih 2002, p. 62.
45. "Advice for Geraldine on Her Miscellaneous Birthday." Available in Bob Dylan, *Lyrics 1962-1985*, London: Jonathan Cape, 1987, pp. 124-125.
46. *Rolling Stone*, January 20, 1978, p. 43.
47. The following comment by Dylan, made at the Los Angeles press conference, on December 16, 1965, would also seem relevant:
   Q. Is it true that you changed your name? If so, what was your other name?
   A. Knezivitch. I changed it to avoid obvious relatives who would come up to me in different parts of the country and want tickets for concerts and stuff like that. Knezivitch, yeah.
   Q. Was that your first or last name?
   A. That was the first name. I don't really want to tell you what the last name was.
48. Roland Barthes, "Textual Analysis: Poe's 'Valdemar,'" in David Lodge and Nigel Wood (eds.), *Modern Criticism and Theory: A Reader* London: Longman, 1992, p.176.
49. It should perhaps be noted here that Stephen Scobie, along with a number of other writers, has heard a reference to "Bob Dylan" in a live performance of "Caribbean Wind" (1981). However, the sound quality of the recording in question renders this hearing somewhat subjective to the listener. Also, the official transcription of the song on Dylan's website would appear to derive from a different version of the song—a version that does not include the line in question. In addition to this, I am disregarding the self-reverential references found within the various song-titles to which Dylan appended his name, for example: "Bob Dylan's Blues," "Bob Dylan's Dream," "Bob Dylan's New Orleans Rag," "Bob Dylan's 115th Dream," and likewise the self-reverential titles of early records: *Bob Dylan, The Freewheelin' Bob Dylan, Another Side of Bob Dylan*.
50. Bob Dylan, *Tarantula*, London: MacGibbon & Kee, 1971, p. 120.
51. Francois Villon, *The Poetry of Francois Villon*, London: n. pub., 1947, p. 66.
52. *Tarantula* 1971, p. 120.
53. One remains uncertain if the reference to "boy dylan" was perhaps originally a misprint, instead of the subtle textual conceit on Dylan's part. Such an enigmatic textual dilemma, "bob dylan" or "boy dylan," with all its psychoanalytical baggage, being reminiscent of a similar textual dilemma James Joyce created in his novel, *Ulysses*. In the novel, Joyce at times deliberately used the word "word" instead of the word "world"—and vice-versa—a carefully crafted textual device, undermined, in some editions, by well-minded editors correcting mistakes that were not mistakes. I only have access to the first edition of *Tarantula*, but as far as can be ascertained this enigmatic textual dilemma remains intact through further editions of the novel.
54. Jacques Lacan, one of Freud's most significant successors, was arguably responsible for psychoanalysis being taken seriously within academic circles. In the Sorbonne, from 1953 to 1980, Lacan gave a series of public seminars each year on the topic. The seminars were popular with both an academic and general audience, regularly gaining an audience of 800 in a lecture theatre designed for 650. As Stephen Trombley noted, it was Lacan, in these seminars, "who was chiefly responsible for making Freud relevant for the late twentieth century" (Stephen Trombley, *Fifty Thinkers Who Shaped the Modern World*, London: Atlantic, 2012, p. 129)
55. Lacan's wit was often lost in translation; for example, was an *"hommelette"* a little man or some broken eggs: was *"pere-version"* the law of the father or a type of behaviour that deviates from the norm—and so on in a number of other examples.
56. Roger Horrocks, *An Introduction to the Study of Sexuality*, London: Macmillan, 1997, p. 68-69.
57. Horrocks 1997, p. 116.
58. Horrocks 1997.
59. Terry Eagleton, *Literary Theory: An Introduction*, Oxford: Basil Blackwell, 1983, p. 168.
60. David Lodge, *Small World: An Academic Romance*, London: Secker & Warburg, 1984, pp. 26-27.
61. This may appear as an "aberrant decoding," to employ Umberto Eco's phrase, but it would seem difficult to argue against the idea that a reader's interpretation was any less valid

than the original author's—every encoding is another decoding—as Morris Zapp would put it, and so on without end.

62. Lynn Segal, *Straight Sex,* London: Virago, 1994, p. 225.

63. As far as being unspeakable goes, it is obviously relevant that what is arguably our most obscene word, "cunt," literally signifies the vagina, although as a term of extreme abuse it more commonly applies within other descriptive arenas.

64. Norman Mailer, *The Prisoner of Sex,* London: Macmillan, 1971, p.145. Camille Paglia has described the vagina as "lurid in color, vagrant in contour and architecturally incoherent," while on the other hand, Paglia saw the male genitals as having a "rational mathematical design, a syntax" (Camille Paglia, *Sexual Personae,* New Haven: Yale University Press, 1990, p. 24).

65. Roger Horrocks, *Masculinity in Crisis,* London: Macmillan, 1994, p. 83.

66. Cited in Segal 1994, p. 249.

67. In psychoanalysis, the term "cathexis" might be defined as the investment of emotional energy towards another person, or idea, often to a deleterious extent. One notes, within this context, that Judith Butler has suggested: "all gender identity is founded on a primary, forbidden homosexual cathexis or desire" (cited in Salih 2002, p. 55).

68. Rimbaud was one of the very few poets who had the foresight to stop writing poems at a young age; Rimbaud ceased any form of writing when he was aged only twenty-one. As such, the comparison to Dylan was of interest; in other words, what if Dylan had done this—what if Dylan had ceased working as an artist after the motorcycle accident in 1966? Would his reputation as a songwriter have been enhanced? Possibly so, as Robert Frost once observed: most poets are dead by their late twenties.

69. Dylan himself makes this connection in the liner notes accompanying the *Biograph* (1985) collection, in which he commented: "I don't think of myself as Bob Dylan. It's like Rimbaud said, 'I is another.'"

70. Shepard's comment may have been a deliberate reference to Hamlet's retort to Rosencrantz and Guildenstern: "You would pluck out the heart of my mystery." *Hamlet* III. 2. 356-357.

71. Untitled liner notes to *Highway 61 Revisited,* available on the album sleeve and reprinted in *Lyrics,* pp. 209-210.

72. As noted at the start of this chapter, there was, in any case, a strong sense in which Robert Allen Zimmerman "created" Bob Dylan. Hence a biographical reading of Dylan's work would appear, from the outset, to have been built upon flawed and unstable assumptions.

Closing Remarks

1. Terry Eagleton, *Literary Theory: An Introduction* (Second Edition), Oxford: Basil Blackwell, 1996, pp. 193 and 203.

2. The argument referred to here would point towards Betsy Bowden's ideas that Dylan's work was "performed literature" and that literary critics were therefore hindered, at least to a certain degree, in being able to deal only with the textual elements of such an art, in having to leave aside the musical and performance elements of Dylan's artistic creations. See Bowden's *Performed Literature: Words and Music by Bob Dylan,* Bloomington: Indiana University Press, 1982.

3. Cited in Simon Reynolds and Joy Press, *The Sex Revolts: Gender, Rebellion and Rock 'n' Roll,* London: Serpent's Tail, 1995, p. 211.

4. This idea of keeping running, of not stopping, has, of course, a sense of reflective logic in Dylan's own history, in Bob Dylan's own story. In other words, there are obvious biographical comparisons to be made; insomuch as Bob Dylan, himself, has been "on the road" for a large part of his adult life. In a specific sense, one is referring here to the so-called "Never Ending Tour," the title of which being one of Dylan's most playful acts of hubris. Such a way of life could be seen as living out some of the ideological aspects of his work; the "Never Ending Tour," this iconic tour, which has currently been running for more than thirty years, from June 7, 1988, to the present day—will, of course, eventually prove to be nothing of the sort, it will eventually be forced to betray its own hubristic title. The naming of the tour may not have been Dylan's, but it nonetheless remains a satiric title; insomuch as this tour *will* end. It will end either when Dylan decides he can no longer continue touring at such a pace, or—and this is a delicate proposition—it will end should he die on stage, which would not seem impossible—and—in a certain sense would have a kind of logic all of its own. Stephen Scobie, writing some years ago, asked the following question: "Why should

a 52-year-old man drag himself around this horrendous schedule, playing three to four concerts a week for months on end, crossing and recrossing America, crossing and recrossing the Atlantic, playing in smaller halls to a couple of thousand people?" (Scobie 2004, p. 105). This was a good question—and the issue has been compounded up to the present time—now approaching his middle seventies, perhaps Dylan has nothing else to do than to live out this way of life.

5. Cited in Michel Foucault's, "Truth and Power," in Paul Rainbow (ed.), *The Foucauldian Reader*, Harmondsworth: Penguin, 1991, p. 73.

6. Terry Eagleton, *Literary Theory: An Introduction*, Oxford: Basil Blackwell, 1983, p. 201.

7. Mark Simpson, *It's a Queer World*, London: Vintage, 1996, p. 17.

8. Jean François Lyotard, *The Postmodern Condition: A Report on Knowledge*, Minneapolis: University of Minnesota Press, and Manchester: Manchester University Press, 1984, p. xxiv. (Note: the original French edition of Lyotard's book, *La Condition Postmodern: Rapport sur le Savoir*, was originally published in France in 1979, but was not translated into English until 1984.)

9. This would not be to discount the influence of a Christian ideology at other periods in Dylan's life and career, merely to suggest that this point in time showed a much more extreme acceptance of such a way of thinking. Incidentally, on November 3, 2017, the latest installment of the Bootleg Series, *Trouble No More—The Bootleg Series, Vol. 13, 1979-1981*, was released. This release being a retrospective—an eight CD and one DVD box set—covering unreleased studio recordings and live recordings from the so-called Gospel albums and tours of the time. Unsurprisingly, this official release did not include Dylan's racist and homophobic comments from the concert in Hartford.

10. Richard F. Thomas went even further than Ricks, stating that Dylan was "the supreme artist of the English language of my time" (Richard F. Thomas, *Why Dylan Matters*, London: William Collins, 2017, p. 322). Thomas's book deftly described Dylan's debt to such classical writers as Virgil, and Ovid, but otherwise it seemed an almost hagiographical text, unrestrained in its praise and flattery of Dylan's work: Dylan was a "genius" (p. 156), an "innate genius" (p. 215), "the concert was brilliant from start to finish" (p. 268), and so on. In addition, Thomas considered Dylan's Nobel Prize acceptance speech: "a tour de force ... you can add his speech to the rest of his masterpieces" (pp. 304 and 310). Thomas made no reference to the charges of plagiarism in the speech; his book may have gone to press before this news became known. In contrast, Ian Bell is one commentator to have avoided treading the hagiographic path, seeing Dylan's work within a more considered and critical frame. For example, Bell described "Blowin' in the Wind," often seen as Dylan's signature song, as "vacuous in any version, not to say portentous and pretentious and utterly juvenile" (Bell 2013, p. 221); likewise, the song "Masters of War" was an "unaccountably popular dirge ... one of the dullest melodies Dylan ever stole" (Bell 2013, p. 252); Dylan and Joan Baez in duet together, "sounded horrible" (Bell 2013, p. 266); and finally, talking of the liner notes to *The Times They Are A-Changin,*' "Only the blindly devoted could have overlooked the fact that this writer would have remained deep in obscurity had he ever depended on text alone" (Bell 2013, p. 313–314).

11. James Park, *Cultural Icons: Cultural Figures Who Made the 20th Century What It Is*, London: Bloomsbury, 1991, p. 119. However, Park was not completely negative in his criticism, going on to say: "Nevertheless he [Bob Dylan] was immensely significant in the way he fused arrogant teen-energy and folk ... no one should deny that he has transformed rock's attitude to singing."

12. Dylan had his defenders; for example, Sean Wilentz, who carefully and almost pedantically, argued against the charges of plagiarism. Wilentz spoke of "sophisticated borrowing" (Sean Wilentz, *Bob Dylan in America*, London: Bodley Head, 2010, p. 284), that "every artist is, to some extent, a thief" (Wilentz 2010, p. 12) and that, at "the most basic level, the charges of plagiarism were groundless" (Wilentz 2010, p. 309)—that is, many of the sources Dylan had used were out of copyright and in the public domain. Wilentz also suggested that to accuse Dylan of plagiarism was akin to "confuse art with a term paper" (Wilentz 2010, p. 312)—and yet, as discussed in the introduction, why should we not hold an artist, such as Dylan, to the same ethical standards as an academic student? Elsewhere in his book, as with Richard F. Thomas, Wilentz seemed to view Dylan within the tenor of an overly generous critical discourse: speaking, for example, of "new

masterpieces" (Wilentz 2010, p. 96), of "stunning material" (Wilentz 2010, p. 134), of how Dylan was "a national treasure" (Wilentz 2010, p. 304). According to Wilentz the criticism of the film *Masked and Anonymous* (2003) had more to do with "the state of mainstream film criticism" (Wilentz 2010, p. 288) than the shortcomings of the film, and the layered allusions were difficult to comprehend in a single viewing—whereas for many the film seemed so inept as to make even a single viewing problematical. Finally, and perhaps most tellingly, Wilentz found the cover of *The Freewheelin' Bob Dylan* "more arousing than anything I'd glimpsed in furtive schoolboy copies of *Playboy*" (Wilentz 2010, p. 4).

13. Such quotation marks suggest the graphic signs of citational appropriation—but, of course, no such citation was made—or has ever been made by Dylan.

14. There were exceptions, perhaps one of Dylan's most effective examples of subverting a cliché being the phrase: money doesn't talk, it swears—from "It's Alright Ma, I'm Only Bleeding."

15. The use of the word "scapegoat" in "Ballad in Plain D" was of interest. In performance Dylan mispronounces the word as "scrapegoat," and this would not seem to have been a casual mistake, as Dylan repeated the same error in an outtake rendition of the song at the same recording session. Dylan may have been aware of the word via Shirley Jackson's short story "The Lottery" in which the scapegoat ritual was seen to distinguished effect—a figure who suffers for the wrongs of others—however, Dylan does not seem to have been aware of how the word was spelled or pronounced. Incidentally, this mistake was corrected in published versions of the song, telling evidence that Dylan did not have complete authorial control over the transcription of his songs.

16. There were exceptions; for example, Dylan's guitar playing on the original recording of "Don't Think Twice, It's All Right" continues to impress; one might also think, for example, of his piano on "Spanish Is the Loving Tongue," his harmonica on "Mr. Tambourine Man," and so on.

17. www.bobdylan.com. See also, *Time Out of Mind,* New York: Special Rider Music, 1997, p. 45.

Bibliography

Allen, Gary. "That Music: There's More to It than Meets the Ear." *American Opinion* 12, February 1969, pp. 193–213.

Ball, Carolyn. *Bob Dylan: Contemporary Minstrel*. Unpublished Master's Thesis, University of Maryland, 1967.

Ballantine, Christopher. "Say It Straight." *New Society*, June 4, 1970, pp. 967–968.

Barry, Peter. *Beginning Theory: An Introduction to Literary and Cultural Theory*. Manchester: Manchester University Press, 1995.

———. *Beginning Theory: An Introduction to Literary and Cultural Theory* (Second Edition). Manchester: Manchester University Press, 2002.

———. *Beginning Theory: An Introduction to Literary and Cultural Theory* (Third Edition). Manchester: Manchester University Press, 2009.

Barthes, Roland. *Image Music Text*. London: Fontana, 1990.

Bauldie, John (ed.). *The Telegraph* 1–53. Manchester: Wanted Man, 1981–1997.

Bauldie, John, and Michael Gray (eds.). *All Across the Telegraph: A Bob Dylan Handbook*. London: Sidgwick and Jackson, 1987.

Beard, Henry, and Christopher Cerf. *The Officially Politically Correct Dictionary and Handbook*. London: HarperCollins, 1994.

Bell, Ian. *Time Out of Mind: The Lives of Bob Dylan*. Edinburgh: Mainstream, 2013.

Belz, Carl. *The Story of Rock*. New York: Oxford University Press, 1969.

Bicker, Stewart P. *The Red Rose and the Briar: A Commentary on Bob Dylan's Film "Renaldo and Clara."* Bolton: Novaprint, 1984.

Bliss, Carolyn. *Younger Now: Bob Dylan's Changing World and Vision*. Unpublished Master's Thesis, University of Utah, 1972.

Bloom, Fred. "Seeing Dylan Seeing." *Yale Review* 71, Winter 1982, pp. 304–320.

Bordo, Susan. *The Male Body: A New Look at Men in Public and Private*. New York: Farrar, Strauss and Giroux, 1999.

Bowden, Betsy. *Performed Literature: Words and Music by Bob Dylan*. Bloomington: Indiana University Press, 1982.

Bristow, Joseph. *Sexuality*. London: Routledge, 1997.

Brotherton, Rob. *Suspicious Minds: Why We Believe Conspiracy Theories*. London: Bloomsbury Sigma, 2015.

Brownmiller, Susan. *Against Our Will: Men, Women and Rape*. Harmondsworth: Penguin, 1977.

Butler, Andrew. *The Pocket Essentials Film Studies*. Harpenden: Pocket Essentials, 2002.

Butler, Judith. *Gender Trouble: Feminism and the Subversion of Identity*. London: Routledge, 1990.

Cameron, Deborah (ed.). *The Feminist Critique of Language: A Reader*. London: Routledge, 1990.

Campbell, M. "Bob Dylan and the Pastoral Apocalypse," *Journal of Popular Culture* 8, Summer 1975, pp. 696–707.

Carlin, Richard. *The Big Book of Country Music: A Biographical Encyclopaedia*. Harmondsworth: Penguin, 1995.

Cartwright, Bert. *The Bible in the Lyrics of Bob Dylan*. Romford: Wanted Man, 1985.

Castle, Gregory. *The Blackwell Guide to Literary Theory*. Oxford: Blackwell, 2007.

Cawelti, John G. "Reply to Poague." *Journal of Popular Culture* 8, Summer 1974, pp. 57–58.

Clarke, Donald. *The Rise and Fall of Popular Music*. New York: Viking, 1995.

Bibliography

Cott, Jonathan. *Dylan*. London: Vermilion, 1984.

Cuddon, J.A. *The Penguin Dictionary of Literary Terms and Literary Theory*. Harmondsworth: Penguin, 1992.

Culler, Jonathan. *Literary Theory: A Very Short Introduction*. Oxford: Oxford University Press, 1997.

Davey, Frank. "Leonard Cohen and Bob Dylan: Poetry and the Popular Song." *Alphabet* 17, December 1969, pp. 12–29.

Day, Aidan. *Jokerman: Reading the Lyrics of Bob Dylan*. Oxford: Basil Blackwell, 1988.

De Curtis, Anthony (ed.). *Present Tense: Rock and Rock Culture*. London: Duke University Press, 1992.

Dylan, Bob. *Another Side of Bob Dylan*. New York: M. Witmark & Sons, nd.

———. *The Basement Tapes*. London: EMI Music Publishing, 1975.

———. *Blonde on Blonde*. London: B. Feldman, nd.

———. *Blood on the Tracks*. London: EMI Music Publishing, 1975.

———. *Bob Dylan: Anthology*. New York: Amsco, 1990.

———. *Bob Dylan: Anthology 2*. New York: Amsco, 1996.

———. *Bringing It All Back Home*. New York: M. Witmark & Sons, nd.

———. *Chronicles*. London: Simon & Schuster, 2004.

———. *Desire*. London: EMI Music Publishing, 1976.

———. *Empire Burlesque*. New York: Special Rider Music, 1985.

———. *Highway 61 Revisited*. New York: M. Witmark & Sons, nd.

———. *Infidels*. New York: Special Rider Music, 1983.

———. *John Wesley Harding*. London: B. Feldman, nd.

———. *Lyrics 1962–1985*. London: Jonathan Cape, 1987.

———. *Lyrics 1962–1985*. New York: Alfred A. Knopf, 1985.

———. *Nashville Skyline*. London: B. Feldman, 1969.

———. *New Morning*. London: B. Feldman, 1970.

———. *Planet Waves*. London: B. Feldman, 1973.

———. *Saved*. London: EMI Music Publishing, 1980.

———. *Self Portrait*. London: B. Feldman, 1970.

———. *Shot of Love*. London: EMI Music Publishing, 1981.

———. *Slow Train Coming*. London: EMI Music Publishing, 1979.

———. *The Songs of Bob Dylan 1966–1975*. New York: Alfred A. Knopf, 1976.

———. *Street Legal*. London: EMI Music Publishing, 1978.

———. *Tarantula*. London: MacGibbon & Kee, 1971.

———. *Time Out of Mind*. New York: Special Rider Music, 1997.

———. *The Times They Are A-Changin'*. New York: M. Witmark & Sons, nd.

———. *Writings and Drawings*. London: Jonathan Cape, 1973.

———. www.bobylan.com.

Eagleton. Mary (ed.). *Feminist Literary Theory*. Oxford: Blackwell, 1986.

Eagleton, Terry. *After Theory*. London: Penguin, 2004.

———. *Against the Grain: Essays, 1975–1985*. London: Verso, 1985.

———. *Literary Theory: An Introduction*. Oxford: Basil Blackwell, 1983.

———. *Literary Theory: An Introduction* (Second Edition). Oxford: Basil Blackwell, 1996.

Easthope, Antony. *Literary into Cultural Studies,* London: Routledge, 1991.

———. *What a Man's Gotta Do: The Masculine Myth in Popular Culture*. Boston: Unwin Hyman, 1986.

Elliot, Marc. *Rockonomics: The Money Behind the Music*. London: Omnibus, 1989.

Estes, Steve. *I Am a Man: Manhood and the Civil Rights Movement*. Chapel Hill: University of North Carolina Press, 2005.

Fiedler, Leslie. *Love and Death in the American Novel*. New York: Stein and Day, 1966.

———. *Love and Death in the American Novel*. Normal, IL: Dalkey Archive, 1997.

Flanagan, Bill. *Written in My Soul: Rock's Great Songwriters Talk about Creating Their Music*. Chicago: Contemporary, 1986.

Forland, Tor Egil. "Bringing It All Back Home

Bibliography

or Another Side of Bob Dylan: Midwestern Isolationist." *Journal of American Studies* 26, December 1992, pp. 337–355.

Freud, Sigmund. *The Interpretation of Dreams*. Ware, Hertfordshire: Wordsworth Classics, 1997.

Friedlander, Paul. *Rock and Roll: A Social History*. Boulder: Westview, 1996.

Frith, Simon. *Music for Pleasure*. Cambridge: Polity, 1988.

_____. *Performing Rites: On the Value of Popular Music*. Oxford: Oxford University Press, 1996.

Gallop, Jane. *Around 1981: Academic Feminist Literary Theory*. New York: Routledge, 1992.

Garber, Marjorie. *Vice-Versa: Bisexuality and the Eroticism of Everyday Life*. Harmondsworth: Penguin, 1995.

Gay, Peter. *Freud: A Life for Our Time*. New York: W.W. Norton, 1998.

Gill, Andy. *Classic Bob Dylan: 1962–1969 My Back Pages*. London: Sevenoaks, 1998.

Goldberg, Steven. "Bob Dylan and the Poetry of Salvation." *Saturday Review*, May 30, 1970, pp. 43–46.

Goldenson, Robert, and Kenneth Anderson. *The Wordsworth Dictionary of Sex*. Ware, Hertfordshire: Wordsworth, 1994.

Goldwag, Arthur. *Isms and Ologies: 453 Difficult Doctrines You've Always Pretended to Understand*. London: Quercus, 2007.

Gonczy, Daniel J. "The Folk Music of the 1960s—Its Rise and Fall." *Popular Music and Society* 10.1, 1985, pp. 15–31.

Gonzalez, Alberto. "Rhetorical Ascription and the Gospel According to Dylan." *Quarterly Journal of Speech* 69.1, February 1983, pp. 1–14.

Gray, Michael. *Song and Dance Man: The Art of Bob Dylan*. London: Hart-Davis, MacGibbon, 1972.

Gross, Michael. *Bob Dylan: An Illustrated History*. London: Elm Tree, 1978.

Grossman, Edward. "Dylan's Odyssey." *Dissent* 20.4, 1973, pp. 491–493.

Hammond, John. *John Hammond on Record: An Autobiography*. New York: NAL, 1977.

Hampton, Wayne. *Guerrilla Minstrels: John Lennon, Joe Hill, Woody Guthrie, Bob Dylan*. Knoxville: University of Tennessee Press, 1986.

_____. *Working Class Heroes: Counter Cultural Politics and the Singing Hero in 20th Century America*. Unpublished Doctoral Thesis, University of Tennessee, 1986.

Harker, Dave. *One for the Money: Politics and Popular Song*. London: Hutchinson, 1980.

Hatch, David, and Stephen Millward. *From Blues to Rock: An Analytical History of Pop Music*. Manchester: Manchester University Press, 1987.

Hattenhauer, Darryl. "Bob Dylan as Clown and Guru." *Journal of American Culture* 2.2, Summer 1979, pp. 176–18.

_____. "Bob Dylan as Hero: Rhetoric, History, Structuralism and Psychoanalysis in Folklore as a Communicative Process." *Southern Folklore Quarterly* 45, 1981, pp. 69–88.

Herdman, John. *Voice Without Restraint: A Study of Bob Dylan's Lyrics and Their Background*. Edinburgh: Paul Harris, 1982.

Herdt, Gilbert. *Rituals of Manhood*. Berkeley: University of California, 1982.

Heylin, Clinton. *Behind Closed Doors: The Recording Sessions, 1960–1995*. Harmondsworth: Penguin, 1995.

_____. *Dylan: Behind the Shades*. Harmondsworth: Penguin, 1991.

_____. *It's One for the Money: The Song Snatchers Who Carved Up a Century of Pop and Sparked a Musical Revolution*. London: Constable, 2016.

_____. *A Life in Stolen Moments: Bob Dylan Day by Day, 1941–1995*. London: Music Sales, 1996.

_____. *Stolen Moments: The Ultimate Bob Dylan Reference Book*. Romford: Wanted Man, 1988.

Hitchens, Christopher. *God Is Not Great: How Religion Poisons Everything*. New York: Atlantic, 2007.

Hocquenghem, Guy. *Homosexual Desire*. Durham: Duke University Press, 1993.

Hoggart, Richard. *The Way We Live Now*. London: Chatto and Windus, 1996.

Horrocks, Roger. *An Introduction to the Study of Sexuality*. London: Macmillan, 1997.

_____. *Male Myths and Icons: Masculinity in Popular Culture*. London: Macmillan, 1995.

_____. *Masculinity in Crisis*. London: Macmillan, 1994.

Bibliography

Jameson, Frederic. *Postmodernism, or, the Cultural Logic of Late Capitalism.* Durham: Duke University Press, 1990.

Johnson, Thomas S. "Desolation Row Revisited: Bob Dylan's Rock Poetry." *Southwest Review* 62, Spring 1974, pp. 135–147.

Joyce, James. *Ulysses.* Oxford: Oxford University Press, 1993.

Kaiser, Charles. "Encountering Dylan." *Boston Review,* April 1986, pp. 9–10.

Katz, Elia. "Dylan's Unpublished Novel." *Carolina Quarterly* 21, Fall 1969, pp. 34–37.

Katz, Jonathan Ned. *The Invention of Heterosexuality.* New York: Dutton, 1995.

Kelly, Michael (ed.). *French Culture and Society.* London: Arnold, 2001.

Kerouac, Jack. *On the Road.* New York: NAL, 1957.

Khalifa, Jean-Charles. "A Semantic and Syntactic Journey Through the Dylan Corpus." *Oral Tradition* 22/1, 2007, pp. 162–174.

King, Bill. *Bob Dylan: The Artist in the Marketplace.* Unpublished Doctoral Thesis, University of North Carolina, 1975.

Krauss, Lawrence M. *A Universe from Nothing: Why There Is Something Rather than Nothing.* London: Simon & Schuster, 2012.

Lacy, Nick. *Introduction to Film.* Basingstoke: Palgrave Macmillan, 2005.

Larkin, Philip. *All What Jazz: A Record Diary, 1961-68.* London: Faber & Faber, 1970.

LeGuin, Ursula K. *Dancing at the Edge of the World.* London: HarperCollins, 1989.

Lehman, David. *Sign of the Times: Deconstruction and the Fall of Paul de Man.* London: Andre Deutsch, 1991.

Lewis, George H. "The Pop Artist and His Product: Mixed Up Confusion." *Journal of Popular Culture* 4, 1970, pp.327–328

Lhamon, W.T., Jr. "Bicentennial Dylan." *New Republic* 174, February 1976, pp. 23–24.

_____. "A Cut Above." *New Republic* 172, April 1975, pp. 22–24.

_____. "Poplore and Bob Dylan." *Bennington Review,* December 1978, pp. 22–29.

Lindstrom, Naomi. "Dylan—Song Returns to Poetry." *Texas Quarterly* 19, Winter 1976, pp. 136–136.

Lodge, David. *Lives in Writing.* London: Vintage, 2015.

_____. *The Practice of Writing.* London: Secker and Warburg, 1996.

_____. *Small World: An Academic Romance.* London: Secker & Warburg, 1984.

Lodge, David, and Nigel Wood (eds.). *Modern Criticism and Theory: A Reader.* London: Longman, 1992.

London, Herbert. "American Romantics: Old and New." *Colorado Quarterly* 18.1, 1969, pp. 5–20.

Lyon, David. *Postmodernity.* Buckingham: Open University Press, 1995.

Lyotard, Jean-François. *The Postmodern Condition: A Report on Knowledge.* Manchester: Manchester University Press, 1984.

Mailer, Norman. *Advertisements for Myself.* New York, Berkley, 1970.

_____. *The Prisoner of Sex.* London: Macmillan, 1971.

Marcus, Greil. *Invisible Republic: Bob Dylan's Basement Tapes.* London: Picador, 1997.

McDonald, James R. "Bob Dylan: Biograph: A Journey in Life." *Popular Music and Society* 10.3, 1986, pp. 91–94.

McDonough, John William. *Bob Dylan: The Romantic Sensibility in the Modern Cauldron.* Unpublished Master's Thesis, University of North Carolina, 1968.

McGinley, Phyllis. *The Province of the Heart: Some of My Best Friends.* New York: Viking, 1969.

McGregor, Craig (ed.). *Bob Dylan: A Retrospective.* New York. Morrow, 1972.

Medcalf, Lawrence D. *The Rhetoric of Bob Dylan, 1963-66.* Unpublished Doctoral Thesis, Indiana University, 1978.

Meehan, Thomas. "Public Writer No. 1? Bob Dylan: Is He Heir to Faulkner and Hemingway?" *New York Times Magazine,* December 12, 1965, pp. 44–45, 130–136.

Mellers, Wilfrid. *A Darker Shade of Pale: A Backdrop to Bob Dylan.* London: Faber & Faber, 1984.

Middleton, Peter. *The Inward Gaze: Masculinity and Subjectivity in Modern Culture.* London: Routledge, 1992.

Middleton, Richard. *Studying Popular Music.* Buckingham: Open University Press, 1990.

Miles, Rosalind. *The Rites of Man: Life and Death in the Making of the Male.* London: Grafton, 1991.

Bibliography

Miller, Karl. *Doubles: Studies in Literary History.* Oxford: Oxford University Press, 1985.

Mitchell, Juliet. *Psychoanalysis and Feminism.* Harmondsworth: Penguin, 1975.

Moi, Toril (ed.). *French Feminist Thought: A Reader.* Oxford: Blackwell, 1987.

Monaghan, David. "Taking Bob Dylan Seriously: The Waste Land Tradition." *English Quarterly* 6.2, Summer 1973, pp. 165–172.

Monteiro, George. "Dylan in the Sixties." *South Atlantic Quarterly* 1974, pp. 160–172.

Morris, Mary (ed.). *The Virago Book of Women Travellers.* London: Virago, 1996.

Morrison, Toni. *Playing in the Dark: Whiteness and the Literary Imagination.* London: Picador, 1992.

Nelson, James B. (ed.). *Sexuality and the Sacred: Sources for Theological Reflection.* London: Mowbray, 1994.

O'Hara, J.D. "Talking Through their Heads." *New Republic* 20, May 1972, pp. 26–31.

Orman, John. *The Politics of Rock.* Chicago: Nelson Hall, 1986.

Paglia, Camille. *Sex and Violence, or Nature and Art.* London: Penguin, 1995.

_____. *Sex, Art and American Culture.* New York: Vintage, 1992.

_____. *Sexual Personae.* New Haven: Yale University Press, 1990.

Park, James (ed.). *Cultural Icons: Cultural Figures Who Made the 20th Century What It Is.* London: Bloomsbury, 1991.

Parrinder, Patrick. *The Failure of Theory: Essays on Criticism and Contemporary Fiction.* Brighton: Harvester, 1987.

Parrish, Tim. *Walking Blues: Making Americans from Emerson to Elvis.* Amherst: University of Massachusetts Press, 2001.

Pattison, Robert. *The Triumph of Vulgarity: Rock Music in the Mirror of Romanticism.* New York: Oxford University Press, 1987.

Pichaske, David. *The Poetry of Rock: The Golden Years.* Peoria: Ellis, 1981.

Poague, Leland A. "Dylan as Auteur—Theoretical Notes and an Analysis of 'Love Minus Zero/No Limit.'" *Journal of Popular Culture* 8, Summer 1974, pp. 53–58.

Quinn, Edward. *Collins Dictionary of Literary Terms.* Glasgow: HarperCollins, 2004.

Rainbow, Paul (ed.). *The Foucauldian Reader.* Harmondsworth: Penguin, 1991.

Reading, Joseph Donald. *Tears of Rage: A History, Theory and Criticism of Rock Song and Social Conflict Rhetoric, 1965-1970.* Unpublished Doctoral Thesis, University of Oregon, 1980.

Reynolds, Simon, and Joy Press. *The Sex Revolts: Gender, Rebellion and Rock & Roll.* London: Serpent's Tail, 1995.

Ribakove, Sy, and Barbara Ribakove. *Folk Rock: The Bob Dylan Story.* New York: Dell, 1966.

Ricks, Christopher. *The Force of Poetry.* Oxford: Clarendon Press, 1984.

Ricks, Christopher, and Leonard Michaels (eds.). *The State of the Language.* London: Faber & Faber, 1990.

Riley, Tim. *Hard Rain: A Dylan Commentary.* London: Plexus, 1992.

Roos, Michael. "Fixin' to Die: The Death Theme in the Music of Bob Dylan." *Popular Music and Society* 8.3–4, 1982, pp. 103–116.

_____. "Is Your Love in Vain: Dialectical Dilemmas in Bob Dylan's Recent Love Songs." *Popular Music* 7.1, 1987, pp. 36–49.

Ruthven, K.K. *Feminist Literary Studies.* Cambridge: Cambridge University Press, 1984.

Salih, Sara. *Judith Butler* (Routledge Critical Thinkers). London: Routledge, 2002.

Scaduto, Anthony. *Bob Dylan: An Intimate Biography.* London: W.H.Allen, 1972.

Schwenger, Peter. *Phallic Critiques: Masculinity and Twentieth Century Literature.* London: Routledge, 1984.

Scobie, Stephen. *Alias Bob Dylan.* Red Deer, Calgary, Alberta: Red Deer College Press, 1991.

_____. *Alias Bob Dylan Revisited.* Red Deer, Calgary, Alberta: Red Deer College Press, 2004.

Sedgwick, Eve Kosofsky. *Between Men: English Literature and Male Homosocial Desire.* New York: Columbia University Press, 1985.

_____. *Epistemology of the Closet.* Harmondsworth: Penguin, 1994.

Segal, Lynn. *Straight Sex: The Politics of Pleasure.* London: Virago, 1994.

Selden, Raman. *A Reader's Guide to Contemporary Literary Theory.* Hemel Hempstead: Harvester Wheatsheaf, 1993.

Shelton, Robert. *No Direction Home: The Life*

and Music of Bob Dylan. London: New English Library, 1986.
Shepard, Sam. *Rolling Thunder Logbook*. Harmondsworth: Penguin, 1978.
Shewey, Don. *Sam Shepard*. New York: Da Capo, 1997.
Showalter, Elaine. *Sexual Anarchy: Gender and Culture at the Fin de Siècle*. New York: Viking, 1990.
Siann, Gerda. *Gender Sex and Sexuality: Contemporary Psychological Perspectives*. London: Taylor and Francis, 1994.
Simpson, Mark. *It's a Queer World*. London: Vintage, 1996.
_____. *Male Impersonators*. London: Cassell, 1994.
Sloman, Larry. *On the Road with Bob Dylan*. New York: Bantam, 1978.
Snow, Craig Robert. *Folk-Singer and Beat Poet: The Prophetic Vision of Dylan*. Unpublished Doctoral Thesis, Purdue University, 1987.
Sontag, Susan. *Against Interpretation and Other Essays*. New York: Picador, 2001.
Spargo, Tasmin. *Foucault and Queer Theory*. Cambridge: Icon, 1999.
Stokes, Philip. *Philosophy: 100 Essential Thinkers*. London: Arcturus, 2003.
Storey, John. *Cultural Theory and Popular Culture: An Introduction*. Harlow: Pearson, 2001.
Sumner, Carolyn. "The Ballad of Dylan and Bob." *Southwest Review* 66, Winter 1981, pp. 41–54.
Tambling, Jeremy. *What is Literary Language?* Milton Keynes: Open University Press, 1988.
Theweleit, Klaus. *Male Fantasies*. Minneapolis: University of Minnesota Press, 1987.
Thomas, Richard F. *Why Dylan Matters*. London: William Collins, 2017.
Thomson, Elizabeth, and David Gutman (eds.). *The Dylan Companion*. London: Macmillan, 1990.
Tompkins, Jane. *West of Everything: The Inner Life of Westerns*. New York: Oxford University Press, 1992.
Trombley, Stephen. *Fifty Thinkers Who Shaped the Modern World*. London: Atlantic, 2012.
Warhol, Robyn R., and Diane Price Herndl (eds.). *Feminisms: An Anthology of Literary Theory and Criticism*. New Brunswick: Rutgers University Press, 1991.
Watson, Peter. *A Terrible Beauty: A History of the Ideas That Shaped the Modern Mind*. London: Weidenfeld & Nicholson, 2000.
Weedon, Chris. *Feminist Practice and Poststructuralist Theory*. Oxford: Blackwell, 1991.
Wells, John. "Bent Out of Shape from Society's Pliers: A Sociological Study of the Grotesque in the Songs of Bob Dylan." *Popular Music and Society* 6.1, 1978, pp. 39–44.
Wexler, Jerry, and David Ritz. *Rhythm and the Blues: A Life in American Music*. London: Jonathan Cape, 1994.
Whiteley, Sheila (ed.). *Sexing the Groove: Popular Music and Gender*. London: Routledge, 1997.
Wilentz, Sean. *Bob Dylan in America*. London: Bodley Head, 2010.
Williams, Paul. *Bob Dylan: Performing Artist: Book One, 1960–1973*. London: Xanadu, 1990.
_____. *Bob Dylan: Performing Artist: 1974–1986: The Middle Years*. London: Omnibus, 1992.
_____. *Bob Dylan: Watching the River Flow: Observations of His Art in Progress, 1966–1995*. London: Omnibus, 1996.
Willis, Ellen. "The Sound of Bob Dylan." *Commentary* 44, November 1967, pp. 71–78.
Wolff, Janet. *Resident Alien: Feminist Cultural Criticism*. Cambridge: Polity, 1995.
Wood, Michael. *America in the Movies or, Santa Maria, It Had Slipped My Mind*. London: Secker and Warburg, 1975.
_____. "Bob Dylan: Wicked Messenger." *New Society*, 29, February 1968, pp. 314–315.
Woods, Gregory. *A History of Gay Literature: The Male Tradition*. New Haven: Yale University Press, 1998.
Woodward, Kathryn (ed.). *Identity and Difference* London: Sage, 1997, p. 210.

Index

"Abandoned Love" 119–120, 163n
abortion 64, 160n
Achilles and Patroclus 165n
The Adventures of Huckleberry Finn (Twain) 55, 57
"Advice for Geraldine on Her Miscellaneous Birthday" 127
After Theory (Eagleton) 15
"Against Interpretation" (Sontag) 28
AIDS 45, 85
album covers, reverse images 169n
Alias Bob Dylan (Scobie) 116
"All Along the Watchtower" 152n, 153n; as Dylan's most performed song 152n
"All I Really Want to Do" 88
"All You Have to Do Is Dream" 87
"Am I Your Stepchild" 74
America in the Movies (Wood) 40
Another Side of Bob Dylan 133
Any Woman's Blues (Jong) 163n
Armstrong, Neil 78
Aronowitz, Al 117
"Art as a Device" (Shklovsky) 15
"As I Went Out One Morning" 71–72; debt to the folk song, "John Riley" 162n
Auden, W.H. 10

Baez, Joan 117, 161n, 173n
Bakthin, Mikhail 27, 96
"Ballad for a Friend" 166n
"Ballad in Plain D" 149
"Ballad of a Thin Man" 88–90
"The Ballad of Frankie Lee and Judas Priest" 42, 70
"Ballad of Hollis Brown" 153n, 163n
"Ballad of the Ox Bow Incident" 166n
Bangs, Lester 166n
Bardot, Brigitte 89
Barry Peter 16, 17, 18, 154n
Barthes, Roland 25, 26, 27, 116, 150; and the prince of signifiers 127–128
The Basement Tapes 70, 164n; bawdy demeanour of songs in 87, 164n
Baudrillard, Jean 17, 18
Bauldie, John 119, 169n

Behan, Brendan 11
Bell, Ian 151n, 163n, 173n; criticism of www.bobdylan.com 152
Benkert, Karoly Maria 20
Betty Blue 127
the Bible 85, 103, 121; biblical references in Dylan's work 10, 153n; James Joyce's pastiche of 105
"Big City Blues" 156n
The Big Lebowski 166n
"Billy" 60, 70, 132
Billy the Kid 61, 132
Biograph 87, 91, 161n, 169n, 172n
biographical readings of Dylan's work: resistance against 2, 30, 75, 95, 115–116, 117, 136, 162
bisexuality 109
"Black Crow Blues" 148
"Black Diamond Bay" 10, 94, 162n, 165n
Blade Runner 127
"Blind Willie McTell" 10, 68
Blonde on Blonde 91, 94, 108
Blood on the Tracks 36, 95, 165n
Bloom, Leopold 52
Bloom, Molly 52
"Blowin' in the Wind" 6, 32, 152n, 153n, 173n
Blue, David 117, 118
Bob Dylan (album) 162n
"Bob Dylan's Blues" 74
"Bob Dylan's New Orleans Rag" 70
"Bob Dylan's 115th Dream" 93, 98, 159n, 170n
"Boom Boom Mancini" 167n
Boone, Joseph 54
bootleg recordings, ethical considerations 152n
The Bootleg Series 4, 58, 151n, 161n, 164n, 170n, 173n; negative effect on Dylan's artistic reputation 151n
"Boots of Spanish Leather" 67
Bordo, Susan 168n
born-again Christianity 71, 84, 86, 103, 105, 142, 145, 146; and attitudes to sex 101–102
"Born in Time" 134
Bound for Glory 36
"Bound to Lose, Bound to Win" 156n–157n
Bowden, Betsy 7, 81, 87, 157n, 172n

181

boxing, homosocial aspects to 22, 100–101, 166*n*; Dylan's involvement in 167*n*
Branagh, Kenneth 158*n*
Brando, Marlon 62, 108, 168*n*
Bricamont, Jean 17
Bringing It All Back Home 107
Bristow, Joseph 155*n*, 163*n*
Brotherton, Rob 104–105
"Brownsville Girl" 157*n*, 160*n*
Buber, Martin 102
Butler, Judith 22–24, 30, 92, 94, 113, 124, 126, 147, 155*n*, 165*n*, 172*n*

"Can You Please Crawl Out Your Window" 8
capitalism 143
"Caribbean Wind" 6, 171*n*
Carter, Angela 107
castration, fears of 135
Cat on a Hot Tin Roof 164*n*
Challenger Space Shuttle disaster 162*n*
"Champaign Illinois" 74
Chandler, Raymond 159*n*
"Changing of the Guards" 122
charisma 117–119
Chaucer, Geoffrey 81
"Chimes of Freedom" 74
Chodorow, Nancy 40
Christ 71, 79, 104, 105–106, 107, 142, 145; and sexuality 167*n*
"Christabel" 26
Chronicles Volume 1 111, 159*n*
civil rights movement 15, 32
Cixous, Hélène 40; *écriture feminine* 40
Clayton, Paul 11
"Clean Cut Kid" 161*n*
Cohen, Leonard 149, 170*n*
Cohen, Scott 111
cold as indicator of Calvary in Dylan's songs 163*n*, 166*n*
Coleridge, Samuel Taylor 26
concordance of Dylan's work 99
Confessions of a Yakuza 10
Conrad, Joseph 10, 75, 122, 162*n*
conspiracy theories 104–105
Copernicus 110
Corcoran, Neil 6
Cott, Jonathan 127
"Country Pie" 69, 87
"Covenant Woman" 67
Crosby, David 118
cross-dressing in Dylan's songs 94
Crowe, Cameron 87
Cuban Missile Crisis 61
cultural significance of Dylan's work 147–149; abilities as a musician 149, 174*n*; causal use of spelling 147–148, 174*n*; misuse of punctuation 148; other artistic endeavours 149, 173*n*; use of clichés 148, 174*n*; use of rhyme 148; use of tautology 148; worst songs, examples of 149
cultural theory 2, 3, 13, 15, 16, 17, 18–19, 26, 29, 30, 101, 110, 139; Aristotle's *Poetics* and cultural theory 154*n*; Stephen Scobie's comments on 153*n*

"Daddy" (Plath) 26
Dangerous Minds 160*n*
"Dark Eyes" 163*n*
Darwin, Charles 110
Day, Aidan 44, 53, 124
"Dead Man, Dead Man" 97
"The Death of Emmett Till" 59, 99
"The Death of Robert Johnson" 166*n*
"Death of the Author" 25–26, 116
de Beauvoir, Simone 126, 171*n*
deconstruction theory 16, 27, 28, 29
Deleuze, Gilles 18
de Man, Paul 17
"Denise" 69, 133, 161*n*–162*n*
Derrida, Jacques 24, 27–28, 29, 155*n*
Desire 41, 51, 53, 95, 100, 157*n*, 159*n*, 162*n*
"Desolation Row" 95–96; geographical location of 165*n*
dialectical practices in Dylan's songs 25
"Dirty World" 68
"Don't Fall Apart on Me Tonight" 96, 165*n*–166*n*, 174*n*; anxieties of impotence in 97
"Don't Think Twice, It's Alright" 11, 38, 60, 61, 66, 161*n*
"Down Along the Cover" 93
"Down the Highway" 33, 70
drug taking and the feminine 70
"Dusty Old Fairgrounds" 33
Dylan, Sara 115

Eagleton, Terry 13, 15, 16, 21, 30, 90, 103, 132, 138–139, 144, 154*n*, 155*n*
Easthope, Anthony 120
Eat the Document 159*n*, 165*n*
Eco, Umberto 171*n*
Eliot, T.S. 153*n*
Elliot, Rambling Jack 117
Ellis, Havelock 102
"Emotionally Yours" 67
Erikson, Erik 34
eroticism in Dylan's songs 68; lack of an explicit vocabulary 86; lack of sexual candor 86
eschatological discourses in Dylan's songs 103, 105, 106
Esquire 170*n*
Estes, Steve 156*n*
Euripides 10, 102
"Every Grain of Sand" 120

familial constraints 37–38
"Farewell" 157*n*

Index

"Farewell Angelina" 127, 161*n*; and Salvador Dali 157*n*
The Feminine Mystique (Friedan) 64
femininity 64-83
feminism 64, 81, 109, 138, 141, 160*n*; definition of 64; Dylan's hostility to 65
feminist theoretical approach 4-5
Fiedler, Leslie A. 44, 55, 56-58, 155*n*, 158*n*, 159*n*, 160*n*, 165*n*, 168
Finnegans Wake 159*n*
Fish, Stanley 28
flâneur, little presence of in Dylan's work 160*n*
folk tradition, Dylan's usage of 153*n*
"Foot of Pride" 70, 94, 163*n*
Ford, Robert 37
Foucault, Michel 22, 24, 25, 109-110, 141, 142, 143, 168*n*
"4th Time Around" 88
Franklin, Aretha 22
Freud, Sigmund 81, 101, 102, 110, 111, 112, 129, 132, 168*n*, 170*n*, 171*n*; *Beyond the Pleasure Principle* 111; death drive 131; dreams 170*n*; Dylan's attitude to 111-112; Oedipal complex 110, 129, 132, 134, 137
Friedan, Betty 64
"From a Buick Six" 70
Frost, Robert 172*n*
Fuller, Jesse 160*n*
fundamentalist Christian discourse 71

Gagarin, Yuri 78
Gallo, Joey 100, 166*n*
Gallop, Jane 168*n*
Garber, Marjorie 22, 111
"Gates of Eden" and resistance to Freud 168*n*
gender as a performativity construct 30, 32, 83
"George Jackson" 86, 100, 166*n*
Ginsberg, Allen 47, 108, 158*n*, 159*n*; "Kaddish" 164*n*
"Girl from the North Country" 67
"Goin' Goin' Gone" 61
"Goin' to Acapulco" 88
Goldberg, Steven 89
Gordon, John 109
"Gotta Serve Somebody" 126-127
Gottlieb, Bob 5
The Grapes of Wrath (Steinbeck) 36
Gray, Michael 39, 89, 91, 92, 115
Great Expectations 127
Greer, Germaine 80
Griffiths, David 73, 78
"The Groom's Still Waiting at the Altar" 38
Gross, Michael 89
Guartarri, Félix 18
Guthrie, Woody 33, 36, 37, 157*n*
"Gypsy Lou" 40, 151*n*

"Hallelujah" 170*n*
halloween concerts of 1964 and 1975 125
Hammond, John 117
Hampton, Wayne 36
"A Hard Rain's A-Gonna Fall" 10, 61, 153*n*
Hard to Handle 167*n*
Harris, Charles B. 57
Hartford Connecticut May 1980 concert 84
Haynes, Todd 164*n*
Heart of Darkness 75
"Heart of Mine" 71
Hegel, Georg Wilhelm Friedrich 24, 102, 155*n*
Heiman, George 107
Hemingway, Ernest 57
Hendrix, Jimi 140
Hentoff, Nat 106
Herdman, John 7, 44, 53, 73, 89, 95, 106, 124
hermeneutic fallacy 132
"Hero Blues" 70; 1974 concert version 160*n*
heterosexuality 18-20, 23, 24-25, 44-45, 92, 95, 143
Heylin, Clinton 6, 7, 10, 11, 12, 116
"Highlands" 81-83, 150; comparison to Eric Jong's novel, *Any Woman's Blues* 163*n*; and Dylan's inability to "draw" women 83
Highway 61 Revisited (album) 94, 114
"Highway 61 Revisited" (song) 38
hill as indicator of Calvary in Dylan's songs 163*n*
Hitchens, Christopher 104
Hite, Shere 154*n*
Hocquenghem, Guy 21
Hodson, Paul 46
Holiday, Billie 10
"Home on the Range" 56
Homer 55
Homicide: Life of the Streets 58
homoeroticism 46, 88-89, 101, 108, 135, 146, 165*n*
homophobia 22, 84-85
homophonic ambiguity in Dylan's work 8, 136, 158*n*
homosexuality 19-22, 25, 64, 84-85, 101-102, 108, 143, 154*n*, 155*n*
homosociality 4, 22, 56, 58, 100, 101, 105, 119, 135, 143, 146, 155*n*, 169
Horrocks, Roger 23, 49, 108, 130-131, 135
"House of the Risin' Sun" 162*n*
Houston, Cisco 33
Howard, Mel 118
"Huck's Tune" 105
Hume, David 102
Hunter, Robert 151*n*
"Hurricane" 80, 86, 99, 166*n*; scatological inferences in 164*n*

Index

"I Am a Lonesome Hobo" 148
I Am a Man: Manhood and the Civil Rights Movement (Estes) 156n
"I and I" 61, 139, 163n, 170n
"I Can't Leave Her Behind" 59
"I Don't Believe You (She Acts Like We Never Have Met" 88
"I Feel a Change Comin' On" 159n
"I Pity the Poor Immigrant" 148
"I Wanna Be Your Lover" 88
"I'd Hate to Be You on That Dreadful Day" 106
identity 114–137; and twinned self 119–123
Idiot Wind" 75, 163n
"If Not for You" 67
"If You Gotta Go, Go Now" 74
"I'll Be Your Baby Tonight" 92–93
I'm Not There (film) 164n
"I'm Not There" (song) 86, 164n
impotence metaphors in Dylan's songs 96–98
Infidels 78
Intellectual Impostures (Sokal and Bricamont) 17
intertextuality 10, 128; examples of in Dylan's songs 10
Irigaray, Luce 18
"Is Your Love in Vain?" 72–73, 149
Iser, Wolfgang 27, 49
"Isis" 31, 41–58, 79, 140; as American quest narrative 54; and Egyptian myth 50–51, 54; homosocial reading 56, 93; intertextual reference to *Ulysses* 52, 159n; numerical patterning within the song 54, 159n; racial ambiguities 56–57; right and left, right and wrong 158n
Islam 103
"It Ain't Me Babe" 38
"It Takes a Lot to Laugh, It Takes a Train to Cry" 163n
"It's Alright Ma, I'm Only Bleeding" 76

Jackson, Shirley 174n
James, Jesse 37
Jane Eyre 127
Jauss, Hans Robert 27
"Jet Pilot" 91, 165n
"Joey" 80, 100, 163n; Lester Bangs' critique of 166n
"John Wesley Harding" 40, 42, 93, 157n
Johnson, Robert 87, 161n
"Jokerman" 70, 112–113, 120, 163n
Jong, Erica 82, 163n
jouissance 69, 110, 131
Joyce, James 52, 105, 171n; Dylan's awareness of 159n
Jung, Carl 120
"Just Like a Woman" 74, 113
"Just Like Tom Thumb's Blues" 163n

Katz, Jonathan Ned 19, 110
Keats, John 10
Kermode, Frank 154n
Kerouac, Jack 37, 62, 157n
Kerr, Barbara 73, 120
Kinsey, Alfred 21, 154n
Krauss, Lawrence K. 104
Kristeva, Julia 18, 24, 40, 101, 126, 134, 135; the abject 134, 141; and menstruation 134
Krogsgaard, Michael 165n
Kubrick, Stanley 55, 149, 151n

Lacan, Jacques 18, 47–48, 129, 130, 132, 171n; lack and the lost twin in Dylan's work 130; Law of the Father 101; mirror stage 129–130; phallus as ultimate signifier 48
The Last of the Mohicans 57
Lawrence, D.H. 87, 158n, 164n
"Lay, Lady, Lay" 68
Ledbetter, Hughie (Leadbelly) 33
Leed, Eric J. 34
Le Guin, Ursula K. 81
Lehman, David 17
Lennon, John 149
"Lenny Bruce" 160n
"Let Me Die in My Footsteps" 61, 151n
Levi-Strauss, Claude 12
Levy, Jacques 41, 51, 140, 157n, 162n
"License to Kill" 76–80, 81, 162n
"Lily, Rosemary and the Jack of Hearts" 42, 98, 163n
Lingua Franca 17
Linguistics of Writing Conference, Strathclyde University 1987 16
Literary Theory: An Introduction 13
Lodge, David 28, 104, 132–133, 156n
"The Lonesome Death of Hattie Carroll" 75, 166n
"Long Distance Operator" 70
"Long Time Gone" 33
"The Lottery" (Jackson) 174n
Love and Death in the American Novel (Fiedler) 57, 165n
"Love and Theft" 148, 153n, 174n
"Love Is Just a Four Letter Word" 67, 86, 119, 131, 132, 161n
"Lovesick" 98
low record sales by Dylan 151n
Lyotard, Jean François 144
Lyrics (1962-1985) 6, 8, 51, 98, 151n, 161n; preponderance of songs about men in 98–99

MacCabe, Colin 16
"Maggie's Farm" 38
Mailer, Norman 108, 134
the male gaze 133
"The Man in the Long Black Coat" 42
"Man on the Street" 166n

Index

The Man Who Died (Lawrence) 158*n*
Marcus, Greil 107, 125, 164*n*
Marx, Karl 102, 103, 139
Marxism 16, 29, 139
masculinity 1, 4, 21, 23, 31–63, 65, 77, 78, 79, 83, 94, 96, 97, 98, 99, 108, 112, 113, 120, 138, 140, 141, 142; and castration anxiety 96; definition of in Dylan's songs 63; masculine travel 83, 156*n*-157*n*
masks in Dylan's work 124, 125, 126
"Masters of War" 11, 160*n*, 173*n*
McGinley, Phyllis 159*n*
McGregor, Craig 89, 107
Mellers, Wilfrid 44
Melville, Herman 12, 55, 159*n*
Miles, Rosalind 101
"Million Dollar Bash" 87
Milton, John 13
misogyny in Dylan's songs 73–74, 80–81, 138, 145
"Mississippi" 58
Mr. Tambourine Man 174*n*
Mitchell, Joni 153*n*
"Mixed Up Confusion" 121–122
Moby Dick 12, 55
Modern Times 10
the moon, romantic associations in Dylan's songs 163*n*
Moore, Thomas 10
Morris, Mary 156*n*
Morrison, Toni 57, 58
"Most Likely You Go Your Way and I'll Go Mine" 91
most performed songs in concert 152*n*
"Motorpsycho Nitemare" 38, 70
"Mozambique" 74

Nashville Skyline 69, 161*n*
"Neighbourhood Bully" 78
Never Ending Tour 1, 8, 32, 172*n*-173*n*
"New Danville Girl" 42, 160*n*
"New Pony" 68
No Direction Home (film) 31
"No More Auction Block" 58
Nobel Prize for Literature 1, 12, 147, 148, 173*n*
"North Country Blues" 75, 162*n*
"Nottamun Town" 11

Oates, Joyce Carroll 166*n*
"Obviously Five Believers" 93
"Odds and Ends" 87
Odysseus 134
The Odyssey 52, 55
"Oh Sister" 76
On Boxing (Oates) 166*n*
On the Road (Kerouac) 37, 55
"On the Road Again" 37, 62
"One More Cup of Coffee" 75

"One More Night" 39
"One Too Many Mornings" 75
"Only a Pawn in their Game" 59, 99
Orman, John 161*n*
outlaw 36; as epitome of masculinity in Dylan's songs 37, 60, 79–80, 146, 157
"Outlaw Blues" 37
"Oxford Town" 59

Paglia, Camille 56, 172*n*
Park, James 147, 173*n*
Partridge, Eric 156*n*
Pat Garrett and Billy the Kid 42
"Paths of Victory" 33
"The Patriot's Game" 11
"Patty's Gone to Laredo" 42
Peckinpah, Sam 42
Pennebaker, D.A. 148
"Percy's Song" 11, 99
performativity 4, 30, 34, 53, 91, 55, 94, 63, 66, 79, 81, 85, 91, 95, 113, 114, 124–126, 129, 132, 138, 143, 147, 156*n*, 169*n*-170*n*
Perkins, Carl 74
Pfeiffer, Michelle 160*n*
Picasso, Pablo 28
Pichaske, David 33, 122, 170*n*
plagiarism, accusations of 2, 9–12, 147; Dylan as *bricoleur* 12; Dylan's response to 10; and the Nobel Prize 12; opinion of Ian Bell 153*n*; opinion of Stephen Scobie 153*n*
Plath, Sylvia 26
Plato 120, 121, 153*n*
Playboy 31, 64, 84, 89, 106, 123, 155*n*, 170*n*
"Playboys and Playgirls" 86
Playing in the Dark (Morrison) 57
"Please Mrs. Henry" 87
Poe, Edgar Allan 57, 122
"Poor Boy Blues" 166*n*
Pope John Paul II 165*n*
"Positively 4th Street" 108
postmodern theory 12, 17–18, 41, 109, 144, 145; and grand narratives 25, 144
poststructuralism 15, 25, 27, 29, 47, 103, 109, 131–132
"Precious Angel" 6, 67, 103
Prince 161*n*
proper names, significance of 126–129, 165*n*
The Province of the Heart (McGinley) 159*n*
psychoanalysis 111, 128, 129, 135, 137, 139, 171*n*, 172*n*
Publilius Syrus 10

queer theory 24, 25, 109, 110, 138, 165*n*, 168*n*
"Quit Your Low Down Ways" 106

race 32, 56–57, 58–59, 99–100, 156*n*, 159*n*, 161*n*, 166*n*
"Rainy Day Women #12 & 35" 71

185

Index

"Ramblin' Gamblin' Willie" 35, 42; and Wild Bill Hickok 156n
reader response theories 27, 95, 133
reception theories 27
The Red Badge of Courage (Crane) 57
Reed, Lou 167n; the song, "Strawman" and possible reference to Dylan 167n
religion 85, 101–107, 130, 142; and the control of women 146; *Renaldo and Clara* 158n, 164n, 169n, 170n; and sexuality 105–106
Ribakove, Barbara 89
Ribakove, Sy 89
Ricks, Christopher 65, 95, 118, 147, 149, 161n; in love with Dylan 118; resistance to theory 16
The Right Stuff 78
Riley, Tim 107
Rimbaud, Arthur 95, 135, 172n
Robertson, Pat 64, 160n
"Roll on John" 149
Rolling Stone 10, 78
Rolling Thunder Logbook 114
"Romance in Durango" 40, 42
Rosenbaum, Ron 170
Russell, Bertrand 102
Russell, Ken 164n
Russian formalism 15

"Sad Eyed Lady of the Lowlands" 6, 67, 88, 148, 163n
Sahil, Sara 155n
"Sara" 67, 75, 162n
Saved 106, 107
Scobie, Stephen 7, 44, 116, 124, 156n, 161n, 163n, 169n, 171n, 173n; criticism of *Lyrics 1962-1985* 152n
SCUM Manifesto 163n
The Second Sex (de Beauvoir) 171n
"The Secret Sharer" (Conrad) 122
Sedgwick, Eve Kosofsky 22, 155n, 168n
"Seeing the Real You at Last" 134
Segal Lynne 20, 64, 108, 134
Self Portrait 148
"Senor: Tales of Yankee Power" 42
"Series of Dreams" 170n; and Freud 170n
"Seven Curses" 75
sex and gender: distinction between 23
Sexual Behaviour in the Human Male 21
Sexual Persona (Paglia) 56
sexuality 1, 3, 16, 20–22, 24–25, 46, 72, 83, 84–113, 142, 146; fluidity of sexual identity in Dylan's songs 91, 107; as a social and cultural construction 109
Shakespeare, William 26, 136; *Hamlet* 10, 26, 69, 136, 158n, 161n, 172n; *King Lear* 10
"She Belongs to Me" 88
"Shelter from the Storm" 8, 76, 163n
Shelton, Robert 32, 84, 89, 90, 96, 165n

Shepard, Sam 114, 123, 124, 125, 136, 137, 160n, 170n
Shklovsky, Viktor 15
Shot of Love (album) 106, 107
"Shot of Love" (song) 97
"Sign on the Window" 39
signifier and signified 28, 29
"Simple Twist of Fate" 69, 121
Simpson, Mark 144, 154n
"Sitting on a Barbed Wire Fence" 70
"Slow Train" 86
Slow Train Coming 106, 107, 118
Small World (Lodge) 132–133, 156n
Snow, Craig 67, 106; Dylan as Beat poet 163n
Social Text 17
Socrates 102
Sokal, Alan 17
Solanas, Valerie 163n
"Something There is About You" 75
"Song to Woody" 33
Sontag, Susan 28
space travel, reactionary view by Dylan 77–79
"Spanish Harlem Incident" 87
Spanish Is the Loving Tongue 174n
Spargo, Tamsin 110, 168n
Special Rider Music 51
"Standing on the Highway" 33
Steinbeck, John 36
Stevenson, Robert Louis 122
Storey, David 29
The Strange Case of Dr. Jekyll and Mr. Hyde (Stevenson) 122, 127
"structuralism 15, 28, 29, 32, 111
"Sugar Baby" 74
"Sweetheart Like You" 38, 73
Swift, Taylor 151n
The Symposium (Plato) 120

"Talkin' New York 41
"Talkin' World War III Blues" 111, 168n
Tambling, Jeremy 28
"Tangled Up in Blue" 36, 122, 148; derivation of "keep on keeping on" 156n
Tarantula 128–129, 171n; intertextual provenance of 128
The Telegraph (fan magazine) 118–119; male/female ratio of readership 169n; Wanted Man 169n
Tempest 160n
"Temporary Like Achilles" 93
Terkel, Studs 156n
"Terraplane Blues" 161n
Terry, Sonny 33
textual authority of Dylan's songs 5–7, 152n
Thomas, Dylan 61, 127, 160n
Thomas, Richard F. 173n; unrestrained in his praise of Dylan's work 173n
"Tight Connection to My Heart" 59

Index

Till, Paul 169n
Time Out of Mind 33, 81, 98, 123
The Times They Are A-Changin' 9
Timrod, Henry 10
"To Be Alone with You" 149
To Have and Have Not (Hemingway) 57
"To Ramona" 67
"Tom Joad" 36
"Tombstone Blues" 38, 163n
Tomkins, Jane 42, 46, 50, 56, 62, 160n
"Tomorrow Is a Long Time" 161n
Tornonto Sun 73
"Tough Mama" 40
"Train a Travellin'" 106
transcribed and performed texts 6–8
"Transgressing the Boundaries: Towards a Transformative Hermeneutics of Quantum Gravity" (Sokal) 17
Travelling Wilburys 68
Trombley, Stephen 27, 171n
"Trouble" 71
"Troubled and I Don't Know Why" 86
True Dylan (Shepard) 123, 170n
The Turn of the Screw (James) 127
Twain, Mark 55
"Tweeter and the Monkey Man" 94
2001: A Space Odyssey 55, 127, 149
Tyson, Sylvia 118

"The Ugliest Girl in the World" 74
Ulysses (Joyce) 52, 55, 171n
Under the Red Sky 68
"Union Sundown" 78
University of Tulsa, Bob Dylan Archive 152n
"Up to Me" 36

Verlaine, Paul 95, 135
Victory (Conrad) 10, 162n
Vidal, Gore 20–21, 154n
Vietnam War 65, 161n
Villon, Francois 128; "The Testament" 128
The Virago Book of Women Travellers (Morris) 156n
"Visions of Johanna" 88, 98

"Walkin' Down the Line" 33
"Wanted Man" (song) 42, 60, 159n
Warhol, Andy 163n
Weberman, A.J. 93
"Wedding Song" 67, 121
West of Everything: The Inner Life of Westerns 42

Western genre in Dylan's songs 40, 41–43, 46, 47, 49, 50, 56, 60, 62, 160n
Wexler, Jerry 117
What a Man's Gotta Do: The Masculine Myth in Popular Culture (Easthope) 120
"What Kind of Friend is This?" 94, 165n
"Whatcha Gonna Do?" 106
"When He Returns" 148
"When I Paint My Masterpiece" 170n
"When the Night Comes Falling from the Sky" 8
"When You Gonna Wake Up?" 86
"Where Are You Tonight (Journey Through Dark Heat)" 87, 120, 132
"Who Killed Davey Moore" 99, 166n
"Who's Gonna Buy You Ribbons" 11
"The Wife of Bath's Tale" 81
"Wiggle Wiggle" 68
The Wild One 62
Wilde, Oscar 24
Wilentz, Sean 166n; defends charges of plagiarism 173n; effusive critique of Dylan's work 173n-174n; erotic component of *The Freewheelin' Bob Dylan* cover 174n
"William Wilson" (Poe) 122
Williams, Paul 7
Williams, Raymond 154n
Williams, Tennessee 10, 164n
Willis, Ellen 96
"The Wind and the Rain" 11
The Wire 58
"With God on our Side" 11, 160n
Wolfe, Tom 78
Wolff, Janet 34, 35
Women in Love (film) 164n
Wood, Michael 40, 62
Wordsworth, William 10
Writings and Drawings 5, 41; as the most impressive volume of Dylan's work 157n
www.bobdylan.com 8; inferior transcriptions to previous text based sources 8–9, 51, 162n

"You're Gonna Make Me Lonesome When You Go 94, 135
"You're No Good" 160n, 170n

Zapp, Morris 132–133, 172n
Zevon, Warren 167n
Zollo, Paul 170n

www.ingramcontent.com/pod-product-compliance
Ingram Content Group UK Ltd.
Pitfield, Milton Keynes, MK11 3LW, UK
UKHW042012140426
5217IPUK00015B/1134